Menus
for
a
Whole
Year
of
Dinners

PORK ROAST WITH RHUBARB

1 4½-to 5-pound pork loin roast   orange juice
1½ teaspoons salt   3½ pounds rhubarb,* in chunks
½ teaspoon ginger   1 cup granulated sugar
⅛ teaspoon pepper

About 3½ hours before serving: Preheat oven to 325°F. Rub pork with salt, ginger and pepper; insert meat thermometer into center. Place on rack in shallow roasting pan. Roast 2½ to 3 hours or until thermometer reaches 170°F.; baste with ½ cup orange juice.

Meanwhile, in medium saucepan, combine rhubarb with sugar, 4 teaspoons orange juice; simmer 5 minutes or until just tender. Cover; let stand 10 minutes; spoon around roast. Makes 8 servings.
* Or use three 20-ounce packages frozen unsweetened cut rhubarb.

SPRING VEGETABLE PLATTER

¼ cup lemon juice   24 fresh asparagus spears (or 2
6 egg yolks   10-ounce packages frozen
salt   asparagus spears), cooked
dash cayenne (optional)   4 medium tomatoes
butter or margarine   pepper
3 medium white potatoes, cooked

About 45 minutes before serving: Preheat oven to 325°F. To warmed electric-blender container,* add lemon juice, egg yolks, 1 teaspoon salt and cayenne. Cover and blend at low speed until smooth. Switch blender control to high speed. Remove center of cover and very slowly pour in 1 cup butter, melted, in steady stream. Continue blending until well mixed; set aside.

Cut hot potatoes into ¼-inch slices; arrange on greased ovenproof platter. Arrange hot asparagus over potatoes; pour on sauce. Cut tomatoes in half, zigzag fashion; place beside potatoes; sprinkle with salt and pepper; dot with butter. Bake along with pork roast last 30 minutes or until tomatoes are bubbling. Makes 8 servings.
* Or in small bowl of electric mixer, at low speed, blend lemon juice, yolks, pepper and salt until smooth. At high speed gradually pour in 1 cup butter, melted. Beat 5 minutes or until sauce thickens slightly.

EASY CHEESE PIE

2 tablespoons butter or margarine   1 teaspoon Worcestershire
7 slices white bread, crusts removed   ½ teaspoon salt
4 slices process Cheddar cheese   ½ teaspoon dry mustard
2 eggs, slightly beaten   ½ teaspoon paprika
1¼ cups milk

About 3 hours before serving: Butter bread; cut each slice into two triangles. Place 6 triangles, buttered-side down, in greased 9-inch pie plate to cover bottom. Place other triangles, buttered-side up, around sides. Cut each cheese slice into 4 strips; lay over bread in bottom of plate. Beat eggs and remaining ingredients; pour over cheese. Refrigerate 2 hours.

Preheat oven to 325°F. Bake pie 45 minutes. Remove from oven; cool 10 minutes before serving. Makes 6 servings.

SALAD TIP: Add a few red onion rings to avocado slices and orange sections; toss with garlic dressing.

SUNDAY
*Pork Roast
with Rhubarb**
*Spring
Vegetable Platter**
*Cloverleaf Rolls
Minted Melon Balls
Coffee   Tea*

MONDAY
*Hot Tomato Soup
Easy Cheese Pie**
*Avocado-Orange Salad**
*Brownies à la Mode
Coffee   Milk*

SOUP TIP: Top each bowlful of canned onion soup with French-bread slice; sprinkle with cheese; slide under broiler until cheese melts.

SPANISH PEACHES

1 30-ounce can cling-peach halves
3 tablespoons dark brown sugar
2 tablespoons lime juice

¼ cup sherry (optional)
1 tablespoon grated lime peel

At least 2 hours before serving: Drain peaches, reserving ½ cup syrup. In small saucepan, combine syrup, brown sugar, lime juice and sherry; simmer 5 minutes. Meanwhile, place peach halves, flat side down, in serving dish; pour syrup mixture over them. Sprinkle with grated lime peel. Refrigerate until serving time. Makes 8 servings.

———◆———

CHICKEN LIVERS WITH RICE

butter or margarine
3 tablespoons minced onion
1⅓ cups packaged precooked rice
½ pound chicken livers, cut into
   1-inch pieces
¼ cup regular all-purpose flour
½ teaspoon salt

dash pepper
1 10½-ounce can condensed cream-
   of-chicken soup, undiluted
½ cup milk
1 tablespoon chopped parsley
pinch basil

Preheat oven to 375°F. In saucepan, in 1 tablespoon hot butter, sauté onion until tender; add to rice; cook as label directs. Meanwhile, lightly roll chicken livers in mixture of flour, salt and pepper; sauté in same skillet in 3 tablespoons butter until browned.

In 1½-quart casserole, combine soup, rice, livers and rest of ingredients. Bake, uncovered, 30 minutes. Makes 6 servings.

GINGER-BUTTERSCOTCH SAUCE

About 20 minutes before serving: In saucepan over medium heat, bring ¼ cup evaporated milk, undiluted, and ¼ cup light corn syrup to boil, stirring constantly. Remove from heat. Add one 6-ounce package butterscotch pieces; stir until melted. Add 2 tablespoons slivered crystalized ginger. Serve warm over waffles. Makes about 1½ cups.

———◆———

MEAT TIP: After cooking butt, cut one 1-inch slice from each end; cut into ¼-inch cubes. Save for Rice and Ham on page 12.

SMOKED PORK BUTT AND BEANS

1 2½-pound smoked boneless pork
   shoulder butt
¼ cup butter or margarine
½ cup minced onions
1 garlic clove, minced
2 teaspoons brown sugar
¼ cup vinegar

1 teaspoon dry mustard
2 17-ounce cans kidney beans,
   drained
1 16-ounce can green lima beans,
   drained
½ cup catchup
salt and pepper

About 3 hours before serving: Place butt in deep kettle; add boiling water to cover. Simmer, covered, allowing about 50 minutes per pound, or until fork-tender.

About 10 minutes before butt is done, preheat oven to 350°F. In skillet, in butter, sauté onions and garlic 5 minutes or until tender.

Add sugar, vinegar, mustard, beans and catchup; mix well. Taste, then add salt and pepper if needed; set aside.

Drain butt; cut into ¾-inch slices. Pour bean mixture into 2-quart casserole; arrange butt slices on top. Cover and bake 15 minutes; uncover and bake 15 minutes more. Makes 6 servings.

FISH STICKS WITH TOMATO SAUCE

About 20 minutes before serving: Bake one 8- or 9-ounce package frozen breaded fish sticks as label directs. Meanwhile, in small saucepan, combine one 8-ounce can tomato sauce, 1 tablespoon lemon juice, 2 teaspoons light brown sugar. Cook, stirring, until hot. Arrange fish sticks on warm platter; pour on sauce. Garnish with lemon wedges. Makes 4 servings.

RELISH TIP: Try cauliflowerets, cucumber sticks, carrot curls, celery fans and ripe olives. For fans, cut each stalk into 3-inch pieces. Slit each piece, almost to end, into narrow, parallel strips. Chill on ice until ends curl. Pat dry before serving.

JIFFY CHERRIES AND CREAM

1 cup sour cream
1 tablespoon granulated sugar

1 21-ounce can cherry-pie filling

Several hours before serving: In small bowl, with electric mixer at medium speed, beat sour cream with sugar.

Stir pie filling; remove 6 cherries and set aside.

Into each of six 6-ounce parfait glasses, spoon layer of pie filling, then layer of sour-cream mixture. Repeat procedure, ending with sour cream.

Top each dessert with whole cherry; refrigerate until serving time. Makes 6 servings.

MEAT TIP: For economy, buy shoulder lamb chops; today they're tender enough to broil. Serve with herb butter.

SALAD TIP: Into ½ cup bottled or homemade mayonnaise, stir ½ cup French dressing; 1 green pepper, minced; 2 tablespoons chili sauce; and 1 tablespoon minced onion. Blend well for a flavorful Russian dressing to spoon over lettuce wedges. Makes about 1½ cups.

LEMON TART

1⅓ cups wheat germ
⅓ cup butter or margarine, melted
granulated sugar
2 eggs, separated
1 tablespoon grated lemon peel

⅓ cup lemon juice
¼ teaspoon salt
1 envelope unflavored gelatin
½ cup heavy or whipping cream

Preheat oven to 375°F. In bottom of 9-inch flan pan or pie plate, combine wheat germ, butter and 2 tablespoons sugar. Spread over bottom and up sides of pan. Bake for 8 minutes; cool.

In heavy saucepan, combine egg yolks, ¼ cup sugar, lemon peel, lemon juice, salt; cook, stirring, until thickened. In ½ cup cold water in measuring cup, soften gelatin; stir into lemon mixture; cool slightly.

In medium bowl, beat egg whites until soft peaks form; in small bowl, beat cream until soft peaks form; fold both into lemon mixture. Pour into prepared crust; refrigerate. Makes 8 servings.

JIFFY CHERRIES AND CREAM

FRIDAY
*Fish Sticks
with Tomato Sauce**
Frozen Potato Puffs
*Raw Relish Platter**
*Jiffy Cherries
and Cream**
Cookies
Tea   Milk

SATURDAY
*Broiled Lamb Chops**
*Broiled
Tomato Halves
with Cheese*
Whipped Potatoes
*Lettuce Wedges
with Russian Dressing**
*Lemon Tart**
Coffee   Tea

Make, Freeze, Serve This Elegant Party Dinner

Three of the courses in this menu can be made ahead at your leisure, then frozen for later use. Not one bit of flavor is lost in the process. The sausage appetizers are served hot, together with the chilled tomato juice. Chicken Breasts Supreme make a main dish grand enough to please a French chef; for extra flavor the sauce receives a final touch of cheese as it bubbles in the oven. The Brownie Almond Torte, luscious chocolate layers filled with whipped topping, is surprisingly easy to make. Prepare the ham-flavored rice and tossed salad while the frozen dishes are thawing or being warmed in the oven. At the last minute, if you like, pop in two pans of brown-and-serve rolls.

APPETIZER TIP: To each cup of canned tomato juice add some grated cucumber and onion, plus a dash of Worcestershire.

APPETIZER SAUSAGE BALLS IN BLANKETS

1½ cups sifted regular all-purpose flour
2 teaspoons curry
1 teaspoon paprika
¼ teaspoon salt

2 4-ounce packages shredded Cheddar cheese (2 cups)
½ cup butter or margarine
1 pound sausage meat

Up to 1 week before serving: In large bowl, mix flour, curry, paprika, salt and cheese. With pastry blender or 2 knives used scissor-fashion, cut in butter until mixture resembles coarse crumbs; with hands shape into ball; cover and refrigerate.

Meanwhile, shape heaping teaspoons of sausage meat into small balls. In large skillet over medium heat, fry until well browned; drain on paper towels.

Divide dough into as many pieces as sausage balls; shape dough evenly around balls; wrap and freeze.

At serving time: Preheat oven to 400°F. Place frozen sausage balls on cookie sheet; bake 12 to 15 minutes until golden. Serve with toothpicks. Makes 3 dozen.

CHICKEN BREASTS SUPREME

¼ cup regular all-purpose flour
2½ teaspoons salt
1 teaspoon paprika
12 half chicken breasts, skinned
¼ cup butter or margarine
2 teaspoons cornstarch
1½ cups half-and-half or light

cream
¼ cup cooking sherry
1 teaspoon grated lemon peel
1 tablespoon lemon juice
1 cup shredded Swiss cheese
½ cup chopped parsley for garnish

Up to 1 week before serving: On waxed paper, combine flour, salt and paprika; use to coat chicken.

In large skillet, in hot butter, lightly brown chicken breasts on both sides. Add ¼ cup water and simmer, covered, 30 minutes or until almost tender; arrange chicken in freezer- and ovenproof 13″ by 9″ by 2″ baking dish.

Mix cornstarch with ¼ cup half-and-half; stir into drippings in skillet. Cook, stirring, over low heat. Gradually stir in remaining half-and-half, sherry, lemon peel and lemon juice; cook, stirring, until thickened; pour over chicken. Freezer-wrap and freeze.

On serving day: Remove from freezer and thaw about 4 hours or until almost defrosted.

About 50 minutes before serving: Preheat oven to 350°F. Heat, covered, 35 minutes or until sauce is bubbly hot. Uncover; sprinkle with cheese; bake a minute more to melt cheese. Garnish. Makes 12 servings.

RICE AND HAM

About 30 minutes before serving: In large saucepan, in ¼ cup hot butter, sauté ¾ cup minced onions until tender. Add 1 cup cooked ham, cut into ¼-inch cubes, and 2 cups uncooked regular rice; sauté, stirring, a few minutes longer. Add 4 cups chicken broth; simmer, covered, 20 minutes or until broth is completely absorbed by rice and rice is almost tender. Makes 12 servings.

SALAD TIP: Tear chicory, romaine and lettuce into bite-size pieces; add red-onion rings; toss with bottled Italian dressing.

BROWNIE ALMOND TORTE

4 1-ounce squares unsweetened
  chocolate
1¼ cups sifted regular all-
  purpose flour
½ teaspoon double-acting
  baking powder
¼ teaspoon salt
1 cup butter or margarine

1½ cups granulated sugar
4 eggs
1 teaspoon vanilla extract
1 cup finely chopped blanched
  almonds
8 9-inch waxed-paper circles
3 2-ounce packages
  whipped-topping mix

Up to 1 week before serving: Preheat oven to 350°F. In double boiler over hot, *not boiling,* water, melt chocolate. Sift flour with baking powder and salt. In large bowl, with electric mixer at medium speed, cream butter with sugar until fluffy; add eggs, one at a time, beating until light and fluffy. At low speed, beat in chocolate, vanilla, flour mixture, chopped almonds.

Grease large cookie sheet; on it place 2 waxed-paper circles; grease. With broad spatula, spread ½ cup chocolate mixture on each. Bake 10 to 12 minutes; cool 5 minutes; carefully remove to rack; cool. Remove waxed paper. Continue baking layers, making 8 in all.

Prepare whipped-topping mix as label directs. Reserve ¾ cup whipped topping for garnish; spread rest between 7 layers; top with last layer. Garnish top with spoonfuls of topping; freeze to set; freezer-wrap; freeze. *2 hours before serving:* Thaw torte, unwrapped. Makes 12 servings.

CABBAGE WEDGES WITH MUSTARD SAUCE

4 cooked cabbage wedges
1 cup sour cream
1 tablespoon prepared mustard
1 tablespoon minced onion

¼ teaspoon salt
⅛ teaspoon pepper
1 tablespoon chopped green onions
  (optional)

About 15 minutes before serving: While cabbage cooks, in small saucepan over low heat, combine sour cream, mustard, onion, salt and pepper. Heat through. Sprinkle with green onions. Serve over hot, drained cabbage. Makes 4 servings.

SEAFOOD SUPREME

1 10-ounce can frozen condensed
  cream-of-shrimp soup, thawed
½ soup can milk
1 teaspoon paprika
1 to 1½ teaspoons Worcestershire
dash cayenne

2 cups fresh scallops
2 cups shelled, deveined shrimp
¼ teaspoon salt
⅛ teaspoon white pepper
toast triangles

About 1 hour before serving: In medium saucepan over low heat, combine undiluted soup with milk; stir in paprika, Worcestershire and cayenne; heat, stirring, until a smooth and creamy sauce.

Meanwhile, in 1 cup boiling salted water, boil scallops, covered, 10 minutes; drain. Combine scallops with sauce; add shrimp; sprinkle with salt and pepper. Simmer about 3 minutes, stirring occasionally, or until shrimp turn pink. Serve on toast triangles. Makes 4 servings.

MONDAY

*Broiled Thin
Corned-Beef-Hash
Slices
with Poached Eggs*

*Cabbage Wedges
with Mustard Sauce**

Rolls Butter

*Pineapple Cubes
in Wine*

Coffee Tea

TUESDAY

Seafood Supreme*

Mixed-Greens Salad

Brown-and-Serve Rolls

*Strawberry-Banana
Gelatin*

Tea Coffee

SOUP TIP: Heat two 10¼-ounce cans frozen condensed cream-of-potato soup, adding 1 tablespoon chopped parsley with liquid. Makes 8 servings.

HAM STEAKS WITH GINGER SAUCE

1½ cups canned unsweetened
   pineapple juice
½ cup vinegar
¼ cup salad oil

⅓ cup honey
¾ cup fine gingersnap crumbs
2 fully cooked center ham slices,
   each 1-inch thick

About 20 minutes before serving: Preheat broiler if manufacturer directs. In saucepan, combine pineapple juice, vinegar, salad oil and honey; heat. Stir in gingersnap crumbs. Meanwhile, with knife, snip fat edge of ham slices in several places, to keep from curling.

Broil ham for 10 minutes, brushing frequently with sauce. Turn; repeat. Serve with remaining sauce. Makes 8 to 10 servings.

BRUSSELS SPROUTS ROYALE

Cook two 10-ounce packages frozen Brussels sprouts as label directs; drain. Add ¼ cup butter, ¼ cup chopped parsley, dash seasoned salt, sugar. Drain one 5-ounce can water chestnuts; dice. Add to sprouts; heat. Makes 8 servings.

CHICKEN-BROCCOLI SOUP

2 10-ounce packages frozen
   chopped broccoli
2 chicken-bouillon cubes
about 1½ cups milk
2 10½-ounce cans condensed

cream-of-chicken soup
½ teaspoon oregano
2 cups heavy or whipping cream
salt and pepper

About 20 minutes before serving: Cook broccoli as label directs but add bouillon cubes instead of salt; drain well, reserving liquid. Add enough milk to reserved liquid to make 2 cups. In electric-blender container,* place broccoli, undiluted soup, oregano, ½ cup liquid; cover and blend until smooth, about 30 seconds. Pour into large saucepan with rest of liquid and cream; heat but do not boil. Season with salt and pepper. Makes 8 servings.

* Or put cooked broccoli through food mill; combine with rest of ingredients; stir with wire whisk.

Note: If desired, cool, then refrigerate, soup 3 to 4 hours. To serve, thin with a little milk or water.

CORN STICKS AND MUFFINS

About 30 minutes before serving: With salad oil, grease well 1 corn-stick pan and 1 muffin pan. Prepare 1 package corn-muffin mix as label directs, but fold in ½ cup diced pared apples. Bake as directed; serve piping hot with soup. Makes about 7 corn sticks and 8 corn muffins.

VEGETABLE TIP: Cook sliced carrots until tender; drain. Add 1 tablespoon butter, 2½ tablespoons honey; blend. Heat until glazed.

VEGETABLE TIP: Make your favorite scalloped-potato recipe but add ½ teaspoon curry to flour, salt and pepper.

CHICKEN-BROCCOLI SOUP

ORANGE MEDALLION SALAD

3 cups shredded fresh spinach
1 medium head iceberg lettuce,
   shredded
2 tablespoons diced red onion
2 tablespoons diced green pepper
2 large oranges, pared, sliced

2 tablespoons diced pimento
½ medium unpared cucumber,
   scored, sliced
watercress
Honey-Caraway Salad Dressing
   (following)

In large bowl, toss together spinach, lettuce, onion, green pepper, oranges, pimento and cucumber. Garnish with watercress. Refrigerate while you make honey dressing. Toss salad with just enough dressing to moisten greens. Makes 8 servings.

Honey-Caraway Salad Dressing: In small bowl, combine 1 cup mayonnaise or cooked salad dressing with ¼ cup honey and 2 tablespoons lemon juice. Beat smooth with rotary beater; stir in 1½ tablespoons caraway seed. Makes 1¼ cups.

FRIDAY

*Oven-Roasted
Spareribs*

*Curried Scalloped
Potatoes**

Frozen Baby Limas

*Orange Medallion
Salad**

*Butter-Pecan
Ice Cream*

Coffee   Tea

MACARONI AND CHEESE

1 tablespoon salad oil
1 small onion, minced
2 16-ounce cans tomatoes
1 6-ounce can tomato paste
1 teaspoon basil
1 teaspoon salt
½ teaspoon granulated sugar

½ teaspoon ground oregano
1 8-ounce package elbow macaroni
1 8-ounce container cottage cheese
1 8-ounce package process cheese,
   cubed (about 1½ cups)
2 tablespoons butter or margarine

About 50 minutes before serving: In large skillet in hot oil, sauté onion until tender, about 5 minutes. Drain tomatoes (serve liquid as juice if you like); stir in with tomato paste, basil, salt, sugar and oregano. Simmer, covered, over low heat, 20 minutes, stirring occasionally.

Meanwhile, cook macaroni as label directs; drain. Preheat oven to 350°F. Mix macaroni with rest of ingredients. Pour into buttered 2½-quart casserole; bake 30 minutes or until bubbly. Makes 8 servings.

To do ahead: Mix ingredients and refrigerate. Increase baking time to 35 minutes or until mixture is bubbly.

DESSERT TIP: Heat a can or two of apple slices. Sprinkle with salted peanuts. Serve hot with cream.

SATURDAY

*Beef Consommé
with Mushrooms*

Macaroni and Cheese*

Raw Relishes

Italian Green Beans

Apple Dessert*

Coffee

BROILED LEG OF LAMB

1 8-ounce bottle old-fashioned
French dressing
2 bay leaves, crumbled
1 teaspoon peppercorns

1 6- to 8-pound leg of lamb, split
and boned (butterflied)
Avgolemono Sauce (below)
parsley

4 to 24 hours before serving: In large baking dish or roasting pan, combine salad dressing, bay leaves, peppercorns; refrigerate lamb in this marinade, turning occasionally.

About 30 minutes before serving: Preheat broiler if manufacturer directs. Lift lamb from marinade; place on rack in broiler pan; broil 15 minutes; turn over; brush with marinade; broil about 12 minutes for rare, longer for well done. Meanwhile, make Avgolemono Sauce.

Place lamb on large plank; serve with sauce; garnish with parsley. Makes 8 servings plus leftovers for Tuesday, page 18.

Avgolemono Sauce: In small saucepan, with fork or wire whisk, beat together 3 egg yolks, 2 teaspoons cornstarch, 1 teaspoon salt and dash cayenne. Combine 1 envelope instant chicken-broth mix, 1 cup water, 1 tablespoon lemon juice; slowly stir into egg-yolk mixture. Cook over medium heat, *stirring constantly,* until slightly thickened. Keep warm over hot, *not boiling,* water. Makes about 1¼ cups.

SALADE DE TURQUIE

¼ teaspoon instant minced garlic
1 tablespoon vinegar
2 teaspoons salt
½ teaspoon dill seed (or 1
tablespoon snipped fresh dill)

1¾ cups plain yogurt
1 tablespoon olive oil
3 medium cucumbers, pared
mint sprigs

About 10 minutes before serving: In medium bowl, combine garlic, vinegar, salt, dill seed, yogurt and olive oil.

Quarter cucumbers lengthwise; slice thinly. Combine with yogurt mixture; top with mint sprigs. Refrigerate. Makes 8 servings.

BREAD TIP: Stand contents of two 8-ounce packages refrigerated buttermilk biscuits, on edge, in greased 5½-cup ring mold. Brush tops of biscuits with beaten egg; bake and cool as label directs.

CURRIED SPINACH

2 10-ounce packages frozen
chopped spinach
1 teaspoon salt
1½ tablespoons butter or

margarine
⅛ teaspoon pepper
⅛ teaspoon nutmeg
¼ teasoon curry

About 15 minutes before serving: Cook spinach as label directs but add salt.

Meanwhile, in small saucepan, melt butter; remove from heat; stir in pepper, nutmeg and curry.

Drain spinach through fine strainer. Return to original pan; add butter mixture and toss. Makes 4 to 6 servings.

DESSERT TIP: Bake frozen apple pie as label directs. While pie is still warm, top with packaged, shredded Cheddar cheese. Cheese will melt slightly into a delicious tangy topping.

SUNDAY
*Broiled Leg of Lamb
with
Avgolemono Sauce**
Minted Peas
Salade de Turquie**
Biscuits in the Round**
Spice Cake   Coffee*

MONDAY
*Hamburgers
Curried Spinach**
French Fries
Tomato-and-Onion
Ring Salad
Apple Pie**   Coffee*

TUESDAY

Lamb Barbecue*
Hot Buttered Noodles
Cucumber-Lettuce
Salad
with
Creamy Onion Dressing
Mixed-Fruit Shortcake*
Coffee

WEDNESDAY

Oven Fried
Chicken Dinner*
Cranberry-
Gelatin Mold
Parkerhouse Rolls
Peach Vanilla Pudding*
Tea   Coffee

THURSDAY

Baked Pork Sausage*
Rice-Cheese
Continental*
Buttered Broccoli
Applesauce-Topped
Pound Cake*
Coffee   Tea

LAMB BARBECUE

2 tablespoons butter or margarine	1 cup catchup
1 medium onion, sliced	2 teaspoons Worcestershire
2 to 4 tablespoons vinegar	2 cups cut-up cooked roast lamb
1 tablespoon brown sugar	hot buttered noodles

In small saucepan in hot butter, sauté onion until lightly browned. Add vinegar, brown sugar, catchup, ½ cup water, Worcestershire; simmer, covered, 15 minutes. Add lamb; simmer until heated.

Serve over noodles. Makes 4 servings.

DESSERT TIP: Thaw package of frozen mixed fruit; spoon generous amount over sponge-cake layer. Then pile on whipped topping for a quick and easy shortcake.

———◆———

OVEN-FRIED CHICKEN DINNER

½ cup butter or margarine	1 3- to 4-pound broiler-fryer, cut up
¼ cup dry bread crumbs	8 small potatoes
¼ cup cornmeal	8 medium carrots
1½ teaspoons curry	pepper
salt	chopped parsley for garnish

About 1½ hours before serving: Preheat oven to 400°F. Place butter in 13" by 9" by 2" baking pan and set in oven to melt. In pie plate, mix bread crumbs, cornmeal, curry and 2 teaspoons salt; use to coat chicken well.

Place chicken pieces in melted butter in pan; roll potatoes and carrots in butter, and arrange them around chicken. Sprinkle vegetables with salt and pepper to taste.

Bake, uncovered, 45 minutes. Turn chicken and vegetables; bake 20 minutes more. Sprinkle potatoes with parsley. Makes 6 servings.

DESSERT TIP: Chill can of ready-to-serve vanilla pudding. At dessert time, spoon pudding into individual dessert dishes and top each with a few canned cling-peach slices, then a sprinkling of cinnamon.

———◆———

MEAT TIP: Place sausage links in shallow baking pan. Bake at 400°F. along with rice-cheese casserole, turning with tongs until evenly browned, about 20 to 30 minutes.

RICE-CHEESE CONTINENTAL

About 1 hour before serving: Preheat oven to 400°F. In saucepan over low heat, melt 2 tablespoons butter or margarine. Stir in 2 tablespoons regular flour; slowly add 2 cups milk, stirring constantly until smooth and thickened.

Stir in 3 cups cooked white rice, 1 teaspoon seasoned salt, and ¾ cup shredded natural Swiss cheese. Pour into greased 1½-quart casserole.

Combine 1 teaspoon grated Parmesan cheese and 1 teaspoon paprika and sprinkle over top of casserole. Bake 15 to 20 minutes or until golden. Makes 6 servings.

DESSERT TIP: Heat applesauce with a little nutmeg and lemon peel. Spoon onto toasted pound-cake slices. If desired, top with vanilla ice cream, or frozen whipped topping, and a few chopped nuts.

CRÈME CARAMEL

TIP-TOP TUNA CASSEROLE

About 45 minutes before serving: In medium saucepan, in ¼ cup hot butter or margarine, sauté ½ cup chopped onions until limp; add 1 cup chopped green pepper and continue cooking until tender, about 5 minutes. Stir in 2 tablespoons all-purpose flour until blended. Add one 29-ounce can tomatoes, 1 tablespoon Worcestershire, 1 teaspoon dry mustard, ½ teaspoon each salt and sugar and ¼ teaspoon pepper; simmer, covered, 10 minutes. Preheat oven to 375°F. Add two 6½- or 7-ounce cans tuna to sauce and pour into 2½-quart casserole.

Cut each biscuit from one 8-ounce package refrigerated buttermilk biscuits into sixths; arrange on casserole with points up. Brush with egg white, beaten, left from Crème Caramel (below). Bake 25 minutes, covering lightly with foil if biscuits brown too soon. Makes 6 servings.

CRÈME CARAMEL

Prepare two 4½-ounce packages egg-custard mix as labels direct but add extra egg yolk to each. (Use one egg white for Tip-Top Tuna Casserole, above.) Pour into serving bowl and refrigerate until set.

About 1 hour before serving: In small saucepan over medium heat, stir ¼ cup granulated sugar until it melts and turns into an amber syrup. Pour slowly over custard in fine stream. Makes 8 servings.

———◆———

MEXICAN LIVER

About 20 minutes before serving: In large skillet, fry 4 bacon slices; drain; break into pieces. Pour all but 2 tablespoons bacon fat from skillet; sauté 1 medium onion, minced, until tender. Combine 1 tablespoon regular all-purpose flour, 1 tablespoon chili powder; roll 1 pound beef liver, thinly sliced, in mixture. Add liver to onion; brown lightly on each side. Add bacon, one 16-ounce can tomatoes (and their liquid), one 12-ounce can whole-kernel corn, drained, 1 teaspoon salt; simmer 5 minutes or until liver is fork-tender. Makes 4 servings.

FRIDAY
Consommé in Mugs
Tip-Top
*Tuna Casserole**
Hearts-of-Palm Salad
Warmed Italian Bread
*Crème Caramel**
Coffee   Tea

SATURDAY
*Mexican Liver**
Hot Noodles
Frozen Green Beans
in Butter Sauce
Canned-Pears-and-
Cottage-Cheese Salad
Chocolate Eclairs
Tea   Milk

CORNED BEEF AND CABBAGE

1 9-pound corned-beef brisket	1 garlic clove
3 onion slices	2 green-pepper rings
4 cloves	1 stalk celery
6 peppercorns	1 carrot, pared
1 bay leaf	1 head green cabbage
½ teaspoon rosemary	Mustard Sauce (below)

5 to 6 hours before serving: Place brisket in large deep kettle; cover with water. Add onion slices, studded with cloves, peppercorns, bay leaf, rosemary, garlic, pepper rings, celery and carrot. Simmer 5 to 6 hours, or until brisket is fork-tender.

Wash cabbage; cut into quarters or sixths; trim off core, but leave enough to hold cabbage intact.

About 30 minutes before meat is done: Skim fat from top of liquid; arrange cabbage on meat; simmer, covered, 25 to 30 minutes or until cabbage is tender-crisp. Serve meat and cabbage with Mustard Sauce. Makes enough for 8 servings, with meat left for Tuesday.

MUSTARD SAUCE

2 tablespoons butter or margarine	1 tablespoon flour
dash pepper	1 egg yolk, beaten
1 teaspoon salt	¾ cup milk
1 tablespoon prepared mustard	1½ to 3 teaspoons lemon juice

In heavy saucepan, melt butter; stir in pepper, salt, mustard, flour, combined yolk and milk. Cook, stirring, 5 minutes or until smooth and thickened. Remove from heat; add lemon juice. Makes ¾ cup.

IRISH SODA BREAD

½ cup dark seedless raisins	baking powder
2 cups sifted regular all-purpose flour	½ teaspoon salt
½ cup cake flour	3 tablespoons granulated sugar
1 teaspoon baking soda	½ cup butter or margarine
1 teaspoon double-acting	1 cup buttermilk
	egg white

About 2 hours before serving: Preheat oven to 400°F. In small bowl, pour boiling water over raisins; let stand 5 minutes. Meanwhile, into large bowl, sift all-purpose flour and next 5 ingredients. Cut in butter with pastry blender or two knives, used scissor-fashion, until mixture resembles coarse crumbs.

Drain raisins; stir into flour mixture. Add buttermilk all at once; stir vigorously with fork.

Turn mixture onto lightly floured board. Knead gently 8 to 10 times. Shape into ball and place in greased 8-inch pie plate. Brush with slightly beaten egg white.

Bake 15 minutes. Lower heat to 375°F. and bake another 30 minutes or until cake tester inserted in center comes out clean.

Remove from pie plate. Cool 1 hour on rack. Cut into wedges. Makes 10 servings.

DESSERT TIP: Pour hot black coffee, sweetened, if desired, into tall stemmed glasses; spike with Irish whiskey; top with whipped cream. (Sip slowly so that cream and coffee mingle together.)

ASPARAGUS PAR EXCELLENCE

1 onion, chopped
1 green pepper, chopped
2 teaspoons salt
¼ teaspoon pepper
2 10-ounce packages frozen

asparagus spears
2 teaspoons chopped pimiento
½ teaspoon tarragon
2 teaspoons finely chopped parsley
1 hard-cooked egg, sieved

About 20 minutes before serving: In medium skillet, barely cover chopped onion and green pepper, salt and pepper with cold water; bring to boil; simmer 5 minutes.

Add frozen asparagus; cover; simmer 10 to 15 minutes, or until fork-tender; drain.

Serve, surrounded with onion-pepper mixture; sprinkle with pimiento, tarragon and parsley. Garnish with sieved egg. Makes 6 servings.

SALAD TIP: Add chopped stuffed olives and grated raw carrot to shredded cabbage; toss with bottled creamy onion dressing.

DESSERT TIP: Prepare chocolate and vanilla puddings as labels direct. Spoon alternate layers into parfait glasses; cool.

ASPARAGUS PAR EXCELLENCE

CURRIED RICE SALAD

6 cups cold cooked rice
½ cup chopped green pepper
⅓ cup chopped pimiento
2 tablespoons chopped green
   onions
½ cup salad oil

½ cup vinegar
2 tablespoons granulated sugar
2 tablespoons lemon juice
1½ teaspoons curry
1 teaspoon salt
salad greens

Several hours before serving: In large bowl, combine rice with green pepper, pimiento and green onions. In measuring cup, blend together salad oil, vinegar, sugar, lemon juice, curry and salt; toss gently with rice mixture; cover and refrigerate. To serve, arrange rice on salad greens. Makes 8 servings.

WONDERFUL WALNUT TARTS

1 10-ounce package piecrust mix
½ cup packed brown sugar
½ cup butter or margarine,
   softened
¾ cup granulated sugar
3 eggs

¼ teaspoon salt
¼ cup light corn syrup
½ cup light cream
1 cup broken walnuts
½ teaspoon vanilla extract

Make piecrust mix as package label directs; divide into two balls; thinly roll out each one on lightly floured pastry cloth; cut out 9 four-inch circles, making 18 circles in all. Snugly fit each circle into a 2½-inch muffin cup; trim top edges even; refrigerate.

Preheat oven to 425°F. In double boiler, stir together brown sugar and next 6 ingredients. Cook over hot, *not boiling,* water 5 minutes, stirring; add broken walnuts, vanilla. Pour into pastry-lined muffin cups, filling each two-thirds full. Bake at 425°F. for 10 minutes. Lower oven to 350°F; bake 15 to 20 minutes more or until pastry is cooked. Cool on racks 5 minutes; then gently lift from pans and cool thoroughly on racks. Makes 18 tarts.

MONDAY

*Spaghetti
and Meatballs*

*Asparagus
par Excellence**

Rye Bread

*Coleslaw**

*Pudding Parfait**

Coffee

TUESDAY

*Assorted Cold Meats
Platter*

*Curried Rice Salad**

Cheese Cubes   Celery

Breadsticks

*Wonderful
Walnut Tarts**

Tea

Bean-and-Bacon Bake*
Avocado-Onion Salad
Hot French Bread
Orange Pears*
Chocolate Cookies
Milk   Coffee

BEAN-AND-BACON BAKE

2 16-ounce cans pork-and-beans in tomato sauce	2 teaspoons Worcestershire
¼ cup instant minced onion	4 unpeeled orange slices, ¼-inch thick
1 teaspoon chili powder	8 Canadian-bacon slices, ¼-inch thick
1 tablespoon horseradish	
1 tablespoon prepared mustard	¼ cup packed light brown sugar

About 45 minutes before serving: Preheat oven to 350°F. In large bowl, combine pork-and-beans with onion, chili powder, horseradish, mustard and Worcestershire; turn into 2½-quart shallow casserole.

On top of bean mixture, arrange orange and Canadian-bacon slices; sprinkle with brown sugar. Bake 30 minutes or until bubbly. Makes 4 servings.

DESSERT TIP: Drain syrup from canned Bartlett pears; to it, add spoonful of orange marmalade. Heat and pour over pears.

———◆———

MEAT TIP: Cut lamb cubes from shoulder or leg. Thread on skewers. Thread mushrooms and pepper chunks on separate skewers. Brush with bottled dressing. Broil, starting lamb first, then peppers, mushrooms.

COFFEE JELLY

Lamb Shish Kebab*
Herbed Rice
Tomato Aspic
Assorted Hot Rolls
Coffee Jelly*
Coffee

1 envelope unflavored gelatin	1 cup hot coffee
⅓ cup granulated sugar	1 teaspoon lemon juice
⅛ teaspoon salt	sweetened whipped cream

In medium bowl, combine gelatin, sugar and salt. Add ½ cup cold water and the hot coffee; stir thoroughly until gelatin and sugar dissolve. Stir in lemon juice. Leave in bowl; or pour into 4 individual molds. Refrigerate until set. Top with sweetened whipped cream. Makes 4 servings.

———◆———

SHRIMP TIP: Arrange shelled, deveined raw shrimp in shallow pan. Sprinkle with minced garlic, parsley and salt. Dot with butter; broil about 7 minutes on each side.

STRAWBERRY-PINEAPPLE PIE

Garlic-Broiled
Shrimp*
Au Gratin Potatoes
Baby Carrots and Peas
Romaine Salad
Strawberry-Pineapple
Pie*
Tea   Coffee

1 package piecrust mix, or favorite pastry for 2-crust pie	¼ cup cornstarch
	2 tablespoons lemon juice
1 8¾-ounce can crushed pineapple, well drained	½ teaspoon salt
	4 cups washed, hulled strawberries, sliced
¾ cup granulated sugar	

About 4 hours before serving: Make piecrust as label directs. Roll out three-fourths of dough to fit 9-inch pie plate, with ½-inch overhang.

Preheat oven to 425°F. Roll out remaining pastry into rectangle 12 inches long; cut into ¼-inch strips.

In large bowl, mix pineapple, sugar, cornstarch, lemon juice and salt. Add strawberries; turn into pie plate. Using pastry strips, make design on top. Fold pastry overhang over top edge of pie; press flat; finish edge decoratively with tip of teaspoon.

Bake 50 minutes or until crust is golden and fruit bubbling. Remove to rack; serve warm. Makes 6 to 8 servings.

STRAWBERRY-PINEAPPLE PIE

SOUP TIP: Stir 2 tablespoons lemon juice into two 10½-ounce cans condensed beef consommé, heated with 2 soup cans water. Pour into cups; garnish each with quartered lemon slice. Makes 6 servings.

HASH-STUFFED GREEN PEPPERS

6 medium green peppers
2 15½-ounce cans corned-beef hash
1 4-ounce package shredded
   Cheddar cheese (1 cup)

¼ teaspoon pepper
1 10½-ounce can spaghetti sauce
   with mushrooms
2 teaspoons granulated sugar

Early in day: Slice stem end from each green pepper; remove seeds; cut thin slice from bottom of each. In large saucepan, stand peppers on end; cover with boiling water; simmer 5 minutes, uncovered; drain.

In medium bowl, combine corned-beef hash, half of Cheddar cheese, and pepper. Toss well; spoon into green peppers; place peppers in 8″ by 8″ by 2″ baking dish. Combine spaghetti sauce with mushrooms and sugar; pour over peppers. Cover dish with lid or foil; refrigerate.

About 1 hour before serving: Preheat oven to 375°F. Cover, bake, stuffed peppers 30 minutes; uncover; top with remaining cheese; continue baking 15 minutes, uncovered, occasionally spooning sauce over peppers. Makes 4 to 6 servings.

THREE-FRUIT SALAD

Early in day: Cut pears from one 8-ounce can into ¼-inch cubes; combine with one 8¾-ounce can pineapple tidbits, one 11-ounce can Mandarin oranges and their syrups, plus 1 cup ¼-inch unpared apple cubes, and ½ cup each seedless grapes and dark raisins; refrigerate.

Just before serving: Drain fruits well; serve on salad greens. Pass mayonnaise. Makes 8 servings.

PRALINE-TOPPED CAKE

Bake 1 package white- or yellow-cake mix as label directs but pour batter into 13″ by 9″ by 2″ cake pan. Blend ⅓ cup melted butter or margarine with ½ cup packed brown sugar, ¼ cup milk, pinch salt, ½ teaspoon vanilla extract, 1 cup flaked coconut, ½ cup chopped pecans. Remove cake from oven; spread with nut mixture. Increase oven heat to broil. Broil until golden, about 5 minutes.

SATURDAY
Lemon Consommé*
*Hash-Stuffed
Green Peppers**
Three-Fruit Salad*
Sesame Breadsticks
Praline-Topped Cake*
Milk   Coffee

SLICED BEEF À L'ORANGE

SUNDAY

*Sliced
Beef à l'Orange**

*Cold Mixed Vegetables
with French Dressing*

Warmed Cheese Bread

*Chocolate Mousse Pie**

Iced Coffee

2 garlic cloves
1½ teaspoons salt
¾ teaspoon ground cumin
½ teaspoon ground cloves

½ teaspoon ground pepper
1 4-pound top-sirloin beef roast
2 cups orange juice
2 oranges

Day before or early in day: Preheat oven to 325°F. Mash garlic with salt; add cumin, cloves and pepper; mix to paste. With sharp pointed knife, make deep cuts in top and sides of roast; into each cut, with spoon, insert some of garlic paste until all has been used up.

Place roast on rack in uncovered shallow roasting pan; insert meat thermometer into center of thickest part. Roast about 2¼ hours, or to 140°F. on thermometer. Wrap cooked roast in foil; refrigerate.

About 30 minutes before serving: Slice beef into crosswise slices, ¼-inch thick; lay, side by side, in large shallow baking dish; pour orange juice over all; refrigerate. Grate peel from 1 orange, peel a second; remove white membrane; cut oranges into crosswise slices; garnish beef with oranges and grated rind. Makes 8 servings.

CHOCOLATE-MOUSSE PIE

1 baked 9-inch pie shell
1 6-ounce package semisweet-
   chocolate pieces (1 cup)
1 egg
2 egg yolks

1 teaspoon rum
2 egg whites
1¼ cups heavy or whipping cream
½ square unsweetened chocolate,
   shaved

Early in day: Melt chocolate pieces over hot water. Remove from heat; beat in egg and egg yolks, one at a time; add rum. Beat whites until they form stiff peaks; whip 1 cup of the cream; fold egg whites, then cream, into chocolate mixture; spoon into shell; refrigerate. Whip remaining ¼ cup cream. Garnish pie with cream and chocolate. Makes 8 servings.

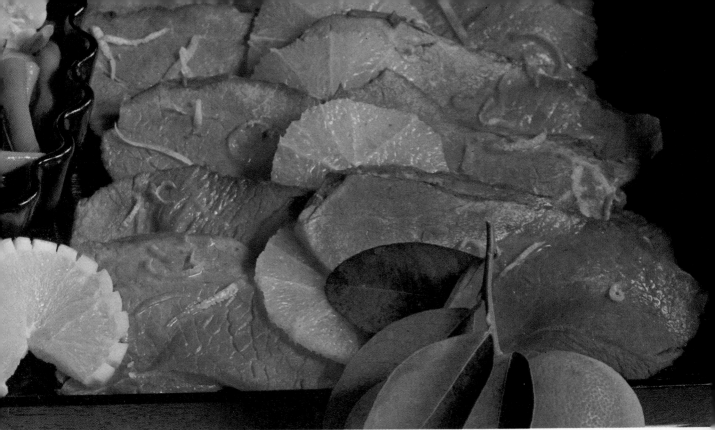

SLICED BEEF À L'ORANGE

SWEET-AND-SOUR MEAT

1 12-ounce can luncheon meat
1 tablespoon butter or margarine
1 tablespoon cornstarch
½ cup orange juice
½ cup packed light brown sugar

¼ cup vinegar
2 teaspoons soy sauce
1 small grapefruit, sectioned and
    cut into chunks
1 3-ounce can chow mein noodles

About 20 minutes before serving: Cut luncheon meat into 6 slices. In large skillet, melt butter or margarine; add meat and sauté until browned; place on warm platter.

   Meanwhile, in small saucepan, blend cornstarch with orange juice, brown sugar, vinegar and soy sauce. Cook over low heat, stirring, until bubbling hot and slightly thickened. Add grapefruit sections and heat through. Pour this sauce over meat. Serve with noodles. Makes 3 or 4 servings.

SALAD TIP: Shred Chinese (or regular) cabbage; toss with drained crushed pineapple and coleslaw dressing.

◆━━◆

OVEN RICE

About 1 hour before serving: Preheat oven to 350°F. In 1- or 1½-quart casserole, dissolve 1 beef-bouillon cube in 1¼ cups boiling water, stirring until dissolved. In medium skillet over medium heat, in 2 tablespoons butter or margarine, sauté ½ cup uncooked regular white rice 5 minutes or until golden brown, stirring constantly.

   To broth in casserole, add rice; ½ cup coarsely chopped onions; ¼ pound fresh mushrooms, sliced; ½ teaspoon salt; ¼ teaspoon pepper and ⅛ teaspoon ground thyme. Bake, covered, stirring occasionally, 40 minutes; then stir in ½ cup coarsely chopped celery and bake, uncovered 5 minutes longer. Makes 4 servings.

MONDAY
Sweet-and-Sour Meat*
Chow Mein Noodles
Chinese Cabbage Slaw*
Vanilla Ice Cream
Fortune Cookies
Tea

TUESDAY
Baked Chicken
Oven Rice*
Waxed Beans
Crusty Rolls
Applesauce
Tea

HAM-AND-CHEESE SANDWICH BAKE

WEDNESDAY

*Ham-and-Cheese
Sandwich Bake**

Big Green Salad

*Blueberry Dessert**

Lemon Cookies

Tea   Milk

2 cups packaged buttermilk-biscuit mix	⅔ cup mayonnaise
3 tablespoons salad oil	1 teaspoon prepared mustard
½ cup milk	1 12-ounce can chopped ham
	4 process American cheese slices

About 45 minutes before serving: Preheat oven to 450°F. With fork, combine biscuit mix, salad oil and milk to make soft dough; beat vigorously until stiff. Press dough into well-greased 13″ by 9″ by 2″ baking dish.

Combine mayonnaise with prepared mustard; spread evenly over dough in baking dish.

Cut ham into 6 crosswise slices, then cut each slice into 2 triangles; arrange on mayonnaise mixture in 2 rows. Bake 15 minutes.

Meanwhile, cut each cheese slice into 3 strips; arrange over ham. Bake a few minutes longer or until cheese is bubbling. Remove from oven; let stand 5 minutes. Cut into rectangles and serve. Makes 12 open-face sandwiches.

DESSERT TIP: Top individual dishes of fresh blueberries with dollop of sour cream; sprinkle with brown sugar.

FRANKFURTERS GARNI

THURSDAY

*Frankfurters Garni**

Oven-Baked Beans

*Sauerkraut Salad**

*Strawberry Cream Cake**

Coffee

1 1-pound package frankfurters	2 tablespoons sherry
2 tablespoons butter or margarine	¼ teaspoon thyme leaves
¾ pound mushrooms	2 bay leaves
1 10¾-ounce can beef gravy	1 15½-ounce can small onions, drained
2 tablespoons instant minced onion	
1 tablespoon granulated sugar	

About 25 minutes before serving: Cut each frankfurter diagonally into 4 pieces. In large skillet over medium heat, in butter or margarine, cook mushrooms until just tender. (If mushrooms are large, cut in half.) Add gravy, onion, sugar, sherry, thyme and bay leaves. Stir in frankfurters and canned onions and heat through. Makes 4 servings.

SALAD TIP: Drain canned sauerkraut; toss with dill seeds; chill. (If you prefer milder flavor, rinse sauerkraut first in cold water; drain.) Or toss kraut with sliced celery, chopped sweet onion or green pepper, diced pimiento or apple cubes.

STRAWBERRY CREAM CAKE

1 envelope unflavored gelatin	1 cup heavy or whipping cream, whipped
2 tablespoons confectioners' sugar	
½ teaspoon almond extract	2 7-inch bakers' spongecake layers
1 10-ounce package frozen sliced strawberries, thawed	1 cup flaked coconut

Several hours ahead: In double-boiler top, sprinkle gelatin over ½ cup cold water to soften; heat over hot water until dissolved; stir in sugar, extract, berries. Refrigerate until mixture mounds when dropped from spoon. Fold in whipped cream; refrigerate until stiff enough to spread. (Do not allow gelatin-cream mixture to become too stiff.)

Fill and frost spongecake layers; sprinkle with coconut. Refrigerate until served. Makes 8 servings.

CURRIED TUNA CASSEROLE

1 10½-ounce can condensed
   cream-of-celery soup
1 cup milk
1 teaspoon curry
½ teaspoon dry mustard
4 hard-cooked eggs, sliced
2 cups cooked rice

2 6½- or 7-ounce cans tuna,
   drained
1 small onion, chopped
¼ cup bread crumbs
1 tablespoon butter or margarine,
   melted
1 tablespoon chopped parsley

About 1 hour before serving: Preheat oven to 350°F. In large bowl, dilute soup with milk; stir in curry and mustard. Reserve 5 egg slices for garnish; stir remaining egg slices, rice, tuna and onion into soup mixture. Spoon into 5 greased individual casseroles.

Mix bread crumbs, melted butter and parsley; sprinkle on top. Bake 30 to 40 minutes. Garnish with egg slices. Makes 5 servings.

DESSERT TIP: Add few drops of mint extract to jar of marshmallow cream. Spoon over brownie squares.

FRIDAY

*Curried Tuna
Casserole**

Peas and Pearl Onions

Avocado Salad

*Snow-Capped Brownies**

Tea   Milk

BEEF BALLS IN ZESTY SAUCE

1½ pounds ground beef chuck
1 cup fresh whole-wheat bread
   crumbs
¼ cup evaporated milk, undiluted
2 teaspoons Worcestershire
1 teaspoon ground sage
salt
2 tablespoons shortening

2 medium onions, sliced
1 cup applesauce
1 tablespoon horseradish
½ cup canned tomato sauce
⅛ teaspoon oregano
⅛ teaspoon pepper
1 tablespoon lemon juice

About 45 minutes before serving: Combine chuck, crumbs, evaporated milk, Worcestershire, sage and 1½ teaspoons salt; mix well: shape into 1½-inch balls.

In large skillet, in hot shortening, brown beef balls on all sides; pile to one side of skillet. In same skillet, sauté onions until golden. Add applesauce, horseradish, tomato sauce, oregano, 1 teaspoon salt, pepper and lemon juice; heat thoroughly. Makes 6 servings.

VEGETABLE TIP: Toss drained canned yams with pineapple preserves and butter; heat and add dash salt.

SATURDAY

*Beef Balls
in Zesty Sauce**

*Green Beans
in Butter Sauce*

*Pineapple-Preserved
Yams**

Coleslaw

*Fruit-Mint
Sherbet Ring**

Tea   Coffee

FRUIT-MINT SHERBET RING

3 pints lemon sherbet
⅓ cup green crème de menthe
2 pints strawberries, blueberries,
   raspberries or sliced

peaches
shredded fresh or canned flaked
   coconut

Early in day: In large bowl, with electric mixer at medium speed, quickly combine lemon sherbet and crème de menthe. Pack into 5½-cup ring mold; freeze.

To serve: Unmold sherbet by running small spatula around outer and inner edges of ring mold. Invert mold on chilled serving plate; place cloth, wrung out in hot water, on top of it for minute or two; then lift off mold. (If sherbet does not come out, repeat hot-cloth treatment.) Fill center of sherbet ring with fruits; sprinkle lightly with coconut. Makes 10 servings.

PARMESAN VEAL ROAST

2 cups packaged precooked rice	2 eggs, beaten
butter or margarine	1 5-pound boned rump of veal
1 cup drained, chopped cooked spinach	6 to 8 boiled ham slices, 1/8-inch thick
1/2 cup grated Parmesan cheese	bacon slices

About 4 hours before serving: Cook rice as label directs but increase butter to 3 tablespoons. Stir in spinach, cheese and eggs.

Preheat oven to 350°F. Slit veal rump lengthwise almost all the way through. Open up halves flat; cover with slightly overlapping ham slices. Spread with rice mixture; put veal back together; tie.

Lay in open roasting pan; top with bacon slices placed side by side. Roast 2½ hours or to 180°F. on meat thermometer, basting several times with the drippings; lightly cover with foil if needed. If desired, make gravy from drippings. Makes 8 to 10 servings.

SAUCE TIP: A quick sauce for broccoli can be made by heating a can of condensed Cheddar-cheese soup with 1/4 to 1/2 cup milk.

EASY CRÈME BRÛLÉE

1 3¼-ounce package vanilla-pudding-and-pie-filling mix	1/4 cup toasted slivered almonds
1½ cups milk	orange sections
1½ cups heavy or whipping cream	banana chunks dipped in lemon juice
1/2 cup packed light brown sugar	grapes for garnish

Day before: Make pudding as label directs but substitute 1½ cups each of milk and cream for milk called for on label. Pour into 1½-quart shallow baking dish; lay foil on surface of pudding; refrigerate.

1 to 2 hours before serving: Preheat broiler if manufacturer directs. Remove foil from pudding; sift brown sugar over top; sprinkle almonds in ring 1 inch in from edge. Broil *just* until sugar melts; refrigerate. Serve on platter with fruits. Makes 8 servings.

———◆———

BEEF, HUNGARIAN STYLE

2 pounds beef round, 1/4-inch thick	1 green pepper, cut into strips
1 tablespoon butter or margarine	3 medium tomatoes, cut into sixths
1 teaspoon bottled sauce for gravy	1 envelope instant beef-bouillon mix
2 medium onions, sliced	

About 1½ hours before serving: Cut steak into 6 serving-size pieces. In Dutch oven, sauté steaks in butter until well browned. Add bottled sauce for gravy, onions, green pepper, tomatoes, bouillon mix and 1 cup water.

Simmer, covered, about 1 hour or until steaks are fork-tender. Serve with Garlic-Buttered Noodles. (Pile noodles on heated platter; spoon steaks and sauce into center.) Makes 6 servings.

NOODLE TIP: Cook enough medium noodles to make 6 servings. Toss with butter that has been seasoned with garlic salt.

CHEESY BUTTERED SQUASH

In skillet, in 1/4 cup butter, cook 4 cups thinly sliced summer squash; 1 onion, sliced; 1 teaspoon salt; dash pepper; 1/4 cup water, about 12 minutes. Sprinkle with 1/2 cup grated Cheddar cheese. Makes 6 servings.

MINT PATTICAKE

MINT PATTICAKE

At least 2 hours before serving: Preheat oven to 350°F. In large bowl of electric mixer, combine 1 package yellow- or devil's-food-cake mix (2-layer size); one 2-ounce package whipped-topping mix; 4 unbeaten eggs; 1 cup water; 1 teaspoon mint extract. Blend until moistened, then beat at medium speed for 4 minutes. Meanwhile, grease and flour two 9-inch layer pans; divide batter equally between them; bake 30 minutes, or until cake tester inserted in center comes out clean. Cool in pans 15 minutes; then loosen sides and remove layers to rack; finish cooling. Freeze one layer for use later (page 33). Cut the other one in half horizontally. On top of each half, arrange a layer of 12 chocolate-peppermint patties, 1½ inches in diameter. Place on cookie sheet; return to oven for 5 to 8 minutes or until patties are partially melted. Stack layers; serve hot. Makes 6 to 8 servings.

───◆─◆───

MEAT TIP: In salted water with bay leaf and sprig of parsley, simmer 4-pound beef tongue, covered, 3 to 4 hours or until tender. Cool slightly; skin and slice. Save some for tongue salad, page 31.

TUESDAY
Skillet-Fried Chicken
Succotash
Pickled Beets
*Mint Patticake**
Coffee

WEDNESDAY
*Boiled Tongue**
Mashed Potatoes
Lemon-Herbed Broccoli
*Spicy Gingerbread**
Coffee

SPICY GINGERBREAD

2½ cups sifted regular all-purpose flour	¾ teaspoon salt
1½ teaspoons baking soda	½ cup shortening
½ teaspoon ground cloves	½ cup granulated sugar
1 teaspoon cinnamon	1 medium egg, unbeaten
1 teaspoon ginger	1 cup molasses
	1 cup hot water

Preheat oven to 350°F. Grease, then line with waxed paper, bottom of 9″ by 9″ by 2″ pan. Sift flour, soda, cloves, cinnamon, ginger, salt.

In large bowl, with electric mixer at medium speed, mix shortening with sugar, then with egg until *very light and fluffy*—about 4 minutes altogether; beat in molasses. At low speed, beat in alternately, *just until smooth,* flour mixture in fourths and hot water in thirds. Turn into pan. Bake 50 to 55 minutes or until cake tester inserted in center of cake comes out clean.

To cool cake, set pan on rack 10 to 15 minutes. Loosen cake with spatula; place another rack on top. Invert and lift off pan. Finish cooling. Cut into 9 squares.

───◆─◆───

MAN-STYLE BAKED EGGS

3 tablespoons butter or margarine	2 tablespoons fine dried bread crumbs
2 medium onions, thinly sliced	4 packaged process sharp Cheddar-cheese slices
salt and pepper	
4 eggs	

THURSDAY
*Man-Style Baked Eggs**
Broiled Bacon
*Honey-Flavored English Muffins**
Blueberry Turnovers
Milk   Coffee

Preheat oven to 350°F. In skillet, in butter, cook onions about 5 minutes or until just tender. Arrange in 8-inch pie plate; sprinkle with salt and pepper.

Carefully break eggs over onions; sprinkle lightly with salt and pepper, then with crumbs. Top with cheese slices. Bake, uncovered, 10 minutes or until eggs are of desired firmness. Makes 4 servings.

BREAD TIP: Split English muffins with tines of fork. Toast under broiler; butter; drizzle with honey; broil 1 or 2 minutes.

DEVILED-TONGUE SALAD

2 envelopes unflavored gelatin	1 tablespoon prepared mustard
1¼ cups boiling water	¼ cup chopped dill pickle
¼ cup mayonnaise	2 cups chopped, cooked tongue
2 tablespoons horseradish	2 hard-cooked eggs, chopped
1 teaspoon salt	salad greens
¼ teaspoon pepper	

Early in day: Sprinkle gelatin on 1 cup cold water to soften; add boiling water; stir until dissolved; cool. Beat in mayonnaise, horseradish, salt, pepper, mustard. Refrigerate until slightly thickened. Fold in pickle, tongue, eggs. Pour into 9″ by 5″ by 3″ loaf pan. Refrigerate until firm. Unmold; slice. Serve on greens. Makes 8 servings.

PARMESAN BISCUITS

About 20 minutes before serving: Preheat oven to 425°F. Melt 3 tablespoons butter or margarine. On waxed paper, combine 1½ tablespoons grated Parmesan cheese with 1 tablespoon chopped parsley. Slightly flatten each biscuit from one 8-ounce package refrigerated biscuits; brush generously with melted butter. Sprinkle with cheese mixture; fold; press edges together.

Place in greased 9-inch pie plate. Brush with melted butter. Bake 10 to 12 minutes or until golden; serve warm. Makes 10 biscuits.

STRAWBERRY SWIRL

Just before serving: Pour three 10-ounce packages frozen sliced strawberries, thawed, into 1½-quart pitcher; add 1 quart buttermilk or yogurt.

Stir until completely blended; pour into glasses. Serve with spoons. Makes 8 to 10 servings.

SHRIMP-POTATO SALAD

1 1-pound package frozen shelled, deveined shrimp	1 teaspoon salt
	4 pounds medium potatoes, cooked, peeled, cubed
3 tablespoons bottled Italian dressing	1 cup celery slices, cut diagonally
mayonnaise	5 hard-cooked eggs, sliced
¼ cup prepared mustard	pitted ripe olives
2 tablespoons lemon juice	2 tablespoons chili sauce
1 tablespoon instant minced onion	few bottled capers for garnish
¼ teaspoon seasoned pepper	

Early in day: Cook shrimp as label directs. Cool; toss with Italian dressing; refrigerate.

Combine 1 cup mayonnaise, mustard, lemon juice, onion, pepper, salt. With fork, toss dressing with potatoes and celery; refrigerate for at least 1 hour.

At serving time: In salad bowl, toss shrimp with potato mixture. Arrange egg slices and olives around salad. Mix ¼ cup mayonnaise with chili sauce; spoon over eggs. Top with capers. Makes 8 servings.

DESSERT TIP: In double boiler, over hot, *not boiling*, water, melt 20 chocolate-covered peppermints with 2 tablespoons butter or margarine. Thin with light cream. Serve on white-cake slices. Makes 6 servings.

FRIDAY
*Deviled-Tongue Salad**
*Parmesan Biscuits**
*Strawberry Swirl**
Tea   Coffee

SATURDAY
*Shrimp-Potato Salad**
Crusty French Bread
White Cake
*Chocolate-Peppermint Sauce**
Iced Tea

RICOTTA CONDITA

CHEESY POTATOES

4 medium potatoes	1 cup cubed, packaged process
½ cup milk	cheese
1 teaspoon salt	1 tablespoon butter or margarine
¼ teaspoon pepper	1 small onion, coarsely chopped

About 1 hour and 15 minutes before serving: Preheat oven to 350°F. Pare potatoes and cut into large chunks; cover with water; set aside. Put milk and rest of ingredients in electric-blender container.* Cover and blend at medium speed until smooth. Drain potatoes; add half at a time, blending at high speed only until potatoes are grated. Do not overblend. Pour into greased 9-inch pie plate; bake 1 hour. Makes 8 servings.
* Or grate potatoes, cheese and onion; mix all ingredients thoroughly.

BAVARIAN CREAM WITH PEACHES

1 envelope unflavored gelatin	1 cup heavy or whipping cream,
pinch salt	whipped
6 tablespoons granulated sugar	1 teaspoon vanilla extract or
2 eggs, separated	½ teaspoon almond extract
1¼ cups milk	or rum to taste

Early in day: In double-boiler top, combine gelatin, salt, 2 tablespoons sugar; stir in egg yolks; slowly stir in milk. Cook over boiling water, stirring, until mixture coats spoon; remove at once; refrigerate until slightly thicker than unbeaten egg whites. Beat egg whites until moist peaks form; gradually add ¼ cup sugar; beat until stiff. Fold into yolk mixture along with whipped cream, vanilla. Turn into 8 custard cups; refrigerate. Nice topped with peaches.

————◆————

CHICKEN AND CHIVES

1 pint sour cream	2 tablespoons butter, melted
2 tablespoons snipped chives	1 2½- or 3-pound broiler-fryer,
½ teaspoon tarragon	cut up
½ teaspoon salt	salt
2 tablespoons white vinegar	flour
2 teaspoons sugar	paprika

About 1 hour before serving: Preheat oven to 400°F. Combine first 6 ingredients; reserve ½ cup. Pour butter into 13″ by 9″ by 2″ baking dish. Sprinkle chicken with salt; coat with flour; dip into sour-cream mixture, coating each piece well. Arrange in baking dish; sprinkle with paprika. Bake 45 minutes or until fork-tender. Lay on heated platter; top with reserved sour-cream mixture. Makes 4 servings.

SALAD TIP: Chopped hard-cooked eggs and red pimiento strips tossed with bite-sized pieces of romaine turn an ordinary salad into a bouquet.

RICOTTA CONDITA

About 1 hour before serving: In small bowl, with electric mixer at high speed, beat one 15-ounce container ricotta cheese smooth. Then beat in 1 to 3 teaspoons milk to make cheese creamy but still hold its shape. Mix 2 tablespoons sugar and 1 teaspoon instant coffee.

In each of four 4-ounce parfait glasses, place spoonful of ricotta; sprinkle with a little coffee mixture; repeat until glass is full, ending with ricotta. Refrigerate. Makes 4 servings.

SUNDAY
Ham Steak
Spiced Crabapples
Cheesy Potatoes*
Tossed Green Salad
with Herb Dressing
Bavarian Cream
with Peaches*
Milk   Coffee

MONDAY
Chilled
Cran-Apple Juice
Chicken and Chives*
Frozen Squash
Bouquet Salad*
Ricotta Condita*
Tea   Coffee

FRANKFURTER GOULASH

¼ cup butter or margarine
2 cups chopped onions
1 tablespoon paprika
1 1-pound package frankfurters, quartered crosswise
5 or 6 medium potatoes, pared,

cut into 1-inch chunks
1 teaspoon salt
1 teaspoon caraway seed
1 8¼-ounce can peeled whole tomatoes, chopped

About 1 hour before serving: In skillet, in hot butter, sauté onions until golden; stir in paprika and frankfurters.

Sauté 5 minutes; stir in potatoes, salt, caraway seed and tomatoes. Simmer, covered, stirring occasionally, 30 minutes or until potatoes are tender, adding a little water if needed. Makes 4 servings.

DESSERT TIP: Make sundaes with vanilla or chocolate ice cream; top with malted-milk powder or chocolate sprinkles.

CHINESE EGGS FOO YOUNG

SAUCE
2 teaspoons soy sauce
1 teaspoon cornstarch
1 teaspoon sugar

1 teaspoon vinegar
¾ teaspoon salt

EGG MIXTURE:
1 cup drained canned bean sprouts
⅔ cup thinly sliced onions
1 cup cut-up cooked chicken, ham or shrimp

6 eggs
2 tablespoons bacon fat or salad oil
chow mein noodles

About 50 minutes before serving: In saucepan, combine soy sauce, cornstarch, sugar, vinegar, salt; stir in ½ cup cold water; cook over low heat until thickened; set aside.

Combine bean sprouts, onions and chicken. With fork, beat eggs; add bean-sprout mixture. In small skillet, in hot fat, fry about ¼ cup egg mixture at a time, like pancakes, turning once. Fold over; keep hot until all are cooked. Arrange on hot platter; cover with heated sauce. Serve with hot chow-mein noodles. Makes 4 servings.

SOFT-SHELL CRABS

Sprinkle 8 cleaned soft-shell crabs with salt, pepper. In skillet, in ½ cup butter or margarine, sauté crabs, a few at a time, 3 minutes on each side or until just golden. Keep warm.

To butter left in skillet, add 1 tablespoon chopped parsley, 1 teaspoon lemon juice and dash of Worcestershire. Pour over crabs. Serve on toast slices with tartar sauce. Makes 4 servings.

VEGETABLE TIP: Sauté sliced zucchini and onions in some olive oil; cook until tender in tomato juice seasoned with salt and basil.

MINT-CREAM LAYER CAKE

Thaw cake layer left from Mint Patticake (page 30), or use fresh layer; cut in half horizontally. In chilled bowl, with chilled beater blades, whip 1 cup heavy or whipping cream; use to fill and frost cake. Refrigerate until serving time. Makes 6 to 8 servings.

TUESDAY
Frankfurter Goulash*
Green-Bean Salad
Hot Garlic Bread
Dusty Sundaes*
Shortbread Cookies
Milk   Coffee

WEDNESDAY
Hot Chicken Broth
*Chinese
Eggs Foo Young**
Hot Chow Mein Noodles
*Pineapple-Kumquat
Compote*
Almond Cakes
Tea

THURSDAY
Hot Tomato Soup
Soft-Shell Crabs*
*Frozen Crinkle-Cut
French Fries*
Sautéed Zucchini*
*Mint-Cream
Layer Cake**
Coffee

PORK-CHOP DINNER

6 loin or shoulder pork chops, about 1-inch thick
paprika
seasoned pepper
1 tablespoon flour
1/8 teaspoon ground cloves
1 envelope from 2¾-ounce package onion-soup mix
1 medium head Chinese cabbage
1/2 teaspoon salt
1/4 cup butter or margarine
1 20-ounce can chick peas, drained

About 1¼ hours before serving: Trim chops of excess fat. In large skillet, over low heat, brown chops 3 to 5 minutes on one side; sprinkle tops with 1 teaspoon paprika and 1/8 teaspoon seasoned pepper. Turn chops; brown on other side 3 to 5 minutes; sprinkle with 1 teaspoon paprika and 1/8 teaspoon seasoned pepper.

Remove chops from skillet. If necessary, add 1 tablespoon shortening. Stir in flour, cloves and onion-soup mix. Gradually stir in 2¼ cups water; bring to boil. Add pork chops; simmer, covered, 35 to 40 minutes or until chops are fork-tender.

About 15 minutes before chops are done: Slice Chinese cabbage into rounds about 1½-inches thick. Place in second large skillet; add about 1/2 cup water; sprinkle with salt. Cook, covered, 5 to 10 minutes or until tender-crisp; drain; add butter.

When pork is done, add chick peas; heat.

Arrange pork chops on platter; pour over gravy and peas. Surround with border of cabbage. Makes 6 servings.

SAVORY GARLIC BREAD

Preheat oven to 375°F. Slash yard-long or junior-size loaf of French bread into thin, thick or diagonal slices, *almost* through to bottom crust. Cream 1/2 cup butter or margarine with bit of minced or mashed garlic, or with garlic salt; add chopped parsley; use to spread cut surfaces of bread. Sprinkle with oregano, then with grated Parmesan cheese. Wrap loaf in aluminum foil, leaving foil partially open at top. Bake 15 to 20 minutes.

BUBBLY PEARS

1 29-ounce can pear halves, drained
1 tablespoon lemon juice
2 tablespoons dark brown sugar
dash ground nutmeg
2 tablespoons butter or margarine
vanilla ice cream

Preheat broiler if manufacturer directs. Place pear halves in 9″ by 9″ by 2″ baking pan. Sprinkle with lemon juice, brown sugar and nutmeg. Dot pears with butter. Broil until bubbly; divide pears among dessert dishes; top each serving with vanilla ice cream. Makes 6 servings.

———◆———

ANCHOVY-CELERY DIP

2 garlic cloves
1 2-ounce can flat anchovy fillets
2 teaspoons vinegar
celery sticks
radishes, cut in half
green onions, split lengthwise

Mince garlic. Drain oil from anchovy fillets, reserving 2 teaspoons. Mash anchovies with garlic until smooth. Stir in vinegar, then reserved oil.

Spoon into small bowl; surround with raw vegetables. Makes 4 servings.

PORK-CHOP DINNER

SKILLET CHERRY TOMATOES

1 tablespoon butter or margarine   removed
½ teaspoon basil   1 teaspoon sugar
2 small onions, thinly sliced   1 teaspoon salt
3 cups cherry tomatoes, stems

About 10 minutes before serving: In medium skillet, in hot butter and basil, sauté onions until golden.

Add tomatoes; sprinkle with sugar and salt. Sauté, shaking skillet to prevent skins from breaking, until tomatoes are warmed through, about 5 minutes. Makes 4 to 6 servings.

CHEESE-NUT MUFFINS

About 50 minutes before serving: Preheat oven to 350°F. In small bowl, stir one 3-ounce package cream cheese, softened, with 2 tablespoons milk until smooth. Prepare one 17-ounce package nutbread mix as label directs but spoon 2 tablespoons of batter into each of 14 greased and floured 2½-inch muffin-pan cups.

Add 1 rounded teaspoonful cream-cheese mixture to each cup; top with 1 tablespoon batter. Bake 40 minutes or until cake tester inserted in center comes out clean. Cool in muffin pans on rack 10 minutes. Run knife around edge of each muffin. Remove from pans. Serve warm. Makes 14 muffins.

DESSERT TIP: Section grapefruit halves, removing center and membrane. Drizzle with honey; sprinkle with cinnamon. Slide under broiler until bubbling. To garnish, sprinkle each grapefruit half with chopped red maraschino cherries.

SATURDAY
Anchovy-Celery Dip*
Roast Beef
Frozen Corn Niblets
Skillet
Cherry Tomatoes*
Watercress Salad
Cheese-Nut Muffins*
Grapefruit Halves*
Tea   Milk

APPETIZER TIP: Fill juice glasses ⅔ full with pineapple juice; add rounded tablespoon of lime sherbet to each; stir slightly.

POULET BLANC

About 3 hours before serving: In small bowl, mix 4 teaspoons salt and 2 tablespoons sherry; rub into two 3-pound broiler-fryers, halved. Refrigerate 2 hours.

In covered Dutch oven, bring 3 cups cold water to boil. Add chicken, 2 tablespoons sherry, 1 teaspoon salt, ⅛ teaspoon ginger. Bring to boil again; simmer 35 minutes or until chicken is tender. Arrange chicken on heated platter; keep warm.

Strain broth through fine sieve; measure 2 cups. In large skillet, bring it to boil; add 1 pound zucchini, pared and slivered; cook until just tender.

Blend 2 tablespoons cornstarch with ¼ cup cold water until smooth. Stir into zucchini until slightly thickened. Stir in ¼ cup milk until well blended. Spoon mixture on and around chicken; garnish with ¼ cup finely diced cooked ham. Serve immediately. Makes 4 to 6 servings.

VEGETABLE TIP: Cook enough potatoes to provide leftovers for tomorrow's Beef-and-Potato Cakes.

————◆————

BEEF-AND-POTATO CAKES

2½ cups ground, leftover cooked beef	1 teaspoon bottled thick meat sauce
1½ cups cold seasoned mashed potatoes	2 teaspoons minced onion flour
½ teaspoon salt	2 tablespoons salad oil
dash pepper	

Mix together all ingredients except flour and salad oil. Shape into 6 patties or cakes. Roll very lightly in flour; sauté in hot oil until brown on all sides. Makes 4 to 6 servings.

DESSERT TIP: Fold ¼ cup miniature marshmallows into butterscotch pudding; serve with cream.

————◆————

WESTERN SALMON LOAF WITH LEMON SAUCE

1 16-ounce can salmon	salt
¾ cup fresh bread crumbs	⅛ teaspoon pepper
1 egg, slightly beaten	butter or margarine, melted
¾ cup milk	lemon juice
2 tablespoons minced onions	Lemon Sauce (below)

About 1 hour before serving: Preheat oven to 350°F. To drained and flaked salmon, add bread crumbs, egg, milk, onion, ½ teaspoon salt, pepper, 2 tablespoons butter and 3 tablespoons lemon juice; toss with fork. Turn into greased 9″ by 5″ by 3″ loaf pan. Bake 40 to 55 minutes or until done. Serve with Lemon Sauce. Makes 4 servings.

Lemon Sauce: Combine ¼ cup lemon juice; ¼ cup butter, melted; and ⅛ teaspoon salt.

DESSERT TIP: Chill diced oranges, snipped dates, sliced bananas; spoon into dessert glasses. Top each with raspberry sherbet.

SUNDAY
*Lime-Pineapple Shrub**
*Poulet Blanc**
*Mashed Potatoes**
*French Endive
with French Dressing*
Herbed Toast Sticks
Chocolate Cake
Coffee

MONDAY
*Beef-and-Potato
Cakes**
*Hot Spiced
Peach Halves*
Peas   Romaine Salad
*Butterscotch-Marshmallow
Pudding**
Milk   Tea

TUESDAY
*Western Salmon Loaf
with Lemon Sauce**
Succotash
Spiced Beets
Relish Tray   Rolls
*Fruit Cup**
Coffee

WEDNESDAY

Antipasto*

All-American Cheese Lasagna*

Hot Italian Bread

Green Salad

Fruit Tray

Coffee

ALL-AMERICAN CHEESE LASAGNA

1 tablespoon salad oil	¾ teaspoon oregano
⅓ cup minced onion	½ teaspoon basil
3 8-ounce cans tomato sauce	1 16-ounce package lasagna noodles
1 6-ounce can tomato paste	2 8-ounce packages sliced process
2 3-ounce cans mushroom slices, drained	Cheddar cheese
1½ teaspoons salt	1 16-ounce container cottage cheese

About 2 hours before serving: In large saucepan over medium heat, in hot oil, cook onion 5 minutes or until tender. Stir in tomato sauce, tomato paste, mushrooms (reserve a few for garnish), salt, oregano, basil and 1 cup water. Simmer 15 minutes, stirring occasionally.

Cook noodles as label directs; drain. Preheat oven to 375°F. Cut all but 4 cheese slices into halves. Into greased 13″ by 9″ by 2″ baking dish, spoon thin layer of sauce. Arrange 4 lasagna noodles in layer over sauce. Spoon ¼ of cottage cheese over noodles; layer 6 cheese slices on top. Repeat layers 3 times, spooning remaining sauce on top.

Cover; bake 40 to 45 minutes. Cut each remaining cheese slice into 4 strips; arrange on top of sauce in diagonal rows. Garnish with reserved mushrooms. Bake, uncovered, 5 minutes, to melt cheese. Let stand 10 minutes. Makes 8 servings.

———◆———

THURSDAY

Jellied Madrilene

Sausage and Curry*

Mashed Potatoes

Carrots and Peas

Spinach Salad

Pineapple-Cream Cake*

Iced Tea   Coffee

SAUSAGE AND CURRY

1 8-ounce package brown-and-serve sausages	cream-of-celery soup
	½ teaspoon curry
1 10½-ounce can condensed	1 medium apple, pared, sliced

About 20 minutes before serving: In skillet, sauté brown-and-serve sausages until lightly browned; add undiluted celery soup, curry, apple slices.

Over low heat cook until apples are tender, about 10 minutes. Makes 4 servings.

DESSERT TIP: Prepare one package vanilla-pudding-and-pie-filling mix as label directs but use 1½ cups milk; chill. Fold in ½ cup drained canned crushed pineapple; use to fill 9-inch white or yellow layer cake.

———◆———

FRIDAY

Rock-Lobster Rice*

Italian Green Beans

Tossed Salad

Raspberry-Sauced Bananas*

Coffee   Milk

ROCK-LOBSTER RICE

8 5-ounce frozen rock-lobster tails	dash pepper
2 cups cooked rice	2 dashes aromatic bitters
¼ cup butter or margarine	¼ cup sherry
2 tablespoons flour	paprika
1 cup light cream	lime wedges
¾ teaspoon salt	

Boil lobster tails as label directs. Remove meat from shells; reserve shells. Cut meat into 1½-inch chunks. Preheat broiler if manufacturer directs.
Line shells with thin layer of rice.
In small saucepan over medium heat, melt butter; stir in flour, cream, salt, pepper, bitters. Cook, stirring, until thickened; stir in sherry.

RIPPLED CHEESECAKE

Combine sauce, rest of rice and lobster; toss lightly. Pile in shells. Broil 4 minutes or until nicely browned. Sprinkle with paprika; garnish with lime wedges. Makes 4 servings.

DESSERT TIP: Thaw 1 package frozen raspberries; while still icy cold, add few drops lemon juice. Pour over sliced bananas in sherbet glasses.

———◆———

SALAD TIP: Marinate drained cooked mixed vegetables in bottled Italian salad dressing; refrigerate until served.

RIPPLED CHEESECAKE

regular all-purpose flour
granulated sugar
¼ teaspoon salt
¼ cup butter or margarine
3 envelopes (3 ounces) no-melt
  unsweetened chocolate

3 8-ounce packages cream cheese,
  softened
2 teaspoons vanilla extract
6 eggs
1 cup sour cream

Day before: Preheat oven to 400°F. Combine ¾ cup flour, 2 tablespoons sugar, salt. With pastry blender, cut in butter until mixture resembles coarse crumbs; stir in 1 envelope chocolate; press over bottom of 9-inch spring-form pan; bake 10 minutes. Remove from oven; turn oven heat up to 500°F.

Meanwhile, in large bowl, with electric mixer at low speed, blend cream cheese with 1 cup sugar until smooth; blend in ¼ cup flour and vanilla. Add eggs one at a time, beating well after each addition; beat in sour cream.

In small bowl, combine 1½ cups of cheese mixture with rest of chocolate. Pour half of plain cheese mixture over baked crust in pan. Drizzle half of chocolate mixture over top; cover with remaining plain mixture, then drizzle on rest of chocolate mixture. With spatula, cut through batter to marbleize.

Bake 12 minutes; lower oven heat to 200°F.; bake 1 hour. Cool away from drafts 2 to 3 hours; refrigerate at least 8 hours. Remove side of pan. With two spatulas, gently lift cake from bottom of pan to cake plate. To cut, use sharp knife which has been run under hot water. This is a rich cake. Makes 12 servings.

SATURDAY
Fried Liver and Onions
Hashed Brown Potatoes
Marinated
*Mixed Vegetables**
*Rippled Cheesecake**
Tea   Coffee

butter or margarine
1/3 pound mushrooms, sliced
salt
2 green onions
1/2 pound chicken livers
1/4 teaspoon ginger

1/8 teaspoon pepper
1 5-pound canned ham
1 package (2-crust) piecrust mix
1 egg yolk, slightly beaten
parsley sprigs for garnish

Day before or early in day: In medium skillet, in 2 tablespoons hot butter, sauté mushrooms with 1/4 teaspoon salt until tender; set aside.

In same skillet, in 2 tablespoons hot butter, sauté green onions until tender. Add livers, 1/4 teaspoon salt, ginger and pepper; sauté until livers are tender. Drain off fat; discard onions.

In covered electric-blender container, blend livers and mushrooms until almost smooth. (Or in medium bowl, with fork, mash smooth or put through food grinder.)

Slice ham horizontally in half. (Wrap; refrigerate half for Tuesday's meal, plus sandwiches.) Remove any gelatin from remaining half; with spoon, spread liver pâté evenly on top of ham.

Preheat oven to 425°F. Prepare piecrust mix as label directs. Roll it into 18" by 13" oval.

Place ham, *pâté-side down,* in center of oval. Lift edges of pastry to cover top of ham; make an overlapping seam down middle, trimming excess pastry. (Reserve leftover pastry.) Moisten seam edges with water; press down with fork; lightly sprinkle with flour. Line jelly-roll pan with foil; grease. Place ham, seam side down, in pan.

Brush pastry with egg yolk. Cut reserved pastry into petal shapes; arrange on top. Brush with remaining yolk. Bake 1 hour; during baking, cover loosely with foil if crust browns too quickly.

Cool pan on rack 10 minutes; blot any drippings in pan with paper towels. With pancake turner, carefully place ham on serving platter; refrigerate to chill. Garnish with parsley. Makes 8 servings.

VEGETABLE TIP: Blend 2 tablespoons milk with 3-ounce package chive cream cheese; cook over low heat, stirring until sauce is hot. Serve on hot cooked asparagus.

———◆———

BEEF STROGANOFF ON RICE

About 45 minutes before serving: Combine 3 tablespoons all-purpose flour, 1 1/2 teaspoons salt, 1/4 teaspoon pepper. Trim fat from 1-pound beef tenderloin, 1/4-inch thick. Rub beef with 1 cut garlic clove. With edge of plate, pound in flour. Cut into 1 1/2" by 1" strips.

In deep skillet over medium heat, in 1/4 cup butter or margarine, brown meat, turning often. Add 1/2 cup minced onions; sauté until golden. Add 1/4 cup water; stir to dissolve brown bits.

Add one 10 1/2-ounce can condensed chicken-and-rice soup, undiluted, 1 pound fresh mushrooms, sliced. Cook, uncovered, over low heat, stirring occasionally, about 20 minutes or until sauce is thickened and beef is tender.

Just before serving, stir in 1 cup sour cream; heat but *do not boil.* Top with chopped chives. Serve on hot rice. Makes 4 to 6 servings.

VEGETABLE TIP: Drain one 16-ounce can of whole baby carrots. Toss in 1 tablespoon each butter and brown sugar, and a dash or two of salt and ground nutmeg. Heat until nicely glazed.

HAM PATTIES HAWAIIAN

¾ pound cooked ham, ground
¾ cup saltine-cracker crumbs
⅓ cup minced celery
1 egg, beaten
3 tablespoons chopped parsley
½ teaspoon seasoned salt
¼ teaspoon seasoned pepper

2 tablespoons catchup
2 tablespoons minced onion
1 20½-ounce can pineapple slices
¼ cup syrup from pineapple slices
butter or margarine
light brown sugar

About 20 minutes before serving: Preheat broiler if manufacturer directs. In medium bowl, combine ham with cracker crumbs, celery, egg, parsley, seasoned salt, seasoned pepper, catchup, onion and pineapple syrup.

Form ham into 4 patties; press one pineapple slice onto top, one onto bottom, of each patty. Place patties on broiling pan; dot with butter and sprinkle with brown sugar.

Broil patties 5 minutes; turn, dot with butter, sprinkle with brown sugar; broil a few minutes longer. Makes 4 servings.

DESSERT TIP: Toast poundcake slices until golden; top with canned applesauce spiced with cinnamon. Sprinkle with nuts.

———◆———

APPETIZER TIP: To canned tomato juice, add lemon juice, basil and celery salt. Serve with celery-heart stirrers.

BURGERS, GREEK STYLE

About 20 minutes before serving: Preheat broiler if manufacturer directs. In large bowl, mix together 2 pounds ground beef chuck, ½ cup catchup, ½ cup chopped onions, 1 teaspoon salt, ½ teaspoon grated lemon peel, 1 tablespoon lemon juice, 1 teaspoon mint flakes. Shape into 6 patties; arrange on rack in broiler pan.

Broil patties 7 minutes on one side; turn; broil 5 minutes on other side or until of desired doneness.

Meanwhile, in small saucepan, with fork or wire whisk, beat 3 egg yolks with 2 teaspoons cornstarch, ½ teaspoon salt, dash cayenne. In measuring cup, combine 1 cup canned chicken broth and 1 tablespoon lemon juice; slowly stir into egg-yolk mixture.

Cook over medium heat, stirring constantly, until sauce is slightly thickened. Serve over hamburgers. Makes 6 servings.

———◆◆———

RHUBARB CRUNCH

1 cup uncooked rolled oats
regular all-purpose flour
1 cup packed brown sugar
½ cup butter or margarine
3 cups diced, unpeeled young

rhubarb
½ cup granulated sugar
1 teaspoon cinnamon
⅛ teaspoon salt
vanilla ice cream

About 55 minutes before serving: Preheat oven to 350°F. Grease 8″ by 8″ by 2″ pan. Mix oats, ½ cup sifted flour and brown sugar. With 2 knives used scissor-fashion, cut in butter until crumbly. Press half of mixture into pan. In medium bowl, combine rhubarb, granulated sugar, 1 tablespoon flour, cinnamon, salt and 1 tablespoon water. Spoon over oat mixture in pan; top with remaining oat mixture. Bake 45 minutes. Serve hot, with ice cream. Makes 6 to 8 servings.

TOMATO JUICE WITH
CELERY HEARTS

TUESDAY
Ham Patties Hawaiian*
Sweet Potatoes
Big Green Salad Bowl
Peas and Onions
Poundcake Plus*
Milk   Coffee

WEDNESDAY
Tomato Juice
with
Celery Hearts*
Burgers, Greek Style*
Cottage-Cheese
Cucumber Salad
Strawberry-Filled
Patty Shells
Coffee   Tea

THURSDAY
Onion Soup
Baked Haddock
Lemon New Potatoes
Baked Tomatoes
Green Salad
Rhubarb Crunch*
Coffee   Milk

SPARKLING PUNCH

1 2- to 3-pound bunch seedless
   green grapes
3 quarts cranberry juice
¼ cup granulated sugar
8 whole allspice

3 small cinnamon sticks
5 16-ounce bottles club soda,
   chilled
3 drops almond extract

Day before: Freeze grapes in one bunch on cookie sheet overnight. In large kettle, combine cranberry juice, sugar, allspice and cinnamon. Heat to boiling, then simmer 10 minutes; strain, discarding spices. Refrigerate overnight to chill.

   Just before serving: Place frozen grapes in bottom of large punch bowl. Add cranberry mixture, club soda and almond extract. Serve immediately. Makes about 20 one-cup servings.

BREAD TIP: With sharp knife, shave off oval pieces of crust from loaf of French bread. Spread crusts with butter; sprinkle with celery seed. Bake at 375°F. 7 minutes or until bubbly. Use crustless loaf for bread cubes for Quick Blueberry Pudding, Saturday, below.

PATIO PARTY SALAD

1 16-ounce can red kidney beans
1 16-ounce can white kidney beans
1 20-ounce can chick peas
2 tomatoes, sliced medium thick
1 cucumber, pared
1 envelope cheese-garlic

salad-dressing mix
⅓ cup Italian dressing
8 romaine leaves
¼ pound Muenster or Mozzarella
   cheese, cut in slivers
½ pound cooked ham, cut in slices

About 2 hours before serving: Drain beans and chick peas. Halve tomato slices; place in small bowl. Slice cucumber onto tomatoes; sprinkle with 1 tablespoon cheese-garlic salad-dressing mix; refrigerate.

   Layer beans and chick peas in salad bowl, sprinkling each layer with some of remaining salad-dressing mix. Refrigerate.

   About ½ hour before serving: Add Italian dressing to beans and chick peas; toss with cucumbers and tomatoes. Tuck romaine around inside of salad bowl. Arrange strips of Muenster and ham on top. Refrigerate. Makes 12 servings.

———◆———

MEAT TIP: Marinate flank steak in mixture of vegetable oil, vinegar, garlic, salt and pepper. Broil about 12 to 15 minutes total time; slice on diagonal.

QUICK BLUEBERRY PUDDING

1 pint fresh or unsweetened
   thawed frozen blueberries
¼ cup granulated sugar
1 tablespoon lemon juice
dash allspice

2 cups bread cubes
3 tablespoons butter or margarine,
   melted
heavy or whipping cream, whipped

Early in day: In saucepan, heat blueberries, sugar, lemon juice, ¼ cup water and allspice, until berries are juicy but still plump and whole. Toss bread with butter; combine with cooked blueberries. Pour into bowl (3-cup capacity). Refrigerate 4 hours or until firm; unmold. Serve with whipped cream. Makes 4 servings.

RUBY-PEACH ANGEL CAKE

SUNDAY

*Chutney
Chicken Breasts**

Saffron Rice

*Green Beans
with Almonds*

*Tomatoes
with Scallions**

*Ruby-Peach
Angel Cake**

Coffee

MONDAY

*Spicy Italian Omelet**

*Easy Breadsticks**

*Tossed Salad
with Garlic Dressing*

Apple Turnovers

Iced or Hot Coffee

CHUTNEY CHICKEN BREASTS

6 large whole chicken breasts, boned
seasoned salt
seasoned pepper

¼ cup butter or margarine
1 8½-ounce jar chutney
2 tablespoons cornstarch

About 1½ hours before serving: Sprinkle chicken with seasoned salt and seasoned pepper. In Dutch oven in hot butter, sauté chicken quickly until golden; remove. Preheat oven to 325°F. To drippings in Dutch oven, add 2½ cups water, chutney; bring to boil; return chicken. Cover; bake 30 minutes. Remove cover; bake, basting occasionally, 30 minutes or until chicken is fork-tender. Remove to serving platter. Mix cornstarch smooth with a little cold water; stir into sauce in Dutch oven; simmer until thickened. Spoon over chicken. Makes 6 servings.

SALAD TIP: Layer sliced red tomatoes in shallow dish; sprinkle with chopped green onions. Pour over dressing made from olive oil, vinegar, garlic, salt and pepper. Or use prepared Italian dressing and sprinkle with oregano.

RUBY-PEACH ANGEL CAKE

1 package angel-food-cake mix
2 10-ounce packages frozen raspberries or strawberries, thawed

1½ teaspoons lemon juice
1½ teaspoons cornstarch
2 peaches, peeled, sliced

Early in day: Bake cake in 10-inch tube pan as label directs; cool.

In medium saucepan, place raspberries and juice, reserving a few raspberries for garnish. Add lemon juice; bring to boil, stirring constantly to mash raspberries. In cup, combine cornstarch with 1½ teaspoons cold water; slowly stir into raspberry mixture. Cook and stir until slightly thickened. Sieve; discard seeds. Refrigerate.

Just before serving: Place cake on serving platter; arrange peach slices on top, pinwheel fashion. Garnish with reserved raspberries. Spoon part of syrup over peaches, letting some drizzle down sides. Pass remaining syrup. Makes 12 servings.

———◆———

SPICY ITALIAN OMELET

1 tablespoon butter
1 slice onion, ¼-inch thick, in rings
6 eggs
¼ teaspoon salt

8 slices salami (about ¼ pound)
2 tomatoes, sliced ½-inch thick
chopped parsley

About 15 minutes before serving: In attractive skillet over low heat, melt butter; sauté onion rings until tender. Remove and set aside.

Beat eggs with salt and 1 tablespoon water, just until blended; pour into skillet, over low heat. As egg sets at edge, with fork draw it toward center, tilting skillet as necessary, so uncooked portion flows to bottom. Occasionally shake skillet to keep egg from sticking.

When eggs are set but surface is still moist, top with salami slices, then onion, then tomato slices, each cut into fourths; sprinkle on parsley. Serve from skillet. Makes 4 servings.

BREAD TIP: Cut frankfurter rolls in fourths, lengthwise; spread with butter or margarine. Sprinkle with garlic salt, oregano or thyme; toast in broiler until golden.

POT ROAST WITH VEGETABLES

1 4-pound beef bottom round
    roast
2 teaspoons instant meat tenderizer
flour
seasoned salt
seasoned pepper

2 tablespoons butter or margarine
6 or 8 small potatoes, pared
4 or 6 carrots, scraped, halved
    crosswise
8 or 10 small onions, peeled

About 3 hours before serving: Sprinkle roast with meat tenderizer as label directs; sprinkle lightly with flour, seasoned salt and seasoned pepper. In Dutch oven, in hot butter, brown roast on all sides. Add 2 cups water; simmer, covered, 2½ to 3 hours or until tender.

Meanwhile, prepare potatoes, carrots and onions. About 1 hour before roast is done, add vegetables. Continue simmering, covered, until meat is done, vegetables tender-crisp. Remove meat and vegetables; thicken gravy.

Serve meat on heated platter, surrounded by vegetables; pass gravy. Makes 6 servings. (Save leftovers for Thursday dinner, below.)

DESSERT TIP: In parfait glasses, layer tapioca pudding with prune puree (use the baby-food kind).

———◆———

SALAD TIP: For croutons, in medium skillet over medium heat, melt 6 tablespoons butter with ½ teaspoon seasoned salt. When butter is hot, but not yet smoking, sauté 1 cup bread cubes until lightly browned on all sides. Drain on paper toweling. Toss with salad.

AVOCADO-SPINACH SALAD WITH CROUTONS

¾ pound fresh spinach, in bite-size
    pieces
½ head iceberg lettuce, in bite-size
    pieces
4 hard-cooked eggs, each cut into 4
    wedges
1 cup croutons
¼ pound Swiss cheese, shredded

¼ pound Swiss cheese, cut into
    ¼-inch strips
2 ripe avocados, peeled, cut in half,
    sliced crosswise
½ red onion, peeled, thinly sliced
1 envelope cheese-garlic salad-
    dressing mix

About 20 minutes before serving: In large salad bowl, toss spinach with lettuce, eggs, croutons, cheeses, avocados and onion.

Make dressing as label directs; pass with salad. Makes 4 main-dish servings.

———◆———

MEAT TIP: Heat leftover pot roast, cubed, in canned mushroom gravy. Serve over hot buttered noodles.

ALMOND CREAM WITH PEACHES

At least one hour ahead: Prepare one 3½-ounce package vanilla-flavor whipped-dessert mix as label directs but substitute all water for milk and water and add ½ teaspoon almond extract during last minute of beating. Refrigerate in 2-quart loaf pan.

At serving time: With knife, cut dessert into cubes. Lift out of pan with spatula; arrange in 4 sherbet glasses. Top with sliced peaches. (Or you can use blueberries or halved strawberries.) Makes 4 servings.

TUESDAY

*Pot Roast
with Vegetables**

*Hearts of Lettuce
with
Green Goddess Dressing*

Prune Parfait*

Coffee Tea

WEDNESDAY

Cream-of-Mushroom Soup

*Avocado-Spinach
Salad with Croutons**

Hot Buttered Biscuits

Lemon Sherbet

Cookies

Milk Coffee

THURSDAY

*Beef
in Mushroom Gravy**

Hot Buttered Noodles

Broiled Tomatoes

Green Salad

*Almond Cream
with Peaches**

Tea Coffee

APPETIZER TIP: Combine bottled cranberry juice, orange juice and dash of mace for a delightfully tart drink.

CHEESE-AND-RICE SOUFFLÉ WITH SHRIMP SAUCE

<table>
<tr><td>2 tablespoons butter or margarine</td><td>4 eggs</td></tr>
<tr><td>3 tablespoons all-purpose flour</td><td>½ teaspoon salt</td></tr>
<tr><td>¾ cup milk</td><td>dash cayenne</td></tr>
<tr><td>8 ounces process sharp Cheddar cheese, shredded (2 cups)</td><td>1 cup cooked rice
Shrimp Sauce (below)</td></tr>
</table>

About 1 hour before serving: Grease 1½-quart soufflé dish.

In saucepan, melt butter; stir in flour until smooth. Slowly stir in milk and cook, stirring constantly, until thickened. Add cheese; cook, stirring constantly, until cheese melts. Preheat oven to 325°F.

Separate eggs, putting yolks in small bowl, whites in larger bowl. Beat egg yolks slightly with salt and cayenne; stir into cheese sauce. Remove sauce from heat; stir in rice. Turn into large bowl.

Beat egg whites until stiff but not dry. Gently fold into cheese mixture.

Turn gently into greased soufflé dish. To form crown, with spoon, make shallow path about 1 inch in from edge all the way around.

Bake 40 minutes. Serve at once with Shrimp Sauce. Makes 5 servings.

Shrimp Sauce: In saucepan, melt 3 tablespoons butter or margarine; stir in 3 tablespoons flour, 1 teaspoon seasoned salt. Slowly add 1½ cups milk, stirring constantly; cook until smooth and thickened. Stir in 1 pound cooked, shelled, deveined shrimp, split in half if desired.

◆

MEAT TIP: Preheat broiler if manufacturer directs. Brush each frankfurter with salad oil. Broil 4 to 5 minutes, turning once.

SALAD TIP: Combine ¼ cup Italian salad dressing with ¼ cup canned tomato juice; toss this mixture together with 4 cups finely shredded cabbage and ⅔ cup halved seedless green grapes. Sprinkle with poppy seed.

BURNT-SUGAR CAKE

<table>
<tr><td>dark brown sugar</td><td>½ cup butter or margarine</td></tr>
<tr><td>¼ cup boiling water</td><td>6 tablespoons milk</td></tr>
<tr><td>1 package (2-layer size) yellow-cake mix</td><td>1 large package creamy vanilla-frosting mix</td></tr>
</table>

Early in day: In heavy skillet over medium heat, stir ⅓ cup packed brown sugar constantly until melted and smoking. Now slowly add boiling water, continuing to stir until sugar is dissolved. Pour into measuring cup; set aside.

Preheat oven as cake-mix label directs. Make cake as directed but substitute burnt-sugar syrup plus enough water for amount of liquid called for.

Turn batter into two greased 9-inch layer-cake pans. Bake, then cool as label directs.

Meanwhile, in medium saucepan, melt butter; add 1 cup packed brown sugar; then boil over low heat, stirring constantly, 2 minutes. Add milk; stir until boiling. Remove from heat; cool.

Pour into small bowl. With electric mixer at medium speed, gradually add frosting mix, beating until smooth. Use to fill and frost cake layers. Makes 12 wedges.

FRIDAY

Cranberry-Orange Cocktail*

Cheese-and-Rice Soufflé with Shrimp Sauce*

Frozen Green Beans with Almonds

Fresh Fruit Tray

Coffee   Tea

SATURDAY

Broiled Frankfurters*

French Fries

Grape-Poppy Seed Slaw*

Burnt-Sugar Cake*

Coffee

POULTRY TIP: After oven-frying chicken, spread with mixture of canned deviled ham, prepared mustard, drop of Tabasco and chopped parsley. Sprinkle with dried bread crumbs. Broil a few minutes until golden.

ZINGY GREEN-BEAN SALAD

3 16-ounce cans whole green beans, drained
1 medium onion, thinly sliced

½ cup bottled Italian dressing
1 ripe avocado
¼ cup lemon juice

Several hours before serving: In large bowl, toss beans with onion and dressing. Cover; refrigerate. (During refrigeration, uncover and toss once or twice to blend flavors.)

Just before serving: Cut avocado in half lengthwise; peel; remove pit. Slice each half into about 5 wedges; toss in lemon juice. Pile salad on tray; arrange avocado slices around it. Makes 6 to 8 servings.

HOT FUDGE SUNDAE

2 squares unsweetened chocolate
1½ cups light corn syrup
⅛ teaspoon salt

1 teaspoon vanilla extract
chocolate ice cream

In saucepan over low heat, cook chocolate with ½ cup water, stirring 2 minutes or until thick. Remove from heat; gradually add syrup and salt. Simmer 10 minutes, stirring often. Add vanilla. Spoon ice cream into dessert glasses; swirl on sauce. Makes about 2 cups sauce.

———◆———

BEEF-AND-AVOCADO DISH

1 5-ounce jar dried beef, shredded
¼ cup butter or margarine
3 tablespoons flour
2 cups milk

1 teaspoon bottled thick meat sauce
1 avocado
6 slices white toast cut into triangles

Pour boiling water over beef; let stand 1 minute; drain.

In saucepan, melt butter; add beef; cook, stirring, until edges curl. Stir in flour; slowly stir in milk; cook, stirring constantly, until smooth and thickened; add meat sauce. Peel, slice avocado into lengthwise slices.

On platter, arrange toast; top with creamed beef; arrange avocado slices on top. Makes 6 servings.

RELISH TIP: Carrot curls, celery sticks, pimiento-stuffed olives and radishes make a good combination.

———◆———

VEAL SCALLOPINI WITH PIQUANTE SAUCE

8 thin veal cutlets (1½ pounds)
¼ cup regular all-purpose flour
salt
¼ teaspoon pepper
¼ cup salad oil

3 seeded medium green peppers, each cut into 12 pieces
3 8-ounce cans spaghetti sauce with mushrooms
1 tablespoon granulated sugar

About 45 minutes before serving: Cut veal cutlets into 2½-inch pieces; sprinkle on flour, ½ teaspoon salt, pepper; with fork, toss until well coated.

In skillet, in hot salad oil, sauté veal until nicely browned on both sides; drain on paper towels.

SUNDAY

Spiced Apple Juice
Deviled Chicken *
Baked Squash
Zingy Green-Bean Salad *
Onion Rolls
Hot Fudge Sundae *
Coffee   Tea

MONDAY

Beef-and-Avocado Dish *
Raw Vegetable Relishes *
Strawberry Shortcake
Coffee   Milk

TUESDAY

Veal Scallopini with Piquante Sauce *
Hot Noodles
Special Waxed Beans *
Chocolate-Cake Squares *
Coffee   Tea

ZINGY GREEN-BEAN SALAD

In large skillet, combine veal, peppers, spaghetti sauce, sugar, ½ teaspoon salt, ¾ cup cold water. Simmer, over low heat, 10 minutes or until veal is fork-tender; turn occasionally. Makes 4 servings.

VEGETABLE TIP: Drain a can or two of waxed beans, reserving liquid. Boil liquid down to a few tablespoons; add to beans with salt, pepper, butter or margarine; add chopped green onions, diced canned water chestnuts or slivered nuts. Heat through.

DESSERT TIP: Frost chocolate-cake squares with whipped cream or topping mix; drizzle on chocolate or fudge sauce.

LAMBURGERS WITH MUSTARD SAUCE

2 egg yolks, well beaten
¼ cup vinegar
2 teaspoons dry mustard
salt
½ cup mayonnaise

dash Tabasco
1 pound lamb shoulder, ground
1 tablespoon chopped parsley
¼ teaspoon marjoram
2 tablespoons finely chopped onion

In small saucepan, combine egg yolks, vinegar, mustard and 1 teaspoon salt. Cook over low heat, stirring constantly, until thickened.
    Add mayonnaise and Tabasco and blend well.
    Preheat broiler if manufacturer directs. Combine lamb, parsley, marjoram, onion and 1 teaspoon salt; mix well. Shape into 4 patties, 1 inch thick.
    Broil patties 5 minutes; turn; broil 5 minutes or to desired doneness. Serve with sauce. Makes 4 servings.

VEGETABLE TIP: Prepare regular or precooked rice. Heat can of either whole-kernel corn or mixed vegetables; drain; toss with rice and some butter.

WEDNESDAY

*Lamburgers
with Mustard Sauce**
Vegetables with Rice*
Mixed-Greens Salad
Pears   Cheese
Coffee   Tea

TUNA QUADRETTINI

CORN-CHILI CASSEROLE

2 tablespoons butter or margarine
1 cup chopped onion
1 pound ground beef chuck
1 1¼-ounce package chili-
   seasoning mix

2 8-ounce cans tomato sauce
2 cups coarsely crumbled corn
   chips
½ cup sliced ripe olives
1 cup shredded Cheddar cheese

About 45 minutes before serving: In medium skillet, in hot butter, brown onion with chuck. Stir in chili-seasoning mix, tomato sauce and 1 cup water. Simmer 10 minutes, stirring occasionally. Preheat oven to 350°F.

   Grease lightly a 1½-quart casserole. In it, layer half of chuck mixture, corn chips, olives and cheese. Repeat. Bake 20 minutes. Makes 4 servings.

VEGETABLE TIP: Sprinkle cooked asparagus with a few drops lemon juice. Garnish with chopped hard-cooked egg.

———◆———

APPETIZER TIP: Dip rims of glasses first into grapefruit juice, then into granulated sugar, to frost. Fill with fresh fruit and quartered maraschino cherries.

TUNA QUADRETTINI

1 8-ounce package medium noodles
3 10-ounce packages frozen leaf
   spinach
2 6-ounce cans mushroom crowns
3 6½- or 7-ounce cans tuna
1 garlic clove, minced

1 bay leaf
¼ teaspoon basil
2 8-ounce cans tomato sauce
½ teaspoon Tabasco
½ cup grated Parmesan cheese

About 1 hour before serving: Cook noodles as label directs; drain; keep warm. Cook spinach as label directs; drain; keep warm. Drain liquid from mushrooms; reserve. Into medium skillet, drain oil from tuna; in it, sauté mushrooms and garlic about 5 minutes. Add bay leaf, basil, tomato sauce, Tabasco, reserved mushroom liquid, and tuna in chunks; heat all about 10 minutes.

   Preheat oven to 400°F. In oval skillet 13½ inches long, or in 2½-quart casserole, layer half of noodles; sprinkle with half of Parmesan, then

half of spinach; pour on half of tuna mixture. Add rest of noodles, and sprinkle with rest of Parmesan. Top with rest of spinach in two crosswise rows. Pour remaining tuna mixture over noodles but not over spinach. Bake, uncovered, 20 minutes or until hot and bubbly. Makes 8 servings.

BLUE-CHEESE-TOPPED SIRLOIN STEAK

1 sirloin steak, about 3 pounds
1 garlic clove, cut
¼ cup crumbled Danish blue cheese
2 tablespoons butter or margarine
·½ teaspoon Worcestershire

1 teaspoon prepared mustard
1 teaspoon lemon juice
½ teaspoon salt
¼ teaspoon freshly ground pepper

Preheat broiler if manufacturer directs. Remove excess fat from steak. Rub steak with garlic. Broil on first side until browned. Meanwhile, cream together cheese, butter, Worcestershire, mustard, lemon juice, salt and pepper. Turn steak and broil on other side until of desired doneness. (Cut near bone to check rareness; broil longer if necessary.) Spread cheese mixture on steak and broil 5 minutes longer or until topping is golden brown. Serve at once on hot platter. Makes 4 servings.

VEGETABLE TIP: Cook small white onions until tender; drain; heat in 2 tablespoons each of butter and sugar, plus a little water, to glaze.

HORSERADISH-HERB DRESSING

1 cup sour cream
1½ tablespoons horseradish
1 tablespoon tarragon vinegar
1 tablespoon chopped chives

1 tablespoon sugar
1 teaspoon dill weed
¾ teaspoon salt
¼ teaspoon paprika

About 30 minutes before serving: Combine sour cream, horseradish and vinegar; mix until smooth. Stir in remaining ingredients. Refrigerate, covered, at least 15 minutes. Serve over tossed greens, sliced tomatoes or cucumbers. Makes 1 cup.

DESSERT TIP: Top each serving of raspberry gelatin with whipped cream or whipped topping and a spoonful of peach preserves.

SATURDAY

Blue-Cheese-Topped Sirloin Steak*

French Fries

Glazed Onions*

Green Salad with Horseradish-Herb Dressing*

Raspberry Gelatin*

Coffee   Tea

YAMS LOUISIANA

6 medium yams	½ teaspoon salt
1 cup orange juice	¼ cup butter or margarine, melted
1 tablespoon dark brown sugar	½ cup dark raisins
¼ teaspoon cinnamon	

About 1½ hours before serving: Boil yams in jackets in salted water for 30 minutes or until just tender. Remove from water; cool.

Meanwhile, in small bowl, combine orange juice, brown sugar, cinnamon, salt and butter.

Peel yams; slice ½ inch thick. Layer yams and raisins in 12″ by 9″ by 2″ baking dish; add orange-juice mixture. Cover with foil; bake along with turkey (temperature 325°F.) for last half hour, basting occasionally with juice mixture. Makes 6 servings.

SALAD TIP: Toss greens with chilled cooked green beans and bottled Italian dressing to which a dash of basil, salt, and seasoned pepper have been added.

POTS DE CRÈME ÉLÉGANTS

1 6-ounce package semisweet-chocolate pieces (1 cup)	1 2-ounce package whipped-topping mix
6 egg yolks, slightly beaten	1 teaspoon instant coffee
2 teaspoons vanilla extract	1 1-ounce square semisweet chocolate
6 egg whites	

Early in day: In double boiler over hot, *not boiling,* water, melt chocolate pieces; remove from heat. With spoon, beat in egg yolks, vanilla.

In small bowl, with electric mixer at high speed, beat egg whites until stiff but not dry; fold into chocolate mixture. Spoon into six 6-ounce wine or other glasses. Refrigerate at least 4 hours.

Just before serving: Make up whipped-topping mix as label directs but add instant coffee while beating. Spoon some onto each glass.

With vegetable parer, scrape curls from chocolate square onto topping. Makes 6 to 8 servings.

BROILED GINGER-LAMB CHOPS

salad oil	4 lamb rib chops, ¾-inch thick
¾ teaspoon ground ginger	4 medium mushrooms
salt	seasoned pepper
½ teaspoon garlic salt	

Preheat broiler if manufacturer directs.

Combine 1 tablespoon salad oil, ginger, ¼ teaspoon salt, garlic salt; brush on both sides of lamb chops.

Broil chops 5 minutes on one side; turn. Place mushrooms around chops; brush with salad oil; sprinkle with salt; continue broiling until mushrooms are tinged with brown and chops are cooked.

Arrange chops and mushrooms on heated platter; sprinkle with seasoned pepper. Makes 4 servings.

DESSERT TIP: Place peeled bananas in shallow baking pan; brush with melted butter or margarine. Bake in 450°F. oven about 12 minutes. Meanwhile, with fork, stir 1 pint vanilla ice cream until soft; add sherry, almond or brandy extract to taste. Or use coffee ice cream and rum extract to taste. Serve over hot bananas.

SUNDAY
Shrimp Cocktail
Roast Turkey
Fresh Asparagus
Yams Louisiana*
Green Salad Bowl*
Pots de Crème Élégants*
Tea   Coffee

MONDAY
Broiled Ginger-Lamb Chops*
Hot Fluffy Rice
Buttered Mixed Vegetables
Baked Bananas*
Coffee   Milk

LUSCIOUS TURKEY HASH

2 cups cut-up cooked turkey	1 teaspoon salt
4 medium potatoes, pared	1/8 teaspoon pepper
1/2 green pepper	3 tablespoons butter or margarine
1 medium onion	chili sauce
1/4 cup diced pimiento	

About 30 minutes before serving: Put turkey, potatoes, green pepper and onion through food grinder. Mix in pimiento, salt and pepper.

In large skillet, melt butter; add hash. Cook, over low heat, covered, 15 minutes or until hash is browned on bottom. Uncover; let stand 1 minute. Loosen edge with spatula; fold one half over other; turn onto serving platter. Pass chili sauce. Makes 4 servings.

VEGETABLE TIP: Cook frozen Brussels sprouts as label directs. Drain; toss with fresh mushroom slices that have been sautéed in butter.

———◆———

HAM-AND-CHEESE BAKE

1 10-ounce package frozen chopped broccoli	cut in 1-inch cubes
14 thin slices white bread, crusts removed	4 eggs
	2 cups milk
1 8-ounce package process cheese slices	1/2 teaspoon dry mustard
1 12-ounce can chopped ham,	1/2 teaspoon salt
	1 tablespoon butter or margarine

About 1 1/2 hours before serving: Cook broccoli as label directs, just until tender-crisp; drain. In 12" by 8" by 2" baking dish, arrange 6 bread slices; top with cheese, broccoli, ham. Cut remaining bread slices diagonally in half; arrange on top in 2 rows, overlapping a bit.

Preheat oven to 350°F. In medium bowl, beat eggs slightly; combine with milk, mustard, salt; pour over bread slices; dot with butter. Bake 45 to 50 minutes or until egg mixture is set. (If bread browns too quickly, cover with foil.) Let stand 10 minutes before serving. Makes 6 to 8 servings.

DESSERT TIP: Sprinkle butterscotch pudding made from instant mix with chopped filberts that have been toasted in a 350°F. oven 15 to 20 minutes.

———◆———

VEGETABLE TIP: Sauté finely shredded Chinese cabbage in melted butter about 5 minutes. Stir in a little light cream and season to taste. Cook, covered, another 5 minutes.

WALDORF SALAD

2 cups diced, unpared red apples	1/2 cup broken walnuts
2 tablespoons lemon juice	1/2 cup seedless raisins
1/2 cup mayonnaise	lettuce leaves
1 cup thinly sliced celery	

About 1 hour before serving: In bowl, toss apples with lemon juice, 1 tablespoon of the mayonnaise; refrigerate. Just before serving, add celery, rest of mayonnaise, walnuts, raisins. Serve on lettuce. Makes 4 servings.

FRUITED SHRIMP SALAD

1 11-ounce can Mandarin-orange
  sections
1/4 cup cider vinegar
1/4 cup salad oil
salt-
pepper

1 pound peeled, deveined shrimp,
  cooked, chilled
1 9-ounce package frozen artichoke
  hearts, cooked, chilled
6 cups mixed salad greens

Drain syrup from oranges; set oranges aside. To syrup add vinegar, salad oil, 1/2 teaspoon salt, dash pepper; pour over shrimp and artichokes. Refrigerate at least 30 minutes, tossing occasionally.

Just before serving: In large salad bowl, toss salad greens with 1/4 teaspoon salt, dash of pepper, marinated shrimp and artichokes and oranges. Makes 4 servings.

ONION-CHEESE ROUND

2 7-ounce packages refrigerated
  onion crescent flaky rolls

1 cup shredded Cheddar cheese
1 egg, well beaten

Preheat oven to 375°F. On lightly floured pastry cloth, unroll one package rolls; pinch perforations together. Unroll second package rolls; lay on top of first; pinch perforations together. Roll all into 18" by 8" rectangle; sprinkle evenly with cheese; then roll lengthwise, jelly-roll fashion; brush edge with beaten egg; seal. Lay on lightly greased cookie sheet; brush one end with beaten egg; form into ring; seal. With scissors, from top, make diagonal cuts almost through ring about 1 inch apart, all the way around; turn each slice slightly outward from center of circle; brush with beaten egg. Bake 35 minutes or until golden brown. Makes one round, 9 inches in diameter, enough for 10 servings.

MINIATURE ORANGE-MEAT LOAVES

orange juice
5 teaspoons cornstarch
3 tablespoons orange marmalade
1 cup fresh bread crumbs
1 pound cooked ham, ground
1 pound veal shoulder, ground
1 egg, beaten

1 teaspoon salt
1/4 teaspoon pepper
2 tablespoons grated orange peel
2 tablespoons chopped parsley
1/4 teaspoon ginger
2 medium oranges, peeled, cut into
  8 crosswise slices

About 1 hour before serving: In small saucepan, combine 1 1/4 cups orange juice, cornstarch and orange marmalade; over medium heat, cook, stirring, until thickened; set this glaze aside.

Preheat oven to 375°F. In large bowl, soak bread crumbs in 1 cup orange juice about 5 minutes; lightly mix in ham, veal, egg, salt, pepper, orange peel, parsley and ginger.

In each of eight 6-ounce custard cups, place 1 tablespoon orange glaze. Divide meat mixture into 8 equal portions; spoon into cups. Arrange in baking pan. Bake 15 minutes; top each with an orange slice, then orange glaze; bake 15 minutes longer. Makes 8 servings.

SALAD TIP: Toss torn lettuce, romaine, sliced raw zucchini, sliced mushrooms, and chopped green onions with blue-cheese dressing.

DESSERT TIP: Cut watermelon into crosswise slices or wedge-shaped pieces. Or with tablespoon, scoop out medium-sized pieces; arrange 3 or 4 pieces on dessert plate. Sprinkle with lime or lemon juice.

FRIDAY
Vichyssoise
Fruited Shrimp Salad*
Stuffed Eggs
Onion-Cheese Round*
Brownies à la Mode
Iced Tea   Coffee

SATURDAY
*Miniature
Orange-Meat Loaves**
Mashed Potatoes
Yellow Squash
Party Salad Bowl*
Watermelon*
Iced Beverage

POACHED SALMON STEAKS WITH
BEARNAISE SAUCE

SUNDAY

*Poached Salmon Steaks
with Béarnaise Sauce**

Hot Fluffy Rice

*Green Beans
with Onions*

Raspberry Sherbet

Coffee   Tea

MONDAY

*Spiced Cube Steaks**

Buttered Limas

Yellow Squash

*Cottage-Cheese Salad**

*Fresh or Frozen
Strawberries
with Sour Cream*

Coffee

TUESDAY

*Gourmet Veal Loaf**

Herbed New Potatoes

Beets in Orange Sauce

Green Salad

Quick Charlotte Russe

Iced Tea   Coffee

56 / menus for Spring

POACHED SALMON STEAKS WITH BEARNAISE SAUCE

1 carrot, sliced	6 small salmon steaks, about 1 inch
1 onion, sliced	thick
1 stalk celery, sliced	½ cup butter or margarine
1 large lemon, sliced	2 egg yolks
2 bay leaves	1 teaspoon minced onion
4 peppercorns	1 teaspoon tarragon
2 sprigs parsley	1 teaspoon lemon juice
2 teaspoons salt	⅛ teaspoon pepper

About 45 minutes before serving: In large skillet over high heat, combine 3 cups water and first 8 ingredients; heat to boiling. Reduce heat; simmer, covered, 30 minutes. Discard vegetables and lemon. In skillet in this bouillon, cook salmon steaks, covered, over medium heat for 8 minutes or until fish flakes easily with fork.

Meanwhile, make sauce: In small saucepan, melt butter. To electric-blender container,* add egg yolks and next 4 ingredients; cover and blend on high speed a few seconds. Remove cover; continue blending and slowly pour in hot butter. (Sauce will be thin.)

Serve salmon on warm platter garnished with lemon and parsley if desired. Pass sauce. Makes 6 servings.

* Or use electric mixer and small bowl. Beat yolks with lemon juice and pepper until thickened and lemon-yellow. Slowly drizzle in melted butter, beating constantly. Stir in minced onion and tarragon.

SPICED CUBE STEAKS

½ cup soy sauce	2 teaspoons ground ginger
¼ cup chopped onion	8 cube steaks
2 garlic cloves, crushed	butter or margarine
2 tablespoons granulated sugar	radish roses (optional)

Early in day: In large bowl, combine soy sauce, ¼ cup water, onion, garlic, sugar, ginger. Pour this marinade over cube steaks; refrigerate.

About 15 minutes before serving: Drain marinade from steaks; pat dry with paper towels. In large skillet over medium heat, in hot butter or margarine, quickly sauté a few steaks at a time on both sides, draining off all juices. Garnish with radish roses. Makes 8 servings.

SALAD TIP: Fold diced tomato into cottage cheese. Spoon into lettuce leaves on individual salad plates. Sprinkle with paprika.

GOURMET VEAL LOAF

1½ pounds veal shoulder, ground	½ cup dried bread crumbs
2 lightly packed cups shredded raw	1 teaspoon salt
carrots	¼ teaspoon pepper
1 small onion, minced	1 teaspoon bottled thick meat sauce
1 3-ounce can chopped mushrooms,	1 cup sour cream
undrained	chopped parsley for garnish

About 1½ hours before serving: Preheat oven to 375°F. In large bowl, with fork, stir veal, carrots, onion, mushrooms, crumbs, salt, pepper, meat sauce with sour cream. Turn into 9″ by 5″ by 3″ loaf pan. Bake 1¼ hours. Pour off juices; invert loaf on heated platter; sprinkle with parsley. Makes 6 servings.

APPETIZER TIP: Reconstitute frozen grape-juice concentrate with chilled ginger ale instead of water. Add ice, if desired.

LEMON-GLAZED CHICKEN

1 3-pound broiler-fryer, cut up	1/4 teaspoon oregano
1 1/2 teaspoons seasoned salt	2 teaspoons grated lemon peel
1/8 teaspoon pepper	3 tablespoons lemon juice
2 tablespoons butter or margarine	1/2 cup dark corn syrup

About 1 hour before serving: Sprinkle cut-up chicken with seasoned salt and pepper.

In skillet over medium heat, in butter, sauté chicken until golden; add oregano, lemon peel, lemon juice, corn syrup and 1/2 cup water.

Cover and simmer about 45 minutes or until tender, basting several times. Makes 4 servings.

VENETIAN RICE AND PEAS

In heavy skillet, sauté 4 bacon slices, diced, until crisp; remove bacon; pour off fat. In same skillet, in 3 tablespoons butter, cook 1 small onion, minced, with one 10-ounce package frozen peas, 5 minutes; stir often. Add 3/4 cup uncooked regular white rice; cook until well coated with butter. Stir in 2 cups canned chicken broth, 1 teaspoon salt, dash pepper; cover; simmer, covered, stirring frequently, about 20 minutes or until rice absorbs all liquid and is tender. Toss with 1/4 cup grated Parmesan cheese and bacon. Makes 4 servings.

◆◆

FRANKFURTERS WITH BACON-BARBECUE SAUCE

In medium skillet, fry 6 slices bacon until crisp; drain on paper towels. Pour all but 3 tablespoons fat from skillet. Add 1/2 cup chopped onions and 1/2 cup chopped green pepper; cook over medium heat until tender, about 5 minutes.

Stir in one 10 1/2-ounce can condensed tomato soup, 1/2 cup water, 1/4 cup bottled thick meat sauce, 2 teaspoons granulated sugar, 1 teaspoon vinegar and 1/2 teaspoon salt. Cover and simmer 15 minutes, stirring occasionally. Crumble bacon pieces, then add to sauce. Serve over broiled frankfurters. Makes 2 cups.

INTERNATIONAL POTATO SALAD

5 cups sliced cooked potatoes (about 5 medium)	1/2 teaspoon pepper
	1/2 cup mayonnaise
1 9-ounce package frozen cut green beans, cooked	1/4 cup sour cream
	2 tablespoons horseradish
1/2 cup chopped green onions	1/2 cup French dressing
1/2 cup sliced celery	1 8 1/4-ounce can whole beets, well drained and halved
1/2 cup sliced radishes	
1 teaspoon salt	

Early in day: In large bowl, place potatoes, beans, onions, celery and radishes. Sprinkle with salt and pepper. Combine mayonnaise, sour cream, horseradish and French dressing. Toss all lightly; cover; refrigerate. Serve, garnished with beets. Makes 8 servings.

DESSERT TIP: Drain small can of apricots; stir syrup into canned, ready-to-serve rice pudding. Top each serving with apricot halves.

WEDNESDAY

*Grape Sparkler**

*Lemon-Glazed Chicken**

*Venetian Rice and Peas**

Raw Vegetable Tray

Sour Cherry Pie à la Mode

Coffee   Milk

THURSDAY

*Frankfurters with Bacon-Barbecue Sauce**

*International Potato Salad**

Green Beans   Rolls

*Fruited Rice Pudding**

Milk   Coffee

PORK CHOPS SORRENTO

FRIDAY

*Pork Chops Sorrento**

Buttered Noodles

Zucchini

*Herb Puffs**

*Gingered Melon Wedges**

Tea   Milk

1 envelope spaghetti-sauce mix
   with tomatoes
1 4-ounce can mushroom buttons
½ teaspoon seasoned salt
¼ teaspoon seasoned pepper
2 tablespoons salad oil

6 loin pork chops, each ½-inch
   thick
1 8-ounce package Mozzarella
   cheese, cut into 6 slices
1 small green pepper, diced

About 1 hour before serving: In bowl, combine spaghetti-sauce mix, 1½ cups cold water, undrained mushrooms, seasoned salt and pepper.

In large skillet, in hot salad oil, sauté chops until golden. Pour off oil; add spaghetti-sauce mixture; simmer, covered, 40 minutes or until fork-tender, stirring occasionally.

Add green pepper to sauce; simmer, covered, 10 minutes. Top each chop with cheese slice. Heat until melted. Makes 6 servings.

HERB PUFFS

¼ cup salad oil
¼ teaspoon salt
½ cup plus 2 tablespoons regular

all-purpose flour
2 eggs
½ teaspoon tarragon

Preheat oven to 450°F. In small saucepan, heat ½ cup water to boiling. Add salad oil and salt; add flour all at once. Beat rapidly over low heat until mixture leaves sides of pan and forms smooth, compact ball. Remove from heat.

Add 1 egg; beat until shiny and smooth. Add second egg and tarragon; beat until shiny and smooth. (Mixture will be thick and hold its shape.)

On ungreased cookie sheet, drop mixture by tablespoons, about 2 inches apart. Bake 20 minutes. Turn oven heat down to 350°F. and bake 15 minutes longer.

Serve hot. Makes 6.

GINGERED MELON WEDGES

Several hours before serving: Cut large honeydew melon in half and re-move seeds; slice each half into 4 wedges. Slash pulp of wedges crisscross into bite-sized pieces; then cut it loose from rind. Place wedges on tray. In cup, combine 2 tablespoons confectioners' sugar and ½ teaspoon ginger; sprinkle over melon. Cover and refrigerate until serving time. Makes 8 servings.

BAKED TROUT

SATURDAY

*Baked Trout**

Hashed Brown Potatoes

*Coleslaw
with Bacon Bits**

Blueberry Muffins

Butterscotch Sundae

Tea   Coffee

6 to 8 trout
salt and pepper
¼ cup chopped parsley
¼ cup chopped chives
3 tablespoons butter or margarine,

softened
2 tablespoons flour
½ cup fine cracker crumbs
¼ cup shredded process Cheddar
   or Swiss cheese

Preheat oven to 375°F. Season trout with salt and pepper; place on bed of parsley and chives in shallow pan. Blend butter with flour; spread on trout. Combine crumbs with cheese; sprinkle on trout. Bake 15 minutes or until golden and easily flaked with fork. Makes 6 to 8 servings.

SALAD TIP: Toss coleslaw, made with green and red cabbage, with bottled bacon bits. Or dice several bacon slices. Fry in skillet until crisp; drain on paper towels.

SUMMER

Summertime, and the living *can* be easy, if you take advantage of the season's bounty, and also move as much of your cooking as possible outdoors. The menus in this section make full use of fresh fruits and vegetables, never so plentiful or so good as when they come from a nearby truck garden—or your own backyard.

Strawberries, raspberries, blueberries, cherries, peaches, plums and nectarines, melons of many kinds, baby beets, young tender carrots, sweet corn, early cabbage and sun-ripened tomatoes give summer's meals more taste with less work, especially when they're combined with convenience foods.

Fish are jumping, in summertime, too: striped bass, bluefish, snapper and perch; and lobsters and softshell crabs are at their succulent peak. Broil them indoors or out, on a barbecue, portable grill or hibachi (you can even use a metal bucket filled with crumpled newspapers). Franks, hamburgers, lamb chops or steak are naturals for grilling too, with or without charcoal. Cut down kitchen time still further by cooking a roast in the morning to serve cold at night; by making up desserts, in advance, that can be stashed until needed in the freezer; and by deliberately planning for leftovers, to be used, in a different dish, later in the week.

Enough of this—it's time to pick a menu you can serve at the beach!

STUFFING TIP: To your favorite bread stuffing, add orange peel and juice saved from cheesecake, plus a pinch of herbs. Allow ¾ to 1 cup stuffing per pound of bird. Stuff bird, or bake stuffing in greased covered casserole, 45 to 60 minutes.

CHEESECAKE MEDLEY

2 lemons	2 egg yolks
1 orange	5 eggs
regular all-purpose flour	¼ cup heavy or whipping cream
granulated sugar	1 8-ounce can sliced pineapple,
¾ cup butter, softened	drained
1 egg yolk	1½ cups sliced fresh strawberries
5 8-ounce packages soft cream	½ cup halved seedless grapes
cheese	¼ cup apple jelly, melted
¼ teaspoon salt	

Early in day: Grate lemons; reserve half of peel for dough, half for filling. Grate orange and reserve half of peel for filling. (Use rest in stuffing.)

With electric mixer at low speed, mix 1½ cups sifted flour, ¼ cup sugar, butter, 1 egg yolk and half of lemon peel; refrigerate 1 hour. Preheat oven to 400°F. Press ⅓ of dough into bottom of 10-inch springform pan. Bake 8 minutes; cool. Press rest of dough around side up to 1 inch below top.

Increase oven heat to 475°F. In bowl, with electric mixer at low speed, beat cream cheese, 1¾ cups sugar, 3 tablespoons flour, salt and 2 egg yolks until smooth. Beat in eggs, one at a time, until smooth. Stir in cream and reserved peels. Pour into springform pan.

Bake 15 minutes, then reduce heat to 200°F. Bake 1¼ hours. Turn off heat; let stand in oven ½ hour; remove to rack. When cool, remove side of pan; refrigerate cake.

About 1 hour before serving: Cut each pineapple slice into 8 pieces. Arrange on cake with strawberries and seedless grapes. Brush melted jelly over fruit; chill. Makes 12 servings.

———◆———

SALAD TIP: Into large bowl, tear several kinds of salad greens—chicory, Boston lettuce, romaine. Add strips of cooked ham and Swiss cheese (allow ¼ pound meat and ¼ pound cheese per person), along with one sliced hard-cooked egg for every two people. Garnish with cherry tomatoes, stuffed olives and onion rings. Toss with Italian or French dressing.

HOT GARLIC BREAD

Preheat oven to 375°F. Cream ½ cup soft butter with 1 mashed garlic clove and ½ teaspoon seasoned salt. Make diagonal slashes in loaf of French bread. Spread cut surfaces with prepared butter; sprinkle with Parmesan cheese. Bake 15 to 20 minutes. Makes about 10 servings.

TOFFEE CREAM CRUNCH

Several hours before serving: With hammer crush six ¾-ounce chocolate-toffee candy bars, in their wrappers. Make up one 2-ounce envelope whipped-topping mix as label directs but add 2 tablespoons rum; split ladyfingers from one 3-ounce package.

In empty ice-cube tray, lay 8 or 9 split ladyfingers, split-side down; top with half of whipped dessert topping; then sprinkle with half of the toffee bars; repeat. Refrigerate. Makes 6 servings.

SUNDAY
*Twin Roast Ducklings with Stuffing**
Peas
Mixed-Greens-and-Watercress Salad
*Cheesecake Medley**
Coffee

MONDAY
*Chef Salad Bowl**
*Hot Garlic Bread**
Buttered Beets
*Toffee Cream Crunch**
Iced Tea

MEAT TIP: Toss ¾ pound ground beef with 1 cup mashed, drained canned kidney beans. Shape into 4 patties. Fry in a little bacon fat.

MELON SOUFFLÉS

Early in day: Thaw two 1-pound boxes frozen melon balls. In saucepan, sprinkle 2 envelopes unflavored gelatin onto 2 cups cold water; let stand 5 minutes; stir over low heat to dissolve. Drain melon balls; reserve 1 cup juice. Remove gelatin mixture from heat; stir in 2 cans frozen lemonade concentrate, melon juice, ½ cup milk (mixture will curdle). Pour into shallow pan; freeze until 1-inch frozen border forms.

Meanwhile, wrap foil collar, 1½ inches high, around each of 6 individual (⅔ cup) soufflé dishes; fasten with cellophane tape. Cut up all but 6 melon balls; refrigerate.

Transfer frozen mixture to large bowl. With electric mixer at high speed, whip until fluffy; drain cut-up melon balls; fold in. Divide mixture among soufflé dishes; refrigerate until firm.

Garnish with reserved melon balls and fresh mint. Makes 6 servings.

COCONUT MOUNDS

Preheat oven to 350°F. Lightly grease two cookie sheets. In large bowl, with electric mixer at high speed, beat 2 eggs with 1 cup granulated sugar *just until well blended*—about 1 minute; then fold in 3 cups flaked coconut and ¼ cup sifted regular all-purpose flour all at once.

Onto cookie sheets, drop mixture, about 2 tablespoons at a time and 2 inches apart; shape into peaked mounds. Bake 10 to 18 minutes or until golden. (Cookies will be soft to touch, but will firm up when cool.)

Cool on racks; store in tight container—flavor develops upon standing. Makes 1¼ dozen.

———◆———

MEAT TIP: Thread cubes of lamb shoulder on skewers; broil; frequently brush with bottled salad dressing.

ICE CREAM GOURMET

Early in day: With ice-cream scoop, from 2 pints each of vanilla and coffee ice cream form 8 balls of each. Place in jelly-roll pan; freeze.

Mix ½ cup chocolate sauce with ½ cup sour cream; refrigerate, covered.

Just before serving: Arrange balls of ice cream in pretty bowl. Spoon sauce over all. Makes 8 servings.

———◆———

ORANGE CONFECTIONS

1 7½-ounce package vanilla wafers, finely crushed (about 2 cups)	¼ cup frozen orange-juice concentrate, thawed
¾ cup flaked coconut	2 1-ounce squares semisweet chocolate, grated
¾ cup confectioners' sugar	
1 egg white	

Day before: In medium bowl, combine all ingredients except chocolate. Shape mixture into 1-inch balls, then roll in grated chocolate. Store in covered container at least a day to mellow. Makes about 20 balls.

BEVERAGE TIP: Pour boiling water over tea bags; add cinnamon stick and let stand 3 minutes. Remove stick; pour tea over ice in glasses.

TUESDAY
Bean Burgers*
on Toasted Buns
Olives   Pickles
Potato Chips
Melon Soufflés*
Coconut Mounds*
Coffee

WEDNESDAY
Lamb en Brochette*
Corn with Peppers
Tomatoes
Lettuce Wedges
with Russian Dressing
Ice Cream Gourmet*
Coffee

THURSDAY
Fried Chicken
Candied Sweet Potatoes
Buttered Spinach
Mixed-Greens Salad
Orange Confections*
Spiced Iced Tea*

SALMON-CUSTARD CASSEROLES

4 eggs
1 cup undiluted evaporated milk
2 tablespoons chopped chives
1 teaspoon dry mustard
½ teaspoon salt

dash pepper
1 16-ounce can salmon, drained and
   flaked, boned and skinned
paprika
4 lemon wedges

Preheat oven to 350°F. In large bowl, beat eggs slightly; stir in milk, chives, mustard, salt and pepper. Mix in salmon and spoon into 4 well-greased individual 10-ounce casseroles. Sprinkle with paprika.

Set casseroles in shallow pan. Pour hot water into pan until it comes about ¾ of the way up casserole sides. Bake 35 to 40 minutes or until knife inserted in center of custard comes out clean. Serve with lemon. Makes 4 servings.

DESSERT TIP: In saucepan, combine 1½ pounds fresh rhubarb cut in 1-inch pieces, ½ cup water, ⅛ teaspoon salt, ¾ cup granulated sugar; simmer, covered, 10 minutes, or until tender, stirring gently once or twice. Fold in 1 pint sliced fresh strawberries; refrigerate. Makes 5 cups; enough for 8 servings.

BAKED HAM WITH CELERY
AND CARROTS WITH CURRIED
CREAM SAUCE

BAKED HAM WITH CELERY AND CARROTS

½ fully cooked, semi-boneless ham,
   about 5 pounds
½ teaspoon curry
whole cloves

12 medium carrots, sliced
12 stalks celery, sliced
salt and pepper
Curried Cream Sauce (below)

About 2½ hours before serving: Preheat oven to 325°F. Remove any outer casing from ham. Rub ham with curry; stud with cloves; insert meat thermometer in center and place in large, shallow roasting pan. Roast 1½ hours; arrange vegetables around sides and sprinkle with salt and pepper. Continue roasting 1 hour longer or until thermometer reaches 130°F., turning vegetables once during cooking.

Serve ham on warm platter, with vegetables arranged around it. Pass Curried Cream Sauce. Makes 6 servings. Save leftovers for Tuesday, page 65.

Curried Cream Sauce: Drain all but 3 tablespoons drippings from ham roasting pan. Over low heat, stir in 3 tablespoons flour, 1½ teaspoons curry, until blended. Stir in 1½ cups each chicken broth and heavy cream and continue cooking over low heat, stirring until sauce thickens; do not boil.

HURRY-UP LEMON PIE

baked 8″ pie shell
1 15-ounce can sweetened
   condensed milk
1 teaspoon grated lemon peel
½ cup lemon juice

2 egg yolks
2 egg whites
dash salt
¼ teaspoon vanilla extract
4 tablespoons granulated sugar

Preheat oven to 350°F. Blend condensed milk with lemon peel, juice and egg yolks until thickened. Pour into shell. In small bowl, with electric mixer, beat egg whites with salt and vanilla until frothy. Add sugar a little at a time, beating well. Continue to beat until mixture forms peaks; swirl over filling to touch pie shell all around. Bake 12 to 15 minutes. Makes 6 servings.

FRIDAY
Pea Soup in Mugs
Salmon-Custard
Casseroles*
Asparagus
Relish Tray
Stewed Rhubarb
and Strawberries*
Coffee   Tea

SATURDAY
Baked Ham
with
Celery and Carrots*
with
Curried Cream Sauce*
Parsley Potatoes
Hurry-up Lemon Pie*
Tea   Coffee

GARDEN TOMATO SOUP

4 large tomatoes
1 cup canned chicken broth
4 green onions, chopped
1 small cucumber, thinly sliced
½ cup diced green pepper

1 cup canned tomato juice
juice of 1 lemon
2 teaspoons granulated sugar
1 tablespoon seasoned salt
¼ teaspoon seasoned pepper

Early in day: Dip each tomato into boiling water for about 1 minute, then into cold water for 1 minute. With paring knife, slip off skin; cut tomatoes into chunks.

In large saucepan, in chicken broth, simmer green onions, cucumber slices, green pepper and tomatoes, covered, 5 minutes. Add tomato juice, lemon juice, sugar, seasoned salt, and seasoned pepper; simmer, covered, 10 minutes. Transfer to large bowl; cover; refrigerate.

Serve in soup bowls. Makes 6 servings.

VEGETABLE TIP: Toss fresh cooked green beans with melted butter, flavored with crushed garlic.

MINT-ICE-CREAM PIE

Early in day: Preheat oven to 375°F. Combine 3 tablespoons butter or margarine, softened, with 1⅓ cups chocolate-cookie crumbs (about eighteen 2¾″ cookies) until crumbly. Press into 9-inch pie plate. Bake 8 minutes; cool. Fill with mounds of mint ice cream; freeze.

About 15 minutes before serving: Remove pie from freezer. Drizzle with chocolate sauce. Makes 8 servings.

—◆—

CHICKEN WITH ARTICHOKES

1 3½- to 4-pound roasting chicken,
  cut-up
paprika
¼ cup butter or margarine
1 teaspoon salt
1 envelope garlic-salad-dressing

mix
1 10½-ounce can condensed cream-
  of-mushroom soup
1 9½-ounce can artichoke hearts,
  drained

About 1 hour before serving: Sprinkle chicken with paprika; in large skillet, in butter, sauté chicken until golden. Sprinkle with salt and salad-dressing mix. Stir in undiluted soup and ½ soup can of water.

Simmer, covered, 30 minutes; add artichokes; simmer 5 minutes or until hot. Makes 6 servings.

VEGETABLE TIP: Add a little granulated sugar, along with salt, to water in which you cook carrots. It brings out the natural sweetness of the carrots.

GREEN-GODDESS DRESSING

1 garlic clove, minced
½ teaspoon salt
½ teaspoon dry mustard
1 teaspoon Worcestershire
2 tablespoons anchovy paste
3 tablespoons tarragon-wine

vinegar
3 tablespoons snipped chives
⅓ cup chopped parsley
1 cup mayonnaise
½ cup sour cream
⅛ teaspoon pepper

Early in day: Combine all ingredients; refrigerate, covered. Makes 1¾ cups.

SUNDAY
Garden Tomato Soup*
Sirloin Steak
Mashed Potatoes
Green Beans*
Mint-Ice-Cream Pie*
Tea

MONDAY
*Chicken
with Artichokes**
*Buttered
Carrot Strips**
Hot Poppy-Seed Rolls
*Tomato Salad
with
Green-Goddess Dressing**
Chocolate Pudding
Coffee   Tea

GARDEN TOMATO SOUP

PICKLED PEACHES

1 29-ounce can cling peach halves,
  drained
whole cloves
1 cup syrup, drained from peaches

½ cup vinegar
1 3-inch stick cinnamon
½ cup granulated sugar

Early in day: Stud each peach half with 3 cloves. Simmer with remaining ingredients 3 or 4 minutes. Cool; refrigerate. Makes 8 servings.

COLOSSAL STRAWBERRY SHORTCAKE

3 pints strawberries, sliced
granulated sugar
2 cups sifted regular all-purpose
  flour
1 tablespoon double-acting baking
  powder

¾ teaspoon salt
½ cup butter or margarine
¼ cup milk
1 egg, beaten
1 cup sour cream

About 40 minutes before serving: Gently toss strawberries with ½ cup sugar. Refrigerate.

Preheat oven to 450°F. Into large bowl, sift together flour, baking powder, salt and 2 tablespoons sugar. With pastry blender or 2 knives used scissor-fashion, cut butter into flour mixture until like coarse crumbs. Stir in milk and egg.

Pat biscuit dough into greased 8-inch round cake pan. Bake 20 minutes or until golden brown. Cool 10 minutes; loosen edges with spatula and invert onto rack to finish cooling.

Just before serving: Drain strawberries, reserving syrup. In small bowl, combine sour cream with ¼ cup sugar. Split biscuit horizontally. Place bottom layer, cut side up, on serving plate; drizzle with half of syrup from strawberries, allowing syrup to soak in; spread on half of sour-cream mixture and top with half of strawberries. Place second layer, cut side down, on top; top with rest of syrup, sour cream and strawberries. Makes 8 servings.

BEVERAGE TIP: In saucepan, bring 1 quart water to rolling boil. Remove from heat; add 15 tea bags or ⅓ cup loose tea; brew 4 minutes. Strain into pitcher containing 1 quart cold water. To serve, pour into ice-filled glasses. Makes 8 to 10 servings.

TUESDAY
Sliced Baked Ham
*Pickled Peaches**
Macaroni Salad
Colossal
*Strawberry Shortcake**
*Iced Tea**

MEAT TIP: Place each broiled hamburger or cheeseburger on a rusk round. Top with sweet gherkin or chopped olives.

CRUNCHY BEAN SALAD

2 cups thinly sliced celery	2 16-ounce cans barbecue beans,
2 cups thinly sliced, unpared	chilled, drained
radishes	⅓ cup creamy French dressing
1 cucumber, thinly sliced	1 teaspoon salt
2 cups shredded green or red	curly endive
cabbage	

In large bowl, toss together all ingredients except endive. Line salad bowl with endive; pour in bean mixture. Makes 6 servings.

FRESH SOUR-CHERRY PIE

1 to 1½ cups granulated sugar	5 cups pitted fresh sour cherries
½ cup all-purpose flour	pastry for 2-crust 9-inch pie
½ teaspoon salt	1 tablespoon butter or margarine

Preheat oven to 425°F. In large bowl, combine sugar, flour and salt. Add cherries and toss lightly. Turn into pastry-lined 9-inch pie plate. Dot with butter. Adjust top crust; cut steam vents. Bake in 425°F. oven 50 to 60 minutes or until pie crust is golden. Cool on rack. Nice served warm with vanilla ice cream. Makes 6 servings.

GOURMET VEAL CUTLET

1½ pounds thin veal cutlets,	⅓ cup butter or margarine
about 6	1 cup sauterne
6 thin slices natural Swiss cheese	1 cup canned beef gravy
6 paper-thin slices cooked ham	½ cup light cream
2 tablespoons flour	dash salt
½ teaspoon paprika	4 to 6 drops lemon juice

About 1 hour before serving: With edge of heavy plate, pound cutlets well; cut in half. On each of 6 halves, place ½ slice cheese; 1 slice ham, folded over; another ½ slice cheese. Cover with second cutlet half. Fasten with toothpicks. Coat lightly with flour mixed with paprika.

In skillet, in hot butter, brown cutlets on both sides. Add ½ cup sauterne; simmer, uncovered, until liquid is almost completely absorbed. Add ½ cup sauterne, gravy, cream; simmer, covered, 10 minutes, or until fork-tender. Add salt, lemon juice; *remove picks.* Makes 6 servings.

VEGETABLE TIP: Sauté slivered almonds in butter; pour over cooked cauliflowerets just before serving.

CREAMY MUSTARD SAUCE

Mix 1 cup sour cream, 1 tablespoon prepared mustard, 1 tablespoon minced onion, ¼ teaspoon salt, ⅛ teaspoon pepper. Heat over low heat. Sprinkle with 1 tablespoon chopped scallions. Makes 1 cup—enough for 4 servings of broiled fish.

DESSERT TIP: Split ladyfingers; halve crosswise. Place 4 or 5 pieces around insides of dessert dishes. Fill centers with raspberry or lemon sherbet. Drizzle with chocolate sauce.

WEDNESDAY
Open-Faced Hamburgers*
Crunchy Bean Salad*
Fresh Sour-Cherry Pie*
Milk   Tea

THURSDAY
Bisque of Tomato
Gourmet Veal Cutlet*
Nutted Cauliflower*
Peas   Relishes
Fan-Tan Rolls
Custard
Coffee

FRIDAY
Vegetable-Juice
Cocktail
Broiled Flounder
Creamy Mustard Sauce*
Little New Potatoes
Favorite Green Salad
Sherbet Sundae*
Milk   Coffee

PLUM-SAUCED SPARERIBS

APPETIZER TIP: Soften large package cream cheese with mayonnaise and lemon juice. Mix in drop of Tabasco, small can tuna, drained and flaked.

PLUM-SAUCED SPARERIBS

2 tablespoons butter or margarine
1 medium onion, chopped
1 17-ounce can purple plums, pitted
1 6-ounce can frozen lemonade
   concentrate
¼ cup chili sauce
¼ cup soy sauce

1 teaspoon Worcestershire
2 teaspoons prepared mustard
1 teaspoon ground ginger
2 drops Tabasco
10 pounds pork spareribs (4 racks)
1 tablespoon salt

Early in day: In medium saucepan, in butter, sauté onion.

In food mill or sieve, puree plums with syrup; add to onion with lemonade, chili sauce, soy sauce, Worcestershire, mustard, ginger and Tabasco. Simmer, uncovered, 15 minutes; cover; refrigerate.

Cut spareribs into 2- or 3-rib portions; place in large kettle, with salt and water to cover; simmer, covered, 1½ hours or until fork-tender. Drain; cover; refrigerate.

About 1 hour and 15 minutes before serving: Preheat oven to 425°F. Pour plum sauce over spareribs; bake about 1 hour or until of desired brownness, basting often with sauce, and turning at least once as they bake. Makes 10 servings.

For 5 servings: Halve above ingredients, then proceed as directed.

SATURDAY
Tuna Dip*
Crackers
Plum-Sauced
Spareribs*
Hot Dinner Rolls
Corn   Zucchini
Watermelon
Milk   Iced Tea

CHICKEN IN ASPIC

SUNDAY

*Chicken in Aspic**

Noodles Romanoff

*Seasoned Beets**

Coffee-Marshmallow
*Refrigerator Cake**

Milk   Coffee

3 large whole chicken breasts,
   cut in half
½ teaspoon seasoned salt
¼ teaspoon seasoned pepper
1½ teaspoons unflavored gelatin

2 10½-ounce cans condensed
   consommé
2 heads romaine
fresh dill sprigs for garnish
salad dressing

Early in day: Preheat broiler if manufacturer directs. Meanwhile, place chicken in jelly-roll pan, skin-side down. Sprinkle with seasoned salt and seasoned pepper. Broil until golden brown, about 18 minutes; turn; broil until golden brown.

Cool chicken; place, skin-side down, in 11¾″ by 7½″ by 1¾″ baking dish. Meanwhile, in cup, mix gelatin with 1½ tablespoons water; set in hot water and stir gelatin until dissolved. Stir into undiluted consommé; pour over chicken. Place in refrigerator until consommé is partially set.

Turn chicken over; spoon on consommé in pan; refrigerate until consommé sets a bit; spoon more consommé over chicken until chicken is coated.

Just before serving: Arrange chicken on platter. Remove outer leaves of romaine; cut heart into sixths; arrange between chicken breasts; top with dill. Pass salad dressing. Makes 6 servings.

VEGETABLE TIP: Heat drained cooked beets, cut in julienne strips, with 2 tablespoons butter, dash of salt, garlic salt and pepper.

COFFEE-MARSHMALLOW REFRIGERATOR CAKE

Early in day: In saucepan, dissolve 2 tablespoons instant coffee in 1 cup hot water; add one 10½-ounce package miniature marshmallows; cook over low heat, stirring, until marshmallows are melted. Refrigerate until slightly thickened. Whip 1 cup heavy or whipping cream; fold into coffee mixture. Split 18 ladyfingers; use half to line bottom of 10″ by 6″ by 2″ baking dish. Cover with half of coffee mixture. Repeat; refrigerate.

To serve: Whip ½ cup heavy or whipping cream. Spread over top of cake. Garnish with chocolate curls. Cut into 6 to 8 servings.

GOURMET'S PILAF

MONDAY

*Gourmet's Pilaf**

*Broiled Tomatoes**

Escarole Salad Bowl

Fruit Tray

Coffee   Tea

2 6-ounce packages long-grain-and-
   wild-rice mix
1 pound fresh sausage links
butter or margarine
1 pound fresh mushrooms, sliced

½ teaspoon seasoned pepper
salt
1 tablespoon instant minced onion
1 pound chicken livers

About 1 hour before serving: In 4-quart Dutch oven, prepare rice mix as label directs, cooking until all liquid is absorbed.

Meanwhile, in skillet, sauté sausages for 15 minutes, or until golden brown; remove; reserve; pour off fat. In same skillet, in ¼ cup butter, sauté mushrooms until golden. Toss with seasoned pepper, ½ teaspoon salt and instant minced onion; reserve with sausages.

Still in same skillet, in 2 tablespoons butter, sauté chicken livers until brown on outside but still pink inside; sprinkle with ½ teaspoon salt; combine with mushrooms, sausages and rice; arrange in shallow 2-quart serving dish. Makes 6 servings.

VEGETABLE TIP: Toss seasoned bread crumbs with melted butter; use to top tomato halves; broil until crumbs are tinged with brown.

BUTTERSCOTCH PECAN PUDDING

TUESDAY

*Grilled Lamb Patties
with Pears**

*Green Beans
with Almonds*

Tossed Salad

*Apricot Cheesecake**

Coffee

WEDNESDAY

Vichyssoise

*Salmon-Avocado Salad**

Hot Buttered Biscuits

*Butterscotch Pecan
Pudding**

Tea   Coffee

THURSDAY

*Broiled Flank Steak**

Corn on the Cob

Sliced Tomatoes

*Coupe Español**

Iced Coffee

GRILLED LAMB PATTIES WITH PEARS

2 pounds ground lamb shoulder	¼ cup undiluted evaporated milk
1½ teaspoons salt	6 bacon strips
¼ teaspoon pepper	1 29-ounce can pear halves, drained
¼ cup dry bread crumbs	¼ cup mayonnaise

Preheat broiler if manufacturer directs. In bowl, combine lamb, salt, pepper, bread crumbs and milk, mixing lightly; shape into 6 patties.

Wrap each patty with strip of bacon; secure with toothpick. Place on broiler rack, toothpick side up. Broil 6 minutes; remove picks; turn.

Spread pears with mayonnaise; arrange on broiler. Broil 6 to 7 minutes or until meat is of desired doneness. Makes 6 servings.

DESSERT TIP: Just before serving, spread frozen cheesecake, thawed as label directs, with apricot jam.

SALMON-AVOCADO SALAD

1 16-ounce can red salmon, drained	lemon juice
⅔ cup diced celery	salad greens
3 hard-cooked eggs	1 15-ounce can asparagus spears
½ cup mayonnaise	pimiento strips
½ teaspoon curry	paprika
3 avocados	

Remove bones and skin from salmon. In medium bowl, break up salmon into chunks. Add celery and 2 coarsely chopped eggs; toss.

Combine mayonnaise and curry; pour over salmon mixture; toss well; cover; refrigerate.

Peel, halve lengthwise, then pit, avocados; rub all surfaces with lemon juice. Fill with salmon mixture; place on bed of greens. Top each avocado half with hard-cooked egg slice. Arrange a few drained asparagus spears around each; lay pimiento strip diagonally across. Sprinkle egg slices with paprika. Makes 6 servings.

DESSERT TIP: Make up two packages of instant butterscotch pudding as label directs, but fold in a few chopped pecans. Pour into sherbet glasses; top with frozen whipped topping and a whole pecan.

MEAT TIP: Score flank steak in several places. Broil about 6 minutes on each side, brushing occasionally with mixture of softened butter, snipped parsley and celery salt.

COUPE ESPAÑOL

1 orange	1 banana
⅓ cup heavy or whipping cream	½ pint orange sherbet
1 pear	

About 1 hour ahead: With knife, remove thin layer of peel from orange; cut a few pieces into narrow strips. Section orange. Whip cream; refrigerate.

At serving time: Dice cored, pared pear into 4 sherbet glasses; top with diced, peeled banana and orange sections.

Spoon a little whipped cream over each. Top with spoonful of sherbet. Sprinkle orange peel over each. Makes 4 servings.

QUICK RED-FLANNEL HASH

1 15-ounce can roast-beef hash
1 medium onion, chopped
¼ cup chili sauce

1 cup cooked shoestring or diced beets, drained

In bowl, combine hash, onion, chili sauce and beets. Heat in skillet over high heat for 15 minutes or until well browned. Cut into wedges; lift out with spatula. Makes 4 servings.

INSTANT FRENCH BREAD

Preheat oven to 350°F. On ungreased cookie sheet, stand biscuits from 2 cans refrigerated biscuits on edge in one long roll, lightly pressing together and shaping ends to form tapering loaf. Brush with beaten egg white; sprinkle with sesame seed. Bake 30 to 40 minutes, or until golden. Slice between biscuits almost to bottom crust and serve. Or spread a little garlic butter between baked biscuits, pop into oven for a few minutes, and serve.

EASY FUDGE FROSTING

3 squares unsweetened chocolate
2 tablespoons butter or margarine
2¼ cups sifted confectioners' sugar
6 tablespoons undiluted evaporated

milk or light cream
dash salt
1 teaspoon vanilla extract

Melt chocolate with butter over boiling water; blend. Add 1½ cups confectioners' sugar, milk, and salt, all at once; with spoon, beat until smooth. Cook over low heat, stirring, until mixture bubbles well around edges. Remove from heat. Add vanilla and remaining sugar in thirds, beating until smooth after each addition. Set in bowl of ice water until thick enough to spread, stirring occasionally.

Fills and frosts two 8″ cake layers or frosts two 8″ square cakes.

LOBSTER COCKTAIL

1 tablespoon salt
8 ½-pound frozen rock-lobster
tails
4 large lemons
2¼ cups catchup

2 teaspoons Worcestershire
watercress
3 tablespoons chopped parsley
2 8½-ounce cans colossal ripe olives

Day before serving: In large Dutch oven, to 3 quarts boiling water, add salt and lobster tails; bring to boil; cover and simmer 10 minutes. Drain; cover with cold water; drain again. Using kitchen scissors, cut membrane away from each tail; free lobster meat from shell; leave fantail attached. Cover; refrigerate.

Just before serving: Cut lemons in half; squeeze (save juice for next day). Cut thin slice from bottom of each cup. Combine catchup, horseradish and Worcestershire; use to fill lemon cups. On large platter, on bed of watercress, arrange lemon cups and lobster tails. Sprinkle with parsley; garnish with olives. Makes 8 servings.

MEAT TIP: Have butcher bone, roll and tie a leg of lamb for rotisserie. Brush lamb with mixture of salad oil, lemon juice, garlic and dried marjoram or rosemary as it roasts on the rotisserie. (Or use this mixture to coat lamb to be roasted in oven.) For bone-in leg, place on rotisserie starting at shank end above bone, coming out butt end below bone.

LOBSTER COCKTAIL

FRIDAY

Quick
Red-Flannel Hash*

Tossed Salad

Instant French Bread*

Yellow Cake
with
Easy Fudge Frosting*

Coffee   Tea

SATURDAY

Lobster Cocktail*

Leg of Lamb
Rotisserie*

Herb Rice

Peas and Mushrooms

Fresh Figs

Iced Tea   Coffee

SUNDAY

*Lemon Foam Cocktail**

Roast Turkey Roll

Canned Yams

*Gourmet Spinach Salad**

*Summer Apple Pie**

Tea   Coffee

LEMON FOAM COCKTAIL

1 20-ounce can pineapple juice	½ cup water
⅔ cup lemon juice	2 egg whites (use yolks in salad)
⅓ cup granulated sugar	1 cup finely crushed ice

Combine all ingredients in jar or shaker. Cover; shake until frothy. Pour into cocktail glasses. Makes 6 servings.

GOURMET SPINACH SALAD

¼ cup salad oil	1 pound spinach
1 teaspoon salt	2 cups cherry tomatoes
1½ teaspoons Worcestershire	2 tablespoons lemon juice
⅛ teaspoon pepper	1 cup garlic-flavored croutons
2 egg yolks	

In large salad bowl, combine salad oil, salt, Worcestershire, pepper and yolks. Tear spinach into bite-size pieces in salad bowl; cut tomatoes in half and add to spinach. Toss thoroughly.

Sprinkle on lemon juice and croutons; toss again until well mixed. Makes 8 servings.

DESSERT TIP: Allow about 4 pounds apples (7 to 8 cups sliced) for a 9-inch pie. A little grated lemon rind and juice will enhance the flavor of new summer apples.

MONDAY

*Frank-Sauerkraut Goulash**

*Parsley Carrots and Potatoes**

*Angel Cake with Blueberry Sauce**

Coffee   Tea

FRANK-SAUERKRAUT GOULASH

1 pound frankfurters (about 8)	well packed
2 tablespoons butter or margarine, melted	½ cup sour cream
	½ teaspoon paprika
2 tablespoons minced onion	1 tablespoon chopped parsley
2 cups drained, canned sauerkraut,	

About 15 minutes before serving: Cut each frankfurter into 5 diagonal slices. In large skillet over medium heat, cook onion and frankfurter slices in butter 5 minutes or until onion is tender and frankfurter slices slightly brown.

Rinse sauerkraut under running cold water; drain well; add to frankfurters. Simmer, covered, 5 minutes, stirring occasionally. Stir in sour cream, paprika. Serve garnished with parsley. Makes 4 servings.

PARSLEY CARROTS AND POTATOES

2 cups slivered, pared carrots	6 tablespoons melted butter or margarine
2 cups slivered, pared potatoes	
1¼ teaspoons salt	⅛ teaspoon pepper
¾ cup boiling water	½ cup chopped parsley

Cook carrots and potatoes with salt in boiling water, covered, 10 minutes, or until tender. Drain; add rest of ingredients; toss. Or drain; mash; then add butter, pepper and parsley. Makes 4 servings.

DESSERT TIP: In saucepan, combine 1 teaspoon cornstarch with 3 tablespoons granulated sugar, ⅛ teaspoon each salt and cinnamon, 2 tablespoons lemon juice, ¼ cup orange juice and 2 cups fresh blueberries. Stir and simmer until sauce is thickened and deep purple; cool. Makes enough for 6 servings.

VEGETABLE TIP: Add 1 tablespoon prepared mustard to each ½ cup bottled or homemade mayonnaise. Use to fill hollowed-out cherry tomatoes.

BEN'S COFFEE FLUFF

About 2 hours before serving: Sprinkle 1 envelope unflavored gelatin over ¼ cup cold water in glass measuring cup to soften. Set cup in pan of hot water; stir gelatin until completely dissolved. In small bowl, dissolve 4 teaspoons instant coffee in ⅓ cup boiling water; stir into gelatin mixture.

Separate 3 eggs. In small bowl, with electric mixer at high speed, beat egg yolks until thick and lemon-colored. Beat in ½ cup granulated sugar; continue beating at high speed until yolks and sugar are well blended. Slowly pour in coffee-gelatin mixture until well mixed.

In another small bowl, beat egg whites until stiff. Gently fold in egg-yolk mixture until almost blended. Pour into 1½-quart serving dish. Refrigerate at least 1 hour. Makes 5 to 6 servings.

———◆———

APPLE-AND-ONION SOUP

¼ cup butter or margarine
1 large Bermuda onion, thinly sliced
2 large green apples, pared, cored, thinly sliced

3 10½-ounce cans condensed beef consommé
½ teaspoon curry
1 cup heavy or whipping cream

Early in day: In large saucepan, melt butter; sauté onion slices until soft, about 5 minutes. Add apple slices; cook 5 minutes longer. Add undiluted consommé and curry; cover; simmer gently 25 minutes.

Slowly pour some of hot mixture into electric blender; blend at low speed until creamy; then transfer to bowl; repeat until all soup is blended. (Or press through coarse sieve.)

Pour blended mixture back into saucepan; add cream; heat, over low heat, about 5 minutes: Cool; refrigerate. Stir well; serve in chilled mugs. Makes 6 to 8 servings.

SALAD TIP: Cook package of herb rice; cool. Toss with any leftover mixed vegetables, a little onion and mayonnaise thinned with milk.

———◆———

BROCCOLI MIMOSA SALAD

½ cup apple juice
6 tablespoons cider vinegar
2 tablespoons salad oil
½ teaspoon seasoned salt
¼ teaspoon seasoned pepper

½ teaspoon basil
2 10-ounce packages frozen broccoli spears
2 hard-cooked eggs, chopped

About 4 hours before serving: In jar, combine apple juice, vinegar, oil, ¼ cup water, seasoned salt and seasoned pepper, basil; shake well; refrigerate.

Cook broccoli as label directs; cool. Pour some of dressing over broccoli; cover; refrigerate. Toss occasionally. Serve on salad plates; sprinkle with eggs. Pass extra dressing. Makes 6 servings.

DESSERT TIP: Fill baked tart shells with canned apple-pie filling. Top each with ¼ slice of cheese; broil until cheese melts.

MUSTARD MAYONNAISE IN CHERRY TOMATOES

TUESDAY
Cold Sliced Turkey
Mustard Mayonnaise in Cherry Tomatoes*
Marinated Cold Mixed Vegetables
Ben's Coffee Fluff*
Milk   Coffee

WEDNESDAY
Apple-and-Onion Soup*
Brown-and-Serve Sausages
Easy Herb-Rice Salad*
Chocolate Cake
Milk   Coffee

THURSDAY
Minute Steaks
French Fries
Broccoli Mimosa Salad*
Hard Rolls   Butter
Apple Tarts*   Cheese
Coffee

FRIDAY

Fish Fillets
with Green Sauce*

Cottage-Fried
Potatoes*

Stewed Tomatoes

Peach Ice Cream

Pretzels

Milk   Tea

FISH FILLETS WITH GREEN SAUCE

3 tablespoons chopped watercress	1 7-ounce bottle lemon-lime
3 tablespoons chopped parsley	carbonated beverage
2 tablespoons chopped chives	1½ pounds fresh (or thawed,
½ cup mayonnaise	frozen) cod, ocean perch,
½ teaspoon black pepper	haddock or sole fillets

About 20 minutes before serving: Mix watercress, parsley and chives; add ¼ cup of mixture to mayonnaise; place in serving bowl; refrigerate.

In skillet, combine remaining greens, pepper and lemon-lime soda; bring to boil. Add fillets; cover; simmer 10 minutes or until fish flakes easily with fork. Remove fillets to heated platter; serve with mayonnaise sauce. Makes 4 servings.

VEGETABLE TIP: Fry diced cold cooked potatoes in butter until golden on underside; turn and brown other side. Sprinkle with salt and pepper.

———◆———

APPETIZER TIP: Spread crackers with canned deviled ham. Spoon a little sour cream on each and top with half a green grape, if desired.

DAN'S SWEET-AND-SOUR MEATBALLS

5 thin bread slices, cut into ½-inch cubes	¼ cup white vinegar
½ cup milk	¼ cup granulated sugar
1 egg	½ cup sweet-gherkin chunks
2 pounds ground beef round	1 13½-ounce can pineapple chunks, drained
salt	2 small green peppers, cut into bite-size pieces
⅛ teaspoon pepper	
⅛ teaspoon garlic salt	1 large carrot, pared, diagonally sliced
¼ cup regular all-purpose flour	
salad oil	1 16-ounce jar spiced whole crab apples for garnish
1 8-ounce can tomato sauce	

About 1 hour 15 minutes before serving: In large bowl, combine bread cubes, milk and egg; let stand 5 minutes; then, with fork, press together until bread is soaked. Add meat, 1¼ teaspoons salt, pepper, garlic salt. Mix well; shape into about 34 golf-size balls. Roll, one by one, in flour; shake off excess flour; set aside.

In large skillet over medium heat, in ½ cup hot salad oil, brown meatballs until golden; drain on paper towels.

Drain oil from skillet; return meatballs, together with ¾ cup cold water, tomato sauce, vinegar, sugar, 1 teaspoon salt and sweet gherkins. Add all but 6 pineapple chunks. Simmer, over low heat, uncovered, 10 to 15 minutes, turning often or until about two-thirds of liquid evaporates.

Meanwhile, in medium saucepan over medium heat, in 1 tablespoon hot salad oil, sauté green peppers, carrot slices and ¼ teaspoon salt until tender-crisp, about 3 to 5 minutes. Add half of mixture to meatballs.

Spoon into large serving bowl; top with reserved pineapple chunks and rest of green-pepper-and-carrot mixture. Garnish with crab apples and serve. Makes 6 servings.

DESSERT TIP: To tint coconut, blend 1 teaspoon milk or water with drop or so of desired food color. Add 1⅓ cups flaked coconut, also a little peppermint, almond or vanilla extract if desired. Toss with fork until blended. Sprinkle over cake immediately after frosting.

SATURDAY

Tomato Juice

Ham Pick-Ups*

Dan's Sweet-and-Sour
Meatballs*

Buttered Rice

Hot Rolls

Tinted Coconut Cake*

Milk   Coffee

MEAT TIP: Spread lamb chops with a combination of chopped parsley, mashed garlic and butter; broil.

ZUCCHINI, ITALIAN STYLE

Scrub 2 pounds zucchini, Cut off ends; do not pare. Cut in halves lengthwise; cut crosswise into 3-inch long pieces. In skillet, heat ¼ cup olive or salad oil. Add zucchini, with green sides up; sprinkle with 1½ cups sliced onions; lightly brown cut sides over low heat. Turn cut sides up; add 1½ teaspoons salt, ¼ teaspoon pepper and 3 cups canned tomato juice. Cook, covered, over low heat 40 minutes or until zucchini are tender and tomato juice forms thick sauce. Makes 4 servings.

SUNDAY

*Parsley-Buttered Lamb Chops**

Corn on the Cob

*Zucchini, Italian Style**

*Peppermint Chiffon Pie**

Iced Tea

PEPPERMINT CHIFFON PIE

1⅓ cups finely crushed vanilla wafers (24 2-inch)	½ cup finely crushed hard peppermint candies
¼ cup melted butter or margarine	6 eggs, separated
¾ cup milk	1 envelope unflavored gelatin
¼ cup granulated sugar	

Early in day: Preheat oven to 375°F. Mix wafers with melted butter. Press into bottom and sides of 9-inch pie plate. Bake 8 minutes. Cool.

In medium saucepan, scald milk with sugar and crushed peppermint candy; add beaten egg yolks and cook, stirring constantly, over medium heat, until mixture coats spoon.

Meanwhile, sprinkle gelatin on ¼ cup water to soften; stir into hot peppermint mixture. Stir until gelatin dissolves; refrigerate until cool.

Beat egg whites until stiff, not dry. Fold into cooled peppermint mixture; pour into crumb shell; refrigerate.

If desired, garnish pie with whipped cream. Makes one 9-inch pie.

—◆—

SUMMER CHICKEN SALAD

¾ cup mayonnaise	lemon juice
½ teaspoon salt	3 cups cubed cooked chicken
¼ teaspoon white pepper	1 cup sliced celery
¼ teaspoon dry mustard	1 cup halved, seeded green grapes
½ teaspoon granulated sugar	¼ cup pecan halves
1 teaspoon cider vinegar	2 apples, cut into wedges
1 cup cubed, unpared red apple	6 small bunches green grapes

MONDAY

Cold Apple Juice

*Summer Chicken Salad**

Date-and-Nut-Bread Sandwiches

Iced Tea

In small bowl, combine mayonnaise, salt, pepper, mustard, sugar, vinegar.

In large bowl, sprinkle apple cubes with 1 tablespoon lemon juice; toss; add chicken, celery, halved grapes, pecans; stir in dressing; refrigerate.

To serve, arrange on 6 salad plates with apple wedges, dipped in lemon juice, and grape bunches as garnish. Makes 6 servings.

—◆—

MEAT TIP: In skillet, brown ½-inch-thick ham slices; lower heat. Add canned yams with liquid; heat with a little brown sugar and cinnamon.

ORANGE-GLOW SALAD

At least 6 hours before serving: Prepare 3-ounce package orange-flavor gelatin as label directs.

Spoon 1 tablespoon gelatin in each of four 3″ by 1½″ or six 2½″ by 1½″ muffin-pan cups. Refrigerate until firm; lay ¼ orange slice in each cup; spoon a little gelatin over orange; refrigerate.

TUESDAY

*Skillet Ham and Yams**

*Orange-Glow Salad**

English Muffins

Vanilla-Flavor Whipped Dessert

Tea   Coffee

ORANGE-GLOW SALAD

Meanwhile, chill remaining gelatin until partially thickened. Fold in ¼ cup grated carrot; spoon into muffin-pan cups. Tuck 4 banana slices around insides of each cup; refrigerate until set.

At serving time, dip muffin pan just to rim in warm water for about 10 seconds. Invert on wet cookie sheet; unmold. Transfer salads to salad plates. Garnish with few sprigs of parsley.

BLUE-CHEESE BURGERS ON BUTTERED ROLLS

Lightly toss 1 pound ground beef chuck with 1 teaspoon salt, ¼ teaspoon pepper and 2 tablespoons minced onion. Shape into 8 thin patties. Combine ¼ pound crumbled blue cheese, 2 tablespoons mayonnaise, 1 tablespoon Worcestershire and ½ teaspoon dry mustard; spoon onto four of the patties; top with remaining patties. Press edges together; broil to desired doneness. Makes 4 servings.

ROLL TIP: Split hamburger rolls; spread with butter or margarine; sprinkle with seasoned salt and pinch of oregano. Toast.

MACARONI SALAD

1 8-ounce package elbow macaroni	1 small onion, diced
¾ cup mayonnaise	¼ cup diced stuffed olives
¼ cup milk	¼ cup diced pitted ripe olives
few dashes Tabasco	1 6-ounce package cubed Cheddar
¼ teaspoon dry mustard	cheese
½ cup diced celery	lettuce
½ cup diced green pepper	paprika

Early in day: Cook macaroni as label directs; drain. Mix mayonnaise, milk, Tabasco, mustard; pour over macaroni; toss. Cover; refrigerate.

Just before serving: Toss together macaroni, celery, green pepper, onion, stuffed and ripe olives and cheese.

Arrange on lettuce leaves; sprinkle with paprika. Makes 6 to 8 servings.

WEDNESDAY
Blue-Cheese Burgers on Buttered Rolls*
Macaroni Salad*
Sliced Tomatoes and Green Onions
Peach Ice-Cream Sodas

CREOLE LIVER

THURSDAY
Creole Liver*
Mashed Potatoes
Green Beans
Sliced Peaches
and Cream*
Shortbread Cookies
Milk   Tea

4 bacon slices
1 pound beef liver
1 medium onion, sliced
1 medium green pepper, cut into
  strips

¼ teaspoon chili powder
⅛ teaspoon instant minced garlic
½ 2½-ounce envelope tomato-
  vegetable soup mix (¼ cup)
1 tablespoon Marsala wine

About 40 minutes before serving: In skillet, sauté bacon crisp; crumble. Reserve 2 tablespoons fat. Cut liver into 3-inch by ½-inch strips.

In skillet, in reserved fat, sauté liver, onion, pepper, chili powder, garlic, until liver is browned. Add soup mix, ⅓ cup water, bacon, wine. Cover; simmer 10 to 15 minutes or until liver is tender, stirring often. Makes 4 servings.

DESSERT TIP: While main dish cooks, peel and slice peaches; sprinkle with sugar. Pour heavy or whipping cream over each serving; sprinkle with cinnamon or nutmeg.

LEMON FREEZER CREAM

FRIDAY
Fried Shrimp
Yellow Squash
Shoestring Potatoes
Coleslaw
Lemon Freezer Cream*
Tea   Coffee

1⅔ cups undiluted evaporated
  milk
1 7-ounce jar marshmallow whip
1 6-ounce can frozen lemonade

concentrate, thawed
1 10-ounce package frozen
  strawberries, thawed

Several hours before serving: Pour evaporated milk into large bowl; place in freezer for 25 minutes or until crystals form around edges.

Meanwhile, in small bowl, with electric mixer at medium speed, beat together marshmallow whip and lemonade concentrate; set aside.

With mixer at high speed, beat milk until stiff; slowly pour in marshmallow-lemonade mixture, whipping until very stiff. Pour into 10" by 5" by 3" loaf pan; freeze. Serve with strawberries. Makes 12 servings.

VEAL ALOHA

butter or margarine
¼ pound fresh mushrooms, sliced
seasoned salt
seasoned pepper

1 pound thin veal cutlets
3 fresh pineapple slices, halved
¼ cup heavy or whipping cream

In saucepan, in 2 tablespoons hot butter, sauté mushrooms about 3 minutes or until tender; sprinkle with ¼ teaspoon seasoned salt and ⅛ teaspoon seasoned pepper.

Sprinkle cutlets with 1 teaspoon seasoned salt, ⅛ teaspoon seasoned pepper. In large skillet, in ¼ cup hot butter, quickly sauté them until golden; remove to warm platter. In same skillet, brown pineapple slices on both sides, adding more butter if needed; remove to platter.

To skillet add mushrooms, ⅓ cup water and cream; heat through; pour over veal. Makes 4 servings.

SATURDAY
Veal Aloha*
Pimiento Rice
Peas
Raspberry-Apple Parfait*
Coffee

RASPBERRY-APPLE PARFAIT

In bowl, combine one 10-ounce package frozen raspberries, thawed, drained, ½ cup applesauce and ½ teaspoon cinnamon. Into parfait glasses, spoon alternate layers of raspberry mixture and 1 pint soft vanilla ice cream. Top with spoonful of raspberry mixture. Makes 4 servings.

DEVILED EGGS

6 hard-cooked eggs
¼ cup mayonnaise
¼ teaspoon salt
dash pepper

¼ teaspoon prepared mustard
1 teaspoon minced onion
paprika

Cut eggs in half lengthwise. With teaspoon, carefully remove yolks to small bowl; set whites aside.

Mash yolks; blend in mayonnaise, salt, pepper, mustard and onion.

Use to generously refill whites, slightly rounding each. Sprinkle with paprika; refrigerate. Makes 12 servings.

ROAST ROCK-CORNISH HENS

¾ cup butter or margarine
¾ cup dry white wine
dried tarragon
6 frozen Rock-Cornish hens, each
    about 1¼ pounds, thawed

6 garlic cloves, peeled
salt
pepper
garlic salt

About 1 hour and 15 minutes before serving: Preheat oven to 400°F. In saucepan, melt butter; add wine, 1 tablespoon dried tarragon. In each hen, place 1 garlic clove, 1 teaspoon dried tarragon, ¼ teaspoon salt, ⅛ teaspoon pepper. Sprinkle outside liberally with garlic salt. In large shallow open pan, without rack, roast Cornish hens 1 hour or until well browned and drumstick twists easily out of thigh joint, basting several times with sauce. Serve hens with drippings. Makes 6 servings.

BISCUIT BREADSTICKS

Preheat oven to 400°F. Open one 8-ounce can refrigerated biscuits; cut each biscuit in half crosswise; then, between palms of hands, roll each half into pencil-like strip, 6 to 8 inches long. Place on lightly greased cookie sheet; brush with 1 slightly beaten egg white; sprinkle lightly with poppy seed. Bake 15 minutes or until golden. Makes 20.

DESSERT TIP: In sherbet glasses, alternate layers of peeled sliced peaches with confectioners' sugar, flaked coconut. Or use thawed frozen sliced peaches; omit sugar.

CREAMED DRIED BEEF ON TOAST POINTS

¼ pound dried beef
¼ cup butter or margarine
3 tablespoons flour
2 cups milk

1 teaspoon bottled thick meat
    sauce (optional)
toast points

Tear dried beef into medium pieces. If beef seems too salty, pour boiling water over it for 1 minute; drain.

In double-boiler top, over direct heat, melt butter. Add drained beef; cook until edges curl. Stir in flour. Place over boiling water. Add milk slowly, stirring constantly, and cook until smooth and thickened. Add meat sauce. Serve hot on toast points. Makes 4 servings.

VEGETABLE TIP: Peel small white onions. Brown in butter. Add small amount of water; cover, and simmer about 25 minutes; drain. Sprinkle with paprika. (For 4 servings, you'll need 1½ pounds of small onions.)

MEAT LOAF, COMPANY STYLE

1½ pounds ground beef round
1 egg, slightly beaten
1 tablespoon minced onion
salt
⅛ teaspoon pepper
1 10½-ounce can condensed

Cheddar-cheese soup
3 tablespoons milk
2 cups fresh bread crumbs
⅓ cup chopped celery
¼ cup chopped dill pickle

About 1½ hours before serving: In medium bowl, combine meat, egg, onion, ¾ teaspoon salt and pepper. Dilute soup with milk; add ⅓ cup of this to meat mixture. Mix well. On large piece of waxed paper, lightly pat meat mixture into rectangle about 14″ by 9″.

Preheat oven to 375°F. In bowl, mix bread crumbs, celery, pickle and ½ teaspoon salt; sprinkle over meat, leaving 1-inch border.

Starting at narrow end of meat, roll it up, jelly-roll fashion; gently press ends of roll to seal; transfer, seam-side down, to 10″ by 6″ by 2″ baking dish. Bake 50 minutes. Pour remaining cheese soup over loaf; continue baking until sauce is hot. Makes 6 servings.

SALAD TIP: Cooked chilled peas are excellent tossed with bite-size pieces of escarole, Italian dressing, dried basil, salt and pepper.

ESCAROLE SALAD BOWL

SWEET-SOUR TUNA WITH RICE

2 6½- or 7-ounce cans tuna
in vegetable oil
1 green pepper, cut in strips
1 cup diagonally cut celery
5 teaspoons cornstarch

1 20-ounce can pineapple chunks
2 tablespoons vinegar
2 teaspoons soy sauce
1 chicken-bouillon cube
hot fluffy rice

In medium skillet over high heat, in oil from 1 can tuna, cook green pepper and celery about 2 minutes, stirring constantly.

Measure cornstarch into 2-cup measuring cup; gradually stir in syrup from pineapple, vinegar and soy sauce; add water to make 1½ cups. Pour into skillet with tuna, pineapple, bouillon cube. Cook, stirring constantly, until sauce is thickened. Serve with rice. Makes 6 servings.

DESSERT TIP: Fill packaged spongecake shells with sherbet—lime, lemon or orange—and top with fresh berries.

POULTRY TIP: Early in day, melt ¼ cup butter in shallow pan. Coat chicken pieces with seasoned flour; place in butter in pan. Bake in 450°F. oven 30 minutes; turn; bake 15 minutes longer; cool; refrigerate.

CUCUMBER-CREAM SALAD

1 3-ounce package lemon-flavor
gelatin
1 teaspoon salt
1 to 2 tablespoons vinegar
1 teaspoon grated onion

1 cup sour cream
mayonnaise
1 cup drained, finely chopped
cucumbers
salad greens

Early in day: Dissolve gelatin and salt in 1 cup hot water. Add vinegar and onion. Chill until syrupy; then beat in sour cream, ¼ cup mayonnaise and cucumbers. Pour into 6 individual molds. Refrigerate until firm. Unmold on salad greens. Top each with mayonnaise. Makes 6 servings.

BENEDICT-STYLE POACHED EGGS

FRIDAY
Cran-Apple Juice

Spanish Peanuts

*Benedict-Style
Poached Eggs**

*Asparagus Vinaigrette**

*Vanilla Pudding
with Sliced Peaches*

Iced Tea   Coffee

2 tablespoons butter or margarine	⅓ cup milk
½ cup minced onions	6 eggs
1 10½-ounce can condensed cream-of-mushroom soup	3 English muffins, split
	6 thin slices cooked ham

In skillet, in butter, cook onions until tender. Blend in undiluted soup and milk. Heat to boiling; lower heat. Break eggs, one by one, into saucer, then slide into sauce, side by side. Cook, covered, about 10 minutes or until eggs are of desired doneness. Meanwhile, toast and butter muffins.

To serve: Top each muffin half with ham slice, then with egg and some of sauce. Makes 6 servings.

VEGETABLE TIP: Combine 3 tablespoons sweet-pickle relish, 2 tablespoons snipped parsley, ¾ teaspoon sugar, 1 teaspoon salt, 6 tablespoons vinegar and ¾ cup salad oil. Blend with hand beater or electric mixer. Serve on hot or chilled cooked asparagus. Makes about 1 cup dressing.

LUSTY ITALIAN DIP

Several hours ahead, or day before: In bowl, combine 1 pint sour cream (or use one 8-ounce package cream cheese, stirred smooth with ½ cup milk), one 1½-ounce package spaghetti-sauce mix, 1 tablespoon instant minced onion. Refrigerate until served. Makes about 2 cups.

OLD-FASHIONED CLAMBAKE

SATURDAY
*Lusty Italian Dip**

Corn Chips

*Old-Fashioned Clambake**

*Toasted Rolls in Loaf**

Watermelon

Pitcher Root Beer

1 3-pound bluefish	6 to 12 ears of husked fresh corn on the cob
2 to 3 dozen cherrystone clams	
6 1½- to 2-pound live Maine lobsters	1 pound butter or margarine
	salt (optional)
2 to 3 dozen steamer clams	lemon juice (optional)
1 pound seaweed	

About 1½ hours before serving: Rinse bluefish in running cold water; cut into 3 equal pieces; wrap each in cheesecloth, envelope style, then set aside.

Scrub cherrystone clams *well* with stiff brush, under running cold water.

Rinse lobsters, steamer clams and seaweed until free of sand.

In 1 quart boiling water, in very large kettle, arrange lobsters first, then corn, pieces of bluefish, cherrystone clams, steamer clams and seaweed, in that order. Let steam over medium to high heat, covered, 30 to 35 minutes, or until one of pieces of fish is easily flaked with fork, and clams open.

Meanwhile, melt butter; add salt and lemon juice to taste.

With tongs, remove and discard seaweed. Serve steamers and cherrystone clams first; then bluefish, unwrapped, cut in half; then corn and lobsters, along with butter sauce.

Also, if desired, place double layer of cheesecloth over strainer, on top of large bowl; through it, pour liquid (clam broth) from kettle; serve in mugs. Makes 6 servings.

BREAD TIP: Trim crusts from top and sides of loaf of unsliced bread. Cut, almost to bottom, into 1½-inch slices, then lengthwise through middle. Spread cut surfaces, top, and sides with ½ cup butter mixed with ¼ cup minced onion. Bake in shallow pan at 400°F. 15 to 18 minutes.

SPICED FRUIT COMPOTE

SUNDAY

*Saucy Cube Steaks
on Hero Rolls**

Coleslaw

Paradise Pudding*

Milk   Coffee

MONDAY

*Bacon-Wrapped
Grilled Franks*

Yellow Squash

Hashed-Brown Potatoes

Chocolate Cream Roll*

Tea   Coffee

SAUCY CUBE STEAKS ON HERO ROLLS

Sprinkle 4 small cube steaks (about 1 pound) with 1 teaspoon salt, ⅛ teaspoon pepper, 3 tablespoons flour. In skillet, in 3 tablespoons hot fat, brown steaks quickly on both sides. Remove.

To fat left in skillet, add 1 teaspoon dry mustard, 1 teaspoon Worcestershire, 3 tablespoons chili sauce or catchup, 2 tablespoons lemon juice. Heat until boiling, stirring constantly. Spoon over steaks on toasted hero rolls. Makes 4 servings.

PARADISE PUDDING

⅓ cup packaged graham-cracker crumbs
6 3-ounce paper cups
1 cup heavy or whipping cream
1 20-ounce can crushed pineapple, well drained
¼ cup currant jelly

About 3 hours before serving: Place 1 teaspoon graham-cracker crumbs in each paper cup.

In bowl, with electric mixer at high speed, whip cream; fold in pineapple. Drop 1 teaspoon of mixture into each paper cup; sprinkle with some of graham-cracker crumbs; top with jelly. Repeat layering until all cups are filled. Freeze until firm. Makes 6 servings.

CHOCOLATE CREAM ROLL

½ cup sifted cake flour
½ teaspoon double-acting baking powder
¼ teaspoon salt
2 squares unsweetened chocolate
4 eggs
granulated sugar
1 teaspoon vanilla extract
¼ teaspoon baking soda
3 tablespoons cold water
confectioners' sugar
1 cup heavy or whipping cream
¼ teaspoon almond extract

Early in day: Preheat oven to 375°F. Grease 15″ by 10″ by 1″ jellyroll pan; line bottom with waxed paper. Sift together flour, baking powder and salt onto piece of waxed paper. Melt chocolate in double boiler over hot, *not boiling,* water.

In large bowl, combine eggs and ¾ cup sugar; with electric mixer at high speed (or with hand beater), beat until *very thick and light.*

Fold flour mixture and vanilla, all at once, into egg mixture. To melted chocolate, add 2 tablespoons sugar, soda, cold water; stir until thick and light; quickly fold into batter.

Turn into pan. Bake 15 to 20 minutes or just until cake springs back when gently touched with finger.

While cake bakes, place clean dish towel on flat surface; over it, sift thick layer of confectioners' sugar. When cake is done, with spatula, loosen it from sides of pan; invert onto towel. Lift off pan; carefully peel off paper; with very sharp knife, cut any crisp edges from cake, to make rolling easier. Cool exactly 5 minutes.

Fold edge of towel over edge of cake and roll up cake very gently from narrow end, rolling towel up in it (this prevents cake's sticking). Gently lift rolled cake onto rack to finish cooling—about 1 hour.

Just before serving: Whip cream with almond extract. Unroll cake on towel. Spread cake with whipped cream to within 1″ of edges. Roll up cake from narrow end, lifting towel higher and higher with one hand as you guide roll with other hand. Finish with open end of cake on underside. Remove to serving dish. Makes 8 to 10 servings.

HAMBURGER SCRAMBLE ON BUNS

2 tablespoons butter or margarine
1½ pounds ground beef chuck
1 cup chopped onions
1 8-ounce can tomato sauce
1¾ teaspoons salt

¼ teaspoon pepper
¾ teaspoon basil
1 tablespoon brown sugar
3 hamburger buns, split and
   toasted

In large skillet, in butter, sauté chuck until brown. Pour off drippings; stir in onions and next 5 ingredients; simmer 5 minutes.

Top buns with chuck mixture. Makes 6 servings.

SPICED FRUIT COMPOTE

2 oranges
2 29-ounce cans pear halves,
   drained
1 30-ounce can apricots, drained
1½ cups orange juice
¼ cup granulated sugar

2 or 3 cinnamon sticks, 2½-inches
   long
12 whole cloves
½ teaspoon salt
¼ teaspoon ginger (optional)

Day before or early in day: Peel oranges, reserving one peel; cut oranges into large pieces. In large bowl, combine orange pieces, reserved peel, pears and apricots. In medium saucepan, combine remaining ingredients and simmer 5 minutes; pour over fruits, cover bowl and refrigerate overnight or several hours.

At serving time: Remove cinnamon sticks, cloves and peel if you like. Makes 8 servings.

— • —

SALAD TIP: Toss thinly sliced, canned white potatoes with sliced celery, green onions, hard-cooked eggs, bottled Thousand Island dressing, salt and pepper. Garnish with radish roses, if desired.

WINDMILL ROLLS

Preheat oven to 375°F. Unroll half of 1 package of refrigerated crescent dinner-roll dough; press 2 triangles together in rectangle; cut into 4 lengthwise strips; place 2 strips, parallel to each other, 2 inches apart; twist together at center. Repeat with rest of dough, making 8 windmills; place on ungreased cookie sheet.

Brush with beaten egg; sprinkle with poppy, sesame or caraway seed or grated Parmesan cheese mixed with paprika.

Bake 8 to 10 minutes or until golden. Cool. Makes 8 rolls.

— • —

VEAL VIENNESE WITH NOODLES

4 veal chops
2 tablespoons butter or margarine
1 garlic clove, minced or mashed
¼ teaspoon thyme leaves
   (optional)

1 10½-ounce can condensed
   cream-of-mushroom soup
½ soup can water
¼ teaspoon paprika
hot cooked noodles

About 1 hour before serving: Trim excess fat from chops. In skillet in hot butter, brown chops on both sides with garlic and thyme.

Push chops to one side of pan; blend in undiluted soup, water and paprika. Spread chops in pan; cover; simmer over low heat about 45 minutes or until tender. Serve over hot cooked noodles. Makes 4 servings.

WINDMILL ROLLS

TUESDAY
Hamburger Scramble
on Buns*
French Fries
Tossed Green Salad
Spiced Fruit Compote*
Tea Coffee

WEDNESDAY
Sliced
Cold Cuts
Potato Salad*
Tomato Wedges
Windmill Rolls*
Toasted Poundcake
à la Mode
Coffee Tea

THURSDAY
Veal Viennese
with Noodles*
Buttered Zucchini
Hard Rolls
Lemon Sherbet
Tea Coffee

GUMBO SUPREME

½ cup diced bacon
½ cup chopped green onions
1 garlic clove, minced
4 to 5 tablespoons flour
2½ teaspoons salt
½ teaspoon thyme leaves
¼ teaspoon pepper
2 16-ounce cans whole tomatoes, drained

2 bay leaves
1½ cups boiled ham, cut into ¾-inch squares
1 10-ounce package frozen okra, partially thawed
2 pounds medium shrimp, peeled, deveined, split lengthwise
1 6-ounce package frozen Alaska King crab, partially thawed

About 1 hour before serving: In Dutch oven, sauté bacon until crisp; remove and reserve. To drippings, add green onions and garlic; sauté until tender; stir in flour until blended. Gradually stir in 5 cups water; add salt, thyme, pepper, tomatoes, bay leaves, ham; simmer, covered, 30 minutes, stirring occasionally. Cut okra into 1-inch pieces; add to Dutch oven; cook 15 minutes. Add shrimp and crab; simmer, uncovered, 10 minutes or until shrimp turn pink and crab is heated through. Remove bay leaves and sprinkle gumbo with reserved bacon bits.

Serve over hot cooked rice in soup bowls. Makes 8 servings.

BROWN-SUGAR-GLAZED BANANAS

8 bananas, slightly underripe
6 tablespoons butter or margarine
½ cup packed dark brown sugar

1 teaspoon lemon juice
¼ teaspoon cinnamon

About 20 minutes before serving: Peel and cut each banana diagonally into 4 pieces.

In large skillet, melt butter with brown sugar, lemon juice and cinnamon. Add bananas; sauté over low heat, 10 to 12 minutes, basting with sugar mixture. Serve with vanilla ice cream or sour cream. Makes 8 servings.

COLD CHICKEN SOUFFLÉ

2 envelopes unflavored gelatin
½ cup cold water
2 10½-ounce cans condensed cream-of-chicken soup
2 tablespoons curry
6 cups cooked chicken chunks
seasoned salt

pepper
aluminum foil
2 cups heavy or whipping cream
toasted sesame seed
½ cup cooked chicken slivers
bottled chutney

Day before serving: In large bowl, sprinkle gelatin over cold water; set aside to soften. In saucepan, prepare soup as label directs but add curry. Pour hot soup over gelatin; stir until gelatin dissolves. Sprinkle chicken with seasoned salt and pepper; add to soup; chill until mixture mounds slightly.

Meanwhile, make collar by folding 30-inch piece of foil in half lengthwise; lightly grease it. Wrap collar around outside of greased 1½-quart soufflé dish and secure with cellophane tape.

Whip cream. Fold into cooled chicken mixture, then pour mixture into soufflé dish. Refrigerate.

At serving time: With metal spatula, loosen foil collar from soufflé; remove. Sprinkle soufflé with sesame seed; garnish with chicken slivers. Serve with chutney. Makes 8 to 10 servings.

MEAT TIP: Early in day, bake ham (see chart, p. 220). Last half hour of baking, spread ham with mixture of ½ cup honey or corn syrup, 1 cup brown sugar and ½ cup orange juice. Chill; slice.

SPECIAL BAKED POTATOES

About 1 hour before serving: Preheat oven to 450°F. Bake 6 medium baking potatoes on oven rack 45 minutes or until fork-tender.

To serve: Cut 2 deep crisscross slashes on top of each potato; press potatoes from sides to force open. Spoon sour cream from one 8-ounce container sour cream into centers of potatoes; top each with about 1 teaspoon minced dill pickle (you'll need 2 tablespoons in all). Makes 6 servings.

PAN SPINACH

3 10-ounce packages fresh spinach	⅛ teaspoon pepper
1 tablespoon butter or margarine	1 tablespoon flour
1 garlic clove, minced	½ cup milk
1 teaspoon salt	1 teaspoon lemon juice

About 15 minutes before serving: Wash spinach; cook in covered saucepan with water clinging to leaves about 6 minutes. Meanwhile, in small saucepan over medium heat, melt butter; add garlic, salt and pepper. Stir in flour; cook 2 or 3 minutes. Remove from heat; slowly stir in milk, then lemon juice. Return to heat; cook, stirring, until smooth and thickened. Drain spinach well. Pour sauce over spinach; toss well with fork. Makes 6 servings.

SNOWCAPPED PEACHES

8 fresh peaches	2 egg whites
strawberry or currant jelly	¼ cup granulated sugar

Preheat broiler if manufacturer directs. Pare and pit peaches; cut in half. Spoon ½ teaspoon strawberry or currant jelly into center of each peach half.

In small bowl, beat egg whites, adding sugar gradually until they form stiff peaks. Heap meringue over jelly in each peach half. Arrange peaches on broiler rack; broil 1 to 2 minutes or until golden brown. Serve warm. Makes 8 servings.

HONEYDEW-MELON SHERBET

2 large honeydew melons	½ cup fresh lime juice
4 egg whites	mint sprigs
2 cups granulated sugar	

Early in day: Cut melons in half lengthwise; discard seeds. Scoop meat from 1 melon; reserve shells. In electric-blender container,* at high speed, blend melon meat with 2 egg whites (use yolks in scrambled eggs, page 89), 1 cup sugar and ¼ cup lime juice until smooth. Pour into 9-inch square pan; freeze; stir often until firm. Repeat with second melon.

About 1 hour before serving: With large spoon, scoop sherbet into reserved melon shells, then return to freezer. Just before serving, garnish with mint sprigs. Makes 8 to 10 servings.

* Or mash melon meat with potato masher. Beat egg whites until foamy; gradually beat in sugar; continue beating until mixture forms soft peaks. Fold in lime juice and melon. Freeze as above.

SUNDAY
Glazed Baked Ham*
Special Baked Potatoes*
Pan Spinach*
Snowcapped Peaches*
Milk   Coffee

MONDAY
Chicken à la King
on Cornbread
Avocado-Onion Salad
Honeydew-Melon Sherbet*
Spice-Nut Cookies
Coffee

CHIVE-SCRAMBLED EGGS

5 eggs
4 egg yolks
½ teaspoon salt
⅛ teaspoon pepper

6 tablespoons milk
1 6-ounce package chive cream
  cheese, crumbled
2 tablespoons butter or margarine

Combine eggs, yolks, salt, pepper, milk; mix well; stir in cheese.

In 9-inch skillet, melt butter, tilting skillet so bottom and sides are well covered. Pour in egg-cheese mixture. Cook slowly, gently lifting from bottom and sides with spoon as mixture sets, so liquid can flow to bottom. Avoid constant stirring. Cook until set but still moist. Serve at once. Makes 4 servings.

TUESDAY
Chive-Scrambled Eggs*
Sliced Tomatoes
O'Brien Potatoes
Whole-Wheat Toast
Plum Pie
Coffee   Tea

JELLIED HAM LOAF

2 envelopes unflavored gelatin
3 cups finely chopped cooked ham
¼ cup finely chopped green onions
¼ cup finely diced celery
1 cup mayonnaise or salad dressing
2 tablespoons cider vinegar
2 tablespoons prepared mustard

½ teaspoon salt
¼ teaspoon pepper
1 cup heavy or whipping cream
1 small cucumber, thinly sliced
bottled Italian dressing
watercress for garnish

Day before or early in day: Sprinkle gelatin onto ½ cup cold water in cup to soften; set cup in boiling water; stir until gelatin dissolves.

In large bowl, combine ham, green onions, celery, mayonnaise, vinegar, mustard, salt and pepper. Mix in gelatin.

Whip cream until stiff and gently fold into ham mixture. Thoroughly grease 9" by 5" by 3" loaf pan; fill with ham mixture; level top; cover with foil. Refrigerate.

About 30 minutes before serving: In small bowl, toss cucumber and enough dressing to cover; set aside.

Run spatula between ham mixture and sides of loaf pan to loosen ham; then quickly dip pan in hot water. Place platter on top of pan; invert; lift off pan; refrigerate. (If loaf won't unmold, ring out cloth in hot water and cover inverted pan for few minutes.)

To serve: Cut into ½-inch-thick slices; drain cucumber well and arrange around loaf; garnish with watercress. Makes 8 servings.

WEDNESDAY
Jellied Ham Loaf*
Glazed Beets
Parkerhouse Rolls
Peach Shortcake
Coffee

ITALIAN-STYLE GREEN PEPPERS

4 large green peppers halved,
  seeded
olive or salad oil
¼ cup boiling water
salt
1 medium onion, sliced

2 garlic cloves, minced
2 cups canned tomatoes
2 teaspoons sugar
⅛ teaspoon pepper
½ teaspoon basil

About 45 minutes before serving: Cut peppers into 1½-inch strips; halve crosswise. In large skillet, heat 3 tablespoons oil; add peppers; sauté 10 minutes or until slightly browned. Add boiling water, 1 teaspoon salt; simmer, covered, 20 minutes or until tender.

Meanwhile, in saucepan, in 1 tablespoon oil, sauté onion and garlic until golden. Add tomatoes, sugar, 1 teaspoon salt, pepper and basil. Simmer, uncovered, 30 minutes or until thickened. Place drained peppers in serving dish; pour on tomato sauce. Makes 4 servings.

THURSDAY
Broiled Flank Steak
Italian-Style
Green Peppers*
New Potatoes
Escarole Salad
Chocolate Pudding
Milk   Coffee

CUCUMBER-WALNUT FLOAT

FRIDAY

Cucumber-Walnut Float*

*Shrimp Salad
New Orleans**

*French Bread
Half-and-Half**

Butter-Pecan Ice Cream

Tea   Coffee

2 pints plain yogurt	⅓ cup milk
½ teaspoon salt	1 small cucumber, pared, cut into
⅛ teaspoon white pepper	½-inch cubes
¼ teaspoon garlic powder	½ cup walnut halves

Up to 3 hours before serving: In bowl, beat yogurt until smooth; beat in salt, pepper, garlic powder and milk; stir in cucumber cubes. Refrigerate. Serve in mugs, topped with walnuts. Makes 6 servings.

SHRIMP SALAD NEW ORLEANS

1 cup cold cooked rice	2 tablespoons French dressing
¾ pound cooked, cleaned shrimp, cut up (about 1 cup)	1 tablespoon chopped stuffed olives
¾ teaspoon salt	¾ cup diced raw cauliflower
1 tablespoon lemon juice	dash pepper
¼ cup slivered green pepper	⅓ cup mayonnaise
1 tablespoon minced onion	lettuce

Toss together all ingredients but lettuce. Serve in lettuce cups. Makes 4 servings.

BREAD TIP: Split long loaf of French bread lengthwise in half. Slash each half into 1¼-inch diagonal slices, *almost* through to bottom crust. Top halves with ½ cup butter or margarine, softened, mixed with ½ cup crumbled Danish blue cheese and 2 tablespoons chopped chives. (If desired, wrap in foil, leaving foil partially open at top.) Bake at 375°F. 15 to 20 minutes or until golden.

BAKED BEAN CASSEROLE

SATURDAY

Boiled Tongue

Baked Bean Casserole*

Fruit Slaw*

Brown-and-Serve Rolls

Orange Chiffon Cake

Coffee

¼ cup salad oil	2 tablespoons prepared mustard
2 cups thinly sliced onions	4 peeled tomatoes, sliced
2 28-ounce cans New England–style beans	2 teaspoons salt
1 4½-ounce can deviled ham	1 tablespoon brown sugar

About 1 hour and 15 minutes before serving: Preheat oven to 400°F. In large skillet in hot oil, sauté onions until tender. In large bowl, combine beans, ham, mustard; arrange half in 3-quart casserole. Place half of onions and tomatoes over beans; sprinkle with half of salt and sugar. Repeat layers. Cover; bake 45 minutes; uncover; bake 10 minutes longer. Makes 8 to 10 servings.

FRUIT SLAW

1 large head cabbage	drained
¾ cup mayonnaise	1 peach, cut into thin wedges for
2 tablespoons vinegar	garnish
1½ teaspoons salt	2 purple plums, cut into thin
1 teaspoon granulated sugar	wedges, for garnish
1 13½-ounce can pineapple tidbits,	

Spread apart several outer leaves of cabbage. Carefully cut out center of cabbage, leaving outer leaves as "bowl." (Leave cabbage core intact for about an inch high.) Shred cut-out cabbage.

Mix mayonnaise, vinegar, salt, sugar; toss with pineapple and shredded cabbage. Pile into "bowl"; top with fruit wedges. Makes 10 servings.

APPETIZER TIP: Combine equal parts of tomato-juice or vegetable-juice cocktail and clam juice; season with minced onion, salt, pepper.

MOUNTAIN CHICKEN DINNER

2 2½-pound broiler-fryers, cut up	¼ cup granulated sugar
salt and pepper	⅓ cup wine vinegar
6 medium potatoes, pared	1 tablespoon Worcestershire
6 medium onions	3 bay leaves, crushed
6 medium carrots, pared	6 ears husked corn
1 cup butter or margarine	

About 1¾ hours before serving: Season chicken with salt and pepper. In 4- gallon pot, place chicken in center. Surround with potatoes, onions, and carrots; dot with butter or margarine.

Combine 3 cups boiling water and sugar, vinegar, 2 tablespoons salt, Worcestershire, bay leaves and ¼ teaspoon pepper; pour over chicken and vegetables.

Cover and simmer about 1½ hours until chicken is tender. Add corn about 10 minutes before end of cooking. Serve with salt and additional butter. Makes 6 servings.

SHERBET SCOOP

1 pint lemon sherbet	nuts
1 pint orange sherbet	4 teaspoons roasted, diced
1 pint raspberry sherbet	buttered almonds
1 pint lime sherbet	4 teaspoons shredded coconut
4 teaspoons chopped Macadamia	4 teaspoons chocolate sprinkles

Day before or very early in day: With medium (number 16) ice-cream scoop, scoop sherbets into balls and arrange on cookie sheets. Sprinkle tops of lemon balls with Macadamia nuts, orange balls with buttered almonds, raspberry balls with coconut, lime balls with chocolate sprinkles; freeze. Serve in chilled serving dish. Makes 6 to 8 servings.

———◆———

VINAIGRETTE SPINACH

2½ pounds fresh spinach	2 tablespoons lemon juice
6 tablespoons butter or margarine	¾ teaspoon salt
1 teaspoon minced onion	⅛ teaspoon pepper
½ teaspoon prepared mustard	2 hard-cooked eggs, chopped

About 15 minutes before serving: Wash spinach. Cook in covered saucepan with water clinging to leaves about 6 minutes. Drain well; chop. In 1 tablespoon of the butter, sauté onion until tender. Add mustard, lemon juice, salt, pepper, eggs, remaining butter; heat. Pour over spinach; toss. Makes 4 servings.

ORANGE-JELLY BAGATELLE

1 3-ounce package orange-flavor gelatin	⅛ teaspoon nutmeg
1 17-ounce can applesauce (2 cups)	2 teaspoons grated orange peel
	whipped cream or dessert topping

Early in day: In bowl, stir gelatin into ½ cup hot water until completely dissolved. Add applesauce, nutmeg, orange peel. Pour into 9″ by 5″ by 3″ loaf pan; refrigerate until set.

Just before serving: Cut jelly into 1″ squares; heap in 4 sherbet glasses.

SHERBET SCOOP

Top with whipped cream or dessert topping; sprinkle with nutmeg. Makes 4 servings.

SUMMERTIME STEW

3 tablespoons salad oil
2 pounds beef stew meat, cut into 2-inch cubes
1 medium onion, sliced
1 tablespoon salt
¼ teaspoon pepper
6 large carrots, cut into chunks
6 stalks celery, cut into chunks
1 teaspoon dill weed
1 bay leaf

About 30 minutes before serving: In 4-quart pressure cooker, in hot oil, brown meat and onion. Add remaining ingredients and ¾ cup water. (Use 1 cup if recommended in pressure manual.) Bring to 15 pounds pressure as manufacturer directs; cook 15 minutes.

Remove from heat and reduce pressure quickly, as manufacturer directs, before uncovering. Makes 6 servings.

BREAD TIP: Cut corn muffins in halves. Spread with butter or margarine; then sprinkle with sesame seed, poppy seed, grated cheese or thyme leaves; or spread lightly with jelly, jam or apple butter. Broil until golden.

FLUTED ICE-CREAM CAKE

1 package devil's-food-cake mix or double Dutch batter-cake mix
1 pint strawberry-parfait ice cream, slightly softened

At least day before serving: Preheat oven to 325°F. Make cake mix as label directs; pour batter into 2 identical well-greased 3½-cup fluted molds, up to 1¼ inches below rims (use remaining batter for cupcakes). Bake 50 minutes or until cake tester, inserted in center, comes out clean. Cool cakes 10 minutes in molds; invert on rack; remove molds; cool cakes.

Cut thin slice off top side of each cake to level; hollow out scant cup of crumbs from center of each cake. Fill centers with ice cream, leveling it off flat; also dab top edges of cakes here and there with ice cream. Now invert ice cream side of one cake onto other cake. Freezer-wrap; freeze. To serve, cut into wedges. Makes 6 servings.

TUESDAY
Summertime Stew*
Tossed Green Salad
Toasted Corn Muffins*
Fluted Ice-Cream Cake*
Tea   Coffee

WEDNESDAY
Pan-Fried
Smoked Pork Chops
Applesauce
Mashed Potatoes
Cheesy Swiss Chard*
Hard Rolls
Mixed-Fruit Gelatin
Fig Bars
Tea   Coffee

THURSDAY
Lemon-Barbecued
Meat Loaves*
Green Noodles
Buttered Carrots
Relish Tray
Breadsticks
Tapioca Pudding
Coffee

FRIDAY
Eggplant Parmesan*
Corn on the Cob
with Herb Butter
Escarole Salad
Italian Bread
Rainbow Loaf*
Tea   Coffee

CHEESY SWISS CHARD

2 pounds mature Swiss chard	½ cup milk
2 teaspoons salt	¼ pound diced process Cheddar
2 tablespoons butter or margarine	cheese
2 tablespoons flour	

Preheat oven to 325°F. Wash chard; cut stalks into 1-inch pieces; cook in ½-inch boiling water with salt, covered, 5 minutes. Then add torn chard leaves; cover; cook 5 minutes. Drain well.

In saucepan, melt butter; stir in flour, then milk; cook, stirring, over medium heat until thickened. Add cheese; toss with chard. Turn into 1½-quart casserole. Bake, uncovered, 45 minutes. Makes 4 servings.

LEMON-BARBECUED MEAT LOAVES

1½ pounds ground beef chuck	½ cup catchup
4 slices day-old bread, diced	⅓ cup brown sugar
¼ cup lemon juice	1 teaspoon dry mustard
¼ cup minced onion	¼ teaspoon allspice
1 egg, slightly beaten	¼ teaspoon ground cloves
2 teaspoons seasoned salt	6 thin lemon slices

About 50 minutes before serving: Preheat oven to 350°F. In bowl, combine chuck, bread, lemon juice, onion, egg and salt; mix well; shape into 6 loaves; place in greased 13″ by 9″ baking pan. Bake 15 minutes.

In small bowl, combine catchup and next 4 ingredients; cover loaves with this sauce; top each with lemon slice. Bake 30 minutes longer, basting occasionally with sauce from pan. Makes 6 servings.

EGGPLANT PARMESAN

1 large eggplant	½ cup grated Parmesan cheese
3 eggs, beaten	2 teaspoons oregano leaves
1 cup packaged dried bread crumbs	½ pound Mozzarella cheese, sliced
¾ cup olive or salad oil	3 8-ounce cans tomato sauce

About 50 minutes before serving: Preheat oven to 350°F. Pare and cut eggplant into ¼-inch slices. Dip each slice into eggs, then crumbs. Sauté in hot oil until golden on both sides. In 2-quart casserole, place layer of eggplant; sprinkle with some Parmesan, oregano; add some Mozzarella; cover well with some tomato sauce. Repeat, ending with sauce. Top with several slices of Mozzarella. Bake, uncovered, ½ hour or until sauce is bubbly and cheese is melted. Makes 4 to 6 servings.

RAINBOW LOAF

Several days ahead: Stir 1 pint softened orange sherbet until smooth, then pour into a 9″ by 5″ by 3″ loaf pan in a level layer. Cover sherbet with 12 ladyfingers, placed end to end. Stir 1 pint softened raspberry sherbet until smooth. Spread on ladyfingers. Freeze almost solid.

Prepare one 2-ounce envelope whipped-topping mix as label directs; stir in ½ cup mixed candied fruit; spread over raspberry layer. Freeze loaf firm; then freezer-wrap and store.

About 1 hour before serving: Quickly lower loaf pan in and out of hot water. With spatula, loosen loaf from pan; invert serving plate on top; invert both pan and plate; remove pan. Smooth top of sherbet; sprinkle with blanched almonds; return to freezer. Makes 10 to 12 servings.

MINTED MELON BASKETS

VEGETABLE TIP: Early in day, cook scrubbed new potatoes in same water with the corned beef until potatoes are fork-tender; refrigerate. About 15 minutes before serving, peel potatoes; brush with melted butter; sprinkle with salt, pepper, paprika; broil, turning, until golden.

MINTED MELON BASKETS

Several hours before serving: Combine ½ cup light corn syrup, ¼ cup lime juice and 2 tablespoons snipped mint leaves. Refrigerate.

Cut 2 ripe honeydew melons and 3 medium-ripe cantaloupes in half; remove seeds. With small ice-cream scoop, No. 30, make half-balls from 1 honeydew and 1½ cantaloupes, keeping them separate.

Brush half-balls lightly with lime juice; cover; refrigerate. Pare remaining 2 honeydew halves and 3 cantaloupe halves; brush lightly with lime juice; refrigerate these "baskets," covered.

Up to 1 hour before serving: Fill 2 honeydew baskets with cantaloupe half-balls; fill 3 cantaloupe baskets with honeydew half-balls. Garnish with mint. Each honeydew basket, halved crosswise, makes 2 servings; each cantaloupe basket makes 1 serving. Makes 7 servings. Pass mint sauce.

SATURDAY
Corned Beef
*Broiled New Potatoes**
Peas
*Tomatoes
with Fresh Dill*
Rye Bread   Butter
*Minted Melon Baskets**
Tea   Coffee

PEANUT-BUTTER HAM STEAK

1 fully cooked ham slice, 1 inch
thick
¼ cup dark corn syrup

3 tablespoons smooth or crunchy
peanut butter

Preheat broiler if manufacturer directs. Lay ham on rack; brush one side generously with corn syrup; broil 5 minutes.

Turn ham slice over; brush with rest of corn syrup, then broil 3 minutes. Spread with peanut butter; broil 2 minutes. Makes 4 servings.

DUTCH PLUM CAKE

1 cup sifted regular all-purpose
flour
1½ teaspoons double-acting baking
powder
½ teaspoon salt
6 tablespoons granulated sugar
¼ cup shortening
1 egg

¼ cup milk
5 pitted plums, cut into eighths*
1 teaspoon cinnamon
¼ teaspoon nutmeg
3 tablespoons melted butter or
margarine
⅓ cup currant jelly or apricot
jam

About 1 hour before serving: Preheat oven to 400°F. Sift flour, baking powder, salt, 3 tablespoons sugar. With 2 knives used scissor-fashion, or pastry blender, cut in shortening until mixture resembles coarse crumbs. With fork, stir in combined egg and milk.

Spread dough in greased 12" by 8" by 2" baking dish. On top, arrange plums, slightly overlapping, in parallel rows, with pointed edges down. Sprinkle with combined cinnamon, nutmeg, 3 tablespoons sugar, butter. Bake 25 minutes or until plums are tender, cake dry in center.

Beat jelly with enough hot water, about 1 tablespoon, to make syrup; brush over fruit. Serve warm, cut into squares. Makes 6 servings.
* 16 pitted, halved prunes may be substituted for plums.

WONDERFUL HASH

2 cups chopped cooked corned beef
3 cups chopped cold, cooked
potatoes
½ cup minced onions
1 teaspoon salt

¼ teaspoon pepper
¼ cup nonfat dry milk (optional)
⅓ cup milk or undiluted
evaporated milk
2 tablespoons salad oil

In bowl, combine corned beef, potatoes, onions, salt, pepper, dry milk and milk. In large skillet, heat salad oil; spread hash evenly in bottom of skillet; cook over low heat 30 to 40 minutes, or until underside is brown and crusty. Do not stir, but occasionally lift edge of hash to check browning. Run spatula around edge of hash to loosen; fold one half onto other half; remove hash to platter. Makes 4 servings.

PEACH MELBA

About 2 hours ahead: In saucepan, thaw one 10-ounce package frozen raspberries. (Or use 2 cups fresh raspberries and ½ cup granulated sugar.) Mash berries; add ½ cup currant jelly; bring to boil. Add 1½ teaspoons cornstarch mixed with 1 tablespoon water; cook, stirring, until clear. Strain if desired; cool.

Just before serving: Top each serving of vanilla ice cream with ripe fresh or canned peach half; pour on Melba sauce. Makes 4 to 6 servings.

SUNDAY
*Peanut-Butter
Ham Steak**
Browned Potatoes
Green Beans
Piccalilli
*Dutch Plum Cake**
Milk   Coffee

MONDAY
*Wonderful Hash**
Coleslaw
Salt Sticks
*Peach Melba**
Tea   Coffee

SAVORY LIMA BEANS AND BOLOGNA

2 10-ounce packages frozen limas, or 3 cups fresh cooked
1 tablespoon butter or margarine
24 bologna slices (about 1¼ pounds)
1 8½-ounce can pineapple slices, drained
2 medium onions, chopped
1 teaspoon seasoned salt
¼ teaspoon pepper

About 30 minutes before serving: Cook limas as label directs. Meanwhile, in large skillet over high heat, in hot butter, fry bologna until edges just brown; remove and keep warm.

Add pineapple slices to skillet; cook on both sides until golden; remove and keep warm. In same skillet over medium heat, cook onions until golden. Stir in limas, seasoned salt and pepper. Serve lima mixture on warm platter; top with large circle of overlapping bologna slices, surrounding pineapple slices in middle. Makes 4 servings.

━━━◆━━━

POULTRY TIP: To ¼ cup melted butter for brushing chicken, add 3 tablespoons lemon juice, ¼ teaspoon Tabasco and ½ teaspoon paprika. Place broiler-fryers on broiling pan. Brush with butter-lemon mixture. Broil 30 minutes; turn; brush again; broil 15 to 30 minutes more.

SAVORY CARROTS AND GRAPES

1 pound carrots
¼ cup fresh or thawed frozen orange juice
2 tablespoons olive oil
¼ teaspoon salt
¼ teaspoon sugar
dash ginger
½ cup halved and seeded grapes
1 tablespoon chopped parsley

Cut carrots into thick diagonal slices. Place in medium saucepan with orange juice, olive oil, salt, sugar and ginger. Cover and heat to boiling; reduce to medium heat and cook carrots until tender-crisp, about 35 minutes. Add grapes and cook 5 minutes longer to heat grapes; drain. Sprinkle with parsley. Makes 4 servings.

LEMON PIE

pastry for 1-crust pie
1 lemon
granulated sugar
2 tablespoons regular all-purpose flour
dash salt
¼ cup butter or margarine
2 eggs
½ teaspoon cinnamon

Early in day: Line 8-inch pie plate with pastry crust; trim edges and reserve trimmings to make lattice topping later. Preheat oven to 400°F. Grate 1 teaspoon lemon peel, then slice lemon (with remaining peel left on) *paper thin;* reserve.

In small bowl, with electric mixer at medium speed, beat 1¼ cups sugar, flour, salt and butter until mixture is coarsely crumbled. Reserve 1 teaspoon egg white for later use. Slowly beat in remaining eggs, ½ cup water and lemon peel. Fold lemon slices into mixture. Pour lemon mixture into unbaked pieshell.

Make lattice topping on pie with strips of reserved pastry. Tuck overhang under bottom crust; with fingers, press firmly together. Flute edges, if you like. Brush strips and edge with reserved egg white. Mix 2 teaspoons sugar with cinnamon; sprinkle on top. Bake 30 to 35 minutes or until golden. Cool. Makes 6 servings. Refrigerate leftovers.

SAVORY CARROTS AND GRAPES

TUESDAY
Savory Lima Beans and Bologna*
Melba Toast
Big Green Salad
Golden Egg Custard
Tea   Coffee

WEDNESDAY
Broiled Chicken*
Savory Carrots and Grapes*
Mashed Potatoes
Watercress-and-Cucumber Salad
Lemon Pie*
Coffee   Tea

ITALIAN BRAISED LIVER

THURSDAY

Italian Braised Liver*

Italian Green Beans

*Romaine Salad
with Sliced Onions*

Biscuit Tortoni

Instant Espresso

3 tablespoons all-purpose flour
½ teaspoon seasoned salt
¼ teaspoon seasoned pepper
2 pounds beef liver, unsliced
2 tablespoons salad oil
1 pound sweet Italian sausage
   links, cut in ½-inch pieces

1½ cups pizza-flavored catchup
¼ cup sherry
¼ cup Worcestershire
3 medium onions, sliced
2 medium green peppers, seeded,
   sliced

In small bowl, combine flour, seasoned salt and pepper. Use to coat both sides of unsliced beef liver. In large skillet, in hot salad oil, sauté sausage pieces until brown; add liver and brown on both sides.

In medium bowl, blend catchup, sherry, Worcestershire and ½ cup water; pour over meats in skillet; add onions and peppers. Simmer, covered, 50 minutes or until liver is tender, basting occasionally. Spoon off fat. Slice liver thin. Serve with sausage and gravy. Makes 6 servings.

HOT SEAFOOD SANDWICHES

FRIDAY

Apricot Nectar

Hot Seafood Sandwiches*

Sautéed Zucchini

Watermelon Wedges

Tea   Coffee

2 7½-ounce cans King crab
1 10-ounce can frozen condensed
   cream-of-shrimp soup, thawed
¼ cup minced celery
¼ cup minced green pepper
2 tablespoons minced onion
¼ cup mayonnaise

few drops lemon juice
dash salt
dash pepper
4 English muffins, split, toasted
8 tomato slices
grated Parmesan cheese
⅓ cup milk

Preheat oven to 425°F. Remove cartilage from crab; flake. Measure ⅓ cup undiluted soup; mix well with crab, celery, green pepper, onion, mayonnaise, lemon juice, salt and pepper. Place toasted English muffins on cookie sheet; top each with a tomato slice and crab mixture; sprinkle with cheese. Bake 15 minutes or until hot. Combine remaining soup with milk. Heat, stirring; serve over sandwiches. Makes 4 servings.

BEEF ROLLS CONFETTI

SATURDAY

Beef Rolls Confetti*

Onion Buns*

Peach Pie

Lemonade

1 10-ounce package frozen Ford-
   hook limas
1 9-ounce package frozen cut
   green beans
1 10-ounce package frozen peas
¼ cup minced onion
3 tablespoons cider vinegar

1 tablespoon horseradish
dash Tabasco
1⅓ cups bottled Italian dressing
12 thin slices cooked roast beef
1 pimiento, coarsely chopped
watercress for garnish

Early in day: Cook frozen vegetables as labels direct; drain; place in large bowl; add onion, vinegar, horseradish, Tabasco, 1 cup Italian dressing. Cover; refrigerate, tossing occasionally with fork.

Roll up each slice of beef; place, seam-side down, in 12″ by 8″ by 2″ baking dish. Pour over ⅓ cup dressing; refrigerate, turning occasionally.

Just before serving: With slotted spoon, arrange vegetables on platter; top with pimiento, beef rolls; garnish with watercress. Makes 6 servings.

ONION BUNS

Prepare packaged hot-roll mix as label directs but add 4 teaspoons minced onion. Before baking rolls, top with 1 cup chopped onions, sautéed in 2 tablespoons butter; brush with beaten egg. Bake at 400°F. 15 minutes.

COLD STUFFED VEAL ROLL-UPS

SUNDAY

*Cold Stuffed
Veal Roll-Ups**

Broiled Tomatoes

*Lettuce Wedges
with
Creamy Onion Dressing*

*Fresh Fruit Cup
Deluxe**

Tea   Coffee

1 quart fresh bread crumbs
¾ teaspoon salt
2 teaspoons sage leaves
2 tablespoons chopped celery
2 teaspoons chopped parsley
dash pepper
butter or margarine

3 tablespoons minced onion
1¼-pound veal cutlet, ¼-inch thick
¼ cup flour
¾ teaspoon salt
¼ teaspoon pepper
¼ teaspoon paprika
currant or grape jelly

Day before or early in day: Combine crumbs, salt, sage, celery, parsley and pepper. In medium skillet over medium heat, in ¼ cup butter, cook onion until tender; add crumb mixture; heat. Spread crumb mixture on veal; roll up tightly; tie with string.

Preheat oven to 350°F. Meanwhile, combine flour, salt, pepper and paprika. Coat veal with this mixture. In large skillet, sauté veal in 2 tablespoons butter until golden. Place in 1½-quart casserole. Add 1 cup hot water. Cover; bake 1 hour or until fork-tender. Refrigerate.

At serving time: Slice veal roll and serve with currant or grape jelly. Makes 6 servings.

DESSERT TIP: In dessert glasses, arrange assorted fresh fruit or fresh fruit mixed with canned or thawed frozen fruit. Top with chilled ginger ale, ginger ale frozen to mush, grenadine, crème de menthe or wine.

SWISS PIE

Preheat oven to 350°F. Arrange 1 quart toasted ½-inch bread squares in 9-inch pie plate.

Top bread with 2 tomatoes, sliced; then sprinkle all with seasoned salt, seasoned pepper and 2 cups shredded natural Swiss cheese (½ pound).

With fork, mix 2 eggs with ¾ teaspoon salt, ½ teaspoon paprika, ½ teaspoon dry mustard, ⅛ teaspoon pepper and 1½ cups milk; pour over cheese.

Bake 40 minutes or until puffy and brown. Serve hot. Makes 4 servings.

PERFECTION SALAD

MONDAY

*Swiss Pie**

*Buttered Green Beans
with Almonds*

*Perfection Salad**

*Pineapple Sophisticate**

Tea   Coffee

2 envelopes unflavored gelatin
1½ cups boiling water
⅓ cup granulated sugar
1¼ teaspoons salt
¼ cup vinegar
¼ cup lemon juice
⅔ cup chopped ripe olives

¾ cup diced celery
1½ cups shredded cabbage
¾ cup shredded, pared carrot
¼ cup chopped green pepper
2 tablespoons diced pimiento
salad greens
mayonnaise

Early in day: Sprinkle gelatin over 1 cup cold water to soften; add boiling water; stir until dissolved. Stir in sugar, salt, vinegar and lemon juice; cool. Stir in olives and rest of ingredients except greens and mayonnaise; mix well. Pour into 8″ by 8″ by 2″ pan. Chill until firm.

To serve: Cut into 8 pieces. Garnish with greens. Pass mayonnaise. Makes 8 servings.

PINEAPPLE SOPHISTICATE

Quarter fresh pineapple lengthwise through green top. Run knife between shell and meat, loosening but not removing meat; cut meat into ¼- to ½-inch slices. Serve with lime wedges.

INSTANT BORSCHT

1 16-ounce jar red cabbage,
  undrained
1 16-ounce can julienne beets,
  undrained
1 10½-ounce can condensed
  onion soup

1 10½-ounce can condensed beef
  bouillon
2 tablespoons cider vinegar
1 tablespoon light brown sugar
sour cream

In large saucepan, place red cabbage, beets, undiluted onion soup and beef bouillon, vinegar, brown sugar. Heat to boiling. Serve, topped with sour cream. Makes 6 servings.

WIENERWURST SANDWICH

Preheat oven to 375°F. Open one 11¼-ounce can condensed bean-with-bacon soup. Spread layer of soup on each of 4 toasted pumpernickel-bread slices; cover each with layer of drained sauerkraut (1½ cups in all). Top each with 1 frankfurter split lengthwise. Combine ½ cup catchup and 1 tablespoon prepared mustard; spread on frankfurters. Bake about 20 minutes or until hot. Makes 4 servings.

DESSERT TIP: Place your favorite ice cream in tall glass; add chocolate or maple-blended syrup; fill with chilled sparkling water or ginger ale.

SAGE-GINGER CHICKEN BAKE

SAGE-GINGER CHICKEN BAKE

2 2½- to 3-pound broiler-
  fryers, cut up
1 lemon, halved
ground sage
ginger
salt

white pepper
butter or margarine
2 9-ounce packages frozen whole
  green beans
½ pound mushrooms, sliced

Pierce chicken with fork and rub with lemon. In small bowl, blend 4 teaspoons sage, 1 teaspoon ginger, 2¼ teaspoons salt and ¼ teaspoon white pepper; sprinkle over chicken. Place in large shallow baking dish.

Preheat oven to 350°F. In large skillet with heatproof-handle, or Dutch oven over medium heat, melt ¼ cup butter; add chicken and brown. Add 1 cup water; cover; bake 45 minutes or until tender.

About 15 minutes before serving: Blend ½ teaspoon sage, ¼ teaspoon salt and ⅛ teaspoon ginger. Cook beans as package label directs until tender-crisp; drain. In medium skillet, in 2 teaspoons butter, sauté blended spices. Add mushrooms; sauté 3 to 5 minutes or until tender. Add green beans. Serve vegetables over chicken. Makes 6 to 8 servings.

SPINACH-FRUIT SALAD

1 16-ounce can grapefruit sections
3 tablespoons white vinegar
1 tablespoon soy sauce
1 teaspoon granulated sugar
¼ teaspoon salt

½ teaspoon dry mustard
¼ cup salad oil
1 10-ounce package spinach, washed
½ cup sliced canned water chestnuts

Drain grapefruit; reserve 3 tablespoons juice. Combine this juice, vinegar, soy sauce, sugar, salt, mustard and salad oil as dressing.

In large salad bowl, toss spinach with water chestnuts, grapefruit sections and dressing. Makes 6 servings.

TUESDAY
Instant Borscht*
Wienerwurst Sandwich*
*Carrot and Celery
Sticks*
*Make-Your-Own
Ice-Cream Sodas**

WEDNESDAY
*Sage-Ginger
Chicken Bake**
Spinach-Fruit Salad*
*Marbled Cake
with Chocolate Sauce*
Milk   Coffee

DINNER EGGS ON TOASTED ROLLS

THURSDAY
*Dinner Eggs
on Toasted Rolls**

*Lettuce
with
Dried-Beef Dressing**

*Apricots
and Bing Cherries*

Tea   Coffee

8 small white onions, sliced
8 small carrots, pared, sliced
  diagonally
1 teaspoon salt
1 cup milk
1 10½-ounce can condensed cream-
of-mushroom soup
6 hard-cooked eggs, sliced
6 frankfurter rolls, split,
  toasted
butter or margarine
¼ cup chopped parsley

About 30 minutes before serving: In skillet, simmer onions and carrots, salt and ½ cup water, 15 minutes; drain. Add milk and undiluted mushroom soup; stir until blended. Add eggs; simmer, covered, 10 minutes.

Meanwhile, lightly butter hot rolls. With slotted spoon, heap some of egg mixture on each roll; pour sauce over all. Sprinkle with parsley. Makes 6 servings.

LETTUCE WITH DRIED-BEEF DRESSING

1 8-ounce package cream cheese
⅓ cup milk
4 teaspoons horseradish
¼ teaspoon salt
½ cup diced green pepper
½ cup finely chopped dried beef
1 teaspoon minced onion
1 large head iceberg lettuce
¼ cup pitted ripe olives, slivered,
  for garnish

In small bowl, with electric mixer at medium speed, beat cream cheese with milk, horseradish and salt until well mixed. At low speed, beat in green pepper, dried beef and onion.

Cut lettuce into 4 wedges; arrange on platter. Spoon dressing over lettuce and garnish with olives. Makes 4 servings.

CRISSCROSS POTATOES

FRIDAY
*Baked Fish
Crisscross Potatoes**
*Oven Summer Squash**
*English Lemon Cake**
Milk   Coffee

Cut 2 scrubbed large baking potatoes in half, lengthwise. Score cut surface into ½-inch diamonds. Brush potatoes with melted shortening. Place on cookie sheet cut side up. Bake at 425°F. 45 minutes or until fork tender. Makes 4 servings.

OVEN SUMMER SQUASH

Preheat oven to 425°F. Clean 2 pounds summer squash; cut into ½-inch slices. Place in layers in greased 2-quart casserole, sprinkling each layer with some of 1 teaspoon salt, ⅛ teaspoon pepper and 2 tablespoons butter or margarine, until all are used. Bake, covered, 45 minutes or until tender. Makes 4 servings.

ENGLISH LEMON CAKE

Day before: Preheat oven to 350°F. In large bowl, with electric mixer at medium speed, beat ⅔ cup butter or margarine with 2 cups granulated sugar until light and fluffy; add 4 eggs, beating well after each addition.

Sift 3 cups sifted regular all-purpose flour with 2 teaspoons double-acting baking powder and 2 teaspoons salt. At low speed, slowly beat flour into butter mixture with 1 cup milk until just blended. Fold in 4 or 5 tablespoons grated lemon peel (2 lemons), and one 4-ounce can blanched almonds, ground (about 1 cup).

Bake, in ungreased 9-inch tube pan, 65 minutes or until cake tester, inserted in center, comes out clean. Cool in pan 1 hour; remove from pan

DEEP-DISH GRAPE PIE

to cake plate. Brush surface of cake with one-half 6-ounce can frozen lemonade concentrate, thawed, undiluted. Let stand overnight. Just before serving, sprinkle with confectioners' sugar. Makes 12 to 16 servings.

PORK LOIN IN WATERCRESS SAUCE

5-pound pork loin, cracked
1 teaspoon salt
1 teaspoon pepper
1 garlic clove, crushed

2 tablespoons chopped parsley
1 13¾-ounce can chicken broth
½ cup chopped watercress
3 tablespoons cornstarch

About 3 hours before serving: Rub pork with salt and pepper. In Dutch oven, brown pork well on all sides.

Add garlic, parsley and chicken broth; cover; simmer slowly 2½ hours or until pork is fork-tender, basting often with liquid in Dutch oven. Remove pork to heated platter; keep warm.

Skim fat from surface of liquid; add watercress. Blend cornstarch and ¼ cup cold water; slowly stir into liquid and cook until thickened.

To serve: Slice pork between cracked bones. Pass sauce. Makes 8 servings.

DEEP-DISH GRAPE PIE

For filling, in large bowl, mix 8 cups seeded Ribier grapes, 1 cup granulated sugar, 3 tablespoons lemon juice, 2 teaspoons grated orange peel, 2½ tablespoons quick-cooking tapioca. Let stand 20 minutes; pour into 8″ by 8″ by 2″ baking dish. Heat oven to 425°F. Make up 1 package piecrust mix. Lay 6 pastry strips, each 14″ by ¾″ by ⅛″, across top of baking dish, equidistantly apart. Next, starting at left, lay strip at right angles to others; weave it in and out; repeat with 5 more strips. Roll overhang under; press to edge; make dots in it with skewer; brush with milk. Bake 45 minutes. Chill. Makes 12 servings.
Tarts: Make half filling above; spoon into seven 5-ounce soufflé dishes or custard cups. Weave pastry strips, 4½″ by ½″, over top. Bake, on cookie sheet, at 425°F. 30 to 35 minutes. Chill.

SATURDAY
*Pork Loin
in Watercress Sauce**
Buttered Spinach
Mashed Potatoes
*Deep-Dish Grape Pie**
Tea   Coffee

CREAM OF MONGOLE SOUP WITH SHERRY

1 10½-ounce can condensed tomato soup	1 cup light cream
	1 teaspoon sugar
1 10½-ounce can condensed green-pea soup	2 teaspoons Worcestershire
	5 tablespoons sherry

In saucepan, combine undiluted soups and ¾ cup water; heat over very low heat, stirring until smooth. Slowly stir in cream, sugar and Worcestershire. Remove from heat; slowly add sherry. Makes 5 or 6 servings.

CRAB-RICE SALAD

3 cups cold cooked rice	½ cup diced celery
1 teaspoon curry powder	2 6-ounce packages frozen Alaska
½ cup chopped parsley	King crab, thawed, drained
3 tablespoons bottled creamy French dressing	⅓ cup mayonnaise
	1 large ripe pineapple
1 cup quartered ripe olives	

Early in day: In large bowl, toss together rice, curry powder and parsley; over them drizzle French dressing; toss well; fold in olives, celery, crab and mayonnaise; refrigerate.

Cut pineapple in half lengthwise, right through green top. With grapefruit knife, hollow out each half, leaving ½-inch-thick shell; refrigerate shells. Cut meat scooped from pineapple into chunks; measure 1 cup and add to salad mixture. Pile into pineapple halves. (Save remaining pineapple for dessert another day.) Makes 4 main-dish servings.

HASHBURGER DELUXE

1 16-ounce can corned-beef hash	onion rings
1 tablespoon butter or margarine	mustard pickles
1 or 2 3½-ounce cans French-fried	

Open can of hash at both ends; push out in one piece; cut into 4 slices.

In large skillet over medium heat, melt butter; brown hash slices on both sides; arrange onion rings around hash. Heat onions slightly, tossing occasionally with fork. Then top each hash slice with spoonful of mustard pickles. Serve on heated platter. Makes 4 servings.

VEGETABLE TIP: On serving plate, arrange mashed squash in ring; fill with peas; sprinkle with slivered almonds.

WAFER-THIN SESAME CRISPS

Early in day: Preheat oven to 350°F. In bowl, combine 4 cups packaged biscuit mix, 1 teaspoon salt, ½ teaspoon baking soda. Stir in 6 tablespoons melted butter or margarine and ⅔ cup milk. With floured hands, knead dough, right in bowl, just until it holds together.

Break off golf-ball size pieces of dough. With floured stockinette-covered rolling pin, on large ungreased cookie sheet, roll dough into paper-thin circle 6 inches in diameter. Combine 2 egg yolks with teaspoon of water; brush some over circle of dough; sprinkle with sesame seed. Bake 10 to 15 minutes or until golden; remove from cookie sheet; cool on rack. Repeat with rest of dough. (Use several cookie sheets to speed process.) Sprinkle baked crisps with salt. Store leftovers, covered, in dry place. Makes 16.

CHICKEN-GRAPE SALAD

TUESDAY

Cranberry Juice

*Chicken-Grape Salad**

Hot Corn Muffins

Stewed Pears

Tea   Coffee

½ cup mayonnaise
2 tablespoons milk
1 teaspoon salt
½ teaspoon dry mustard
¼ teaspoon pepper

1 tablespoon lemon juice
3 cups cut up cooked chicken
3 cups halved and seeded grapes
1 cup thinly sliced celery

In large bowl, combine mayonnaise, milk, salt, mustard, pepper and lemon juice; stir until smooth. Add chicken, grapes and celery. Toss well. Makes 4 servings.

QUICK SUMMER STEW

WEDNESDAY

*Quick Summer Stew**

*Hearts of Lettuce
with Cottage Cheese
and Sliced
Garden Vegetables*

Cracker Basket

*Cherry Cloud Cake**

Milk   Coffee

3 tablespoons butter or margarine
1 medium onion, chopped
1 pound frankfurters, quartered
    lengthwise
1 tablespoon flour
1½ teaspoons chili powder

1 teaspoon salt
2 15-ounce cans red kidney beans
1 16-ounce can tomatoes
1 12-ounce can whole-kernel corn,
    drained

About 30 minutes before serving: In large kettle or Dutch oven, in hot butter, sauté onion with frankfurters until lightly browned; blend in flour, chili powder and salt; add beans, tomatoes and corn. Simmer, covered, 15 minutes. Makes 6 servings.

CHERRY CLOUD CAKE

1 package white-cake mix
1 envelope unflavored gelatin
⅓ cup granulated sugar
⅛ teaspoon salt
1 cup boiling water

1 2-ounce envelope whipped-
    topping mix
2 16-ounce cans red tart pitted
    cherries, drained

About 4 hours before serving: Bake two 9″ by 1½″ white-cake layers as label directs; cool.

Pour ½ cup cold water into small bowl; over water sprinkle gelatin to soften. Add sugar, salt and boiling water; stir until dissolved. Refrigerate until slightly thickened.

Prepare whipped-topping mix as label directs; when almost stiff, gradually beat slightly thickened gelatin into it.

Set 1 cake layer on cake plate; top with 1 can drained cherries; spread with 1 cup whipped topping. Lay second cake layer on first; top with second can drained cherries; spread topping as before. Chill 2 hours. Makes 10 to 12 servings.

THURSDAY

*Creamed Eggs
on Deviled-Ham Toast**

Mixed Greens Salad

*Melon Tingle**

Iced Tea   Coffee

EGG TIP: Spread toast with deviled ham, then top with creamed eggs.

MELON TINGLE

2 honeydew melons
2 cups grapefruit juice

lemon ice
mint sprigs

Cut melons in halves; remove seeds. Scoop out balls, using fruit-ball cutter. Fill 6 sherbet glasses two-thirds full of melon balls; add ⅓ cup grapefruit juice to each. Top each with small spoonful lemon ice. Garnish with mint. Makes 6 servings.

CHEESY SCALLOPS

2 tablespoons butter or margarine	2 tablespoons lemon juice
2 tablespoons chopped onion	dash pepper
¼ pound small mushrooms, sliced	dash thyme leaves
1 pound fresh sea scallops	dash ground marjoram
1 10¾-ounce can condensed Cheddar-cheese soup	2 tablespoons buttered bread crumbs

Preheat oven to 350°F. In skillet, in butter, sauté onion and mushrooms until light brown. Add scallops; cook 3 or 4 minutes. Place scallops mixture in 10″ by 6″ by 2″ shallow baking dish. Combine undiluted soup, lemon juice and seasonings; pour over scallops. Bake 15 minutes. Stir well; top with crumbs; bake 15 minutes. Makes 4 servings.

TOMATO COLESLAW

In large bowl, combine 4 cups finely shredded cabbage; ½ green pepper, chopped; 1 tablespoon chopped pimiento; 1 teaspoon grated onion; 3 tablespoons salad oil; ⅓ cup white vinegar; 2 tomatoes, quartered; 1 teaspoon salt; ¼ teaspoon pepper; ½ teaspoon dry mustard; 1 teaspoon celery salt and 2 tablespoons granulated sugar. Makes 4 servings.

APRICOT COOL

About 15 minutes before serving: Drain 1 30-ounce can whole peeled apricots, reserving syrup; pit apricots.

In electric-blender container, combine apricots with 1 cup cracked ice and ¾ cup miniature marshmallows; blend at low speed 1 minute. To mixture in blender, gradually add 1 cup milk, ½ cup canned apricot syrup and 2 tablespoons lemon juice; blend until creamy.

Serve in wine glasses; garnish with mint sprigs. Makes 6 to 8 servings.

ICED CHERRY SOUP

2 16-ounce cans pitted red cherries	3 tablespoons cornstarch
½ cup granulated sugar	½ teaspoon red food color
2 tablespoons lemon juice	sour cream for garnish
½ teaspoon anise seed, crushed	mint leaves for garnish

Early in day: Drain cherries, reserving liquid; add water to liquid to make 5 cups. In large saucepan, combine cherries, liquid, sugar, lemon juice, anise seed; cover and heat to boiling. Reduce heat; simmer, covered, 30 minutes.

Press cherries and liquid through coarse sieve; return to pan and heat to boiling. Blend cornstarch with ½ cup water; stir quickly into strained mixture; continue cooking and stirring until clear and thickened. Stir in food color; cover; refrigerate.

Serve garnished with sour cream and mint leaves. Makes 6 servings.

TURKEY TIP: Secure 8- to 10-pound turkey on spit of outdoor rotisserie, following manufacturer's directions. Insert meat thermometer inside thigh muscle; brush bird with salad oil; sprinkle with seasoned salt, seasoned pepper and paprika. Loosely wrap in foil. Rotate over medium heat. When bird is almost done, stop spit; remove foil; save drippings. Continue to rotate and cook bird, basting with drippings, until thermometer registers 185°F.

ICED CHERRY SOUP

FRIDAY
Cheesy Scallops*
Tomato Coleslaw*
Crescent Dinner Rolls
Apricot Cool*
Milk   Tea

SATURDAY
Iced Cherry Soup*
Rotisserie Turkey*
Hot Curried Rice
Carrots and Peas
Chocolate Cream Pie
Tea   Coffee

SAVORY CHUCK STEAK

3½-pound beef chuck steak, about 1½ inches thick
2 tablespoons flour
½ teaspoon salt
⅛ teaspoon pepper
2 tablespoons salad oil

1 1⅜-ounce envelope onion-soup mix
½ cup chili sauce
1 sprig parsley, chopped, for garnish

About 35 minutes before serving: With sharp knife, cut and discard fat and bones from chuck steak; cut meat into strips ¼-inch wide. In large bowl, toss chuck with flour, salt and pepper.

In large skillet over medium heat, in hot salad oil, brown steak. Add onion-soup mix, 1 cup cold water and chili sauce. Simmer, covered, 25 minutes or until meat is tender. Serve, garnished with parsley. Makes 6 to 8 servings.

VEGETABLE TIP: Toss drained cooked broccoli with butter, salt and lemon juice. Sprinkle with grated Parmesan cheese.

DESSERT TIP: Prepare one 3½-ounce package of strawberry-flavor whipped-dessert mix as label directs. Refrigerate. Toast slices of pound-cake in toaster. Serve strawberry whip on cake; top with sliced, sugared fresh strawberries.

TANGY KNACKWURST BUNS

1 27-ounce can sauerkraut, drained
6 knackwurst
6 oblong French rolls

melted butter or margarine
¼ cup prepared mustard
3 tablespoons pickle relish

About 50 minutes before serving: Preheat broiler if manufacturer directs. In saucepan over medium heat, heat sauerkraut 20 minutes.

Place knackwurst in saucepan, with water to cover. Simmer, covered, over medium heat, 5 to 8 minutes; remove from water. Slit each roll lengthwise from top, not quite to bottom; spread apart; brush inside generously with melted butter.

Slit each knackwurst diagonally across, not quite to bottom, twice; arrange, cut side up, in broiling pan. Broil for 10 to 12 minutes on top side; then turn and broil 8 minutes on other side, or to desired doneness. Toast rolls in broiler.

Spoon and stuff sauerkraut into rolls; lay knackwurst on top of each roll. Combine mustard and pickle relish; spread over slits; serve with fork and knife. Makes 6 servings.

CALIFORNIA SALAD

1 small head chicory
1 large head Boston lettuce
2 hard-cooked eggs

1 large ripe avocado
½ cup pecan halves
bottled Italian dressing

Early in day: Separate chicory and lettuce leaves; wash and dry well. Reserve 6 whole lettuce leaves; tear rest of lettuce and chicory into bite-size pieces; refrigerate.

Slice eggs. Peel, pit, avocado; cut crosswise into 10 rings. Around edge of low salad bowl, tuck reserved lettuce leaves. Toss gently bite-size pieces of chicory and lettuce, avocado rings, egg slices and pecan halves; turn into bowl.

Pass Italian dressing. Makes 6 servings.

SUNDAY

Mixed Apple and Orange Juice

Savory Chuck Steak*

Baked Potatoes

Buttered Broccoli*

Carrots

Club Rolls

Strawberry Whipped Dessert*

Tea   Coffee

MONDAY

Tangy Knackwurst Buns*

California Salad*

Orange Sherbet

Iced Fruit Cookies

Tea   Coffee

BAKED NECTAR PUDDING

1 cup sifted regular all-purpose
   flour
2 tablespoons double-acting baking
   powder
½ teaspoon salt
½ cup granulated sugar
½ cup chopped walnuts
½ cup milk

1 teaspoon vanilla extract
2 tablespoons butter or margarine,
   melted
¼ cup packed brown sugar
1 12-ounce can apricot nectar
   (1½ cups)
light cream

Preheat oven to 350°F. Grease 8" by 8" by 2" baking pan. In large bowl, sift together flour, baking powder, salt and sugar. Stir in nuts, milk, vanilla and butter. Pour into pan. Sprinkle on brown sugar. Heat nectar and ¼ cup water until boiling; pour over pudding; don't stir. Bake 35 to 40 minutes. Serve warm with cream. Makes 8 servings.

EASY BEEF COBBLER

Preheat oven to 475°F. In 2½-quart casserole, combine two 24-ounce cans beef stew, one 16-ounce can drained green beans, 1 minced garlic clove and 1 teaspoon thyme leaves. Bake 30 minutes. Meanwhile, bake one 8-ounce package refrigerated biscuits, as label directs, in oven with stew. Arrange baked biscuits on top of hot stew; sprinkle with ½ cup shredded Cheddar cheese; return to oven and bake 2 or 3 minutes to melt cheese. Makes 6 servings.

CRANBERRY CHIFFON

About 1½ hours before serving: Heat 1 cup cranberry juice. Pour over one 3-ounce package lemon-flavor gelatin in small bowl. Stir to dissolve; add ½ cup cranberry juice.

In large bowl, place some ice cubes; set bowl of cranberry mixture on top. Stir mixture constantly until it just begins to thicken.

Whip one 2-ounce envelope whipped-topping mix as label directs; into it stir cranberry mixture. Refrigerate 10 minutes; spoon into six 6-ounce wine glasses, parfait glasses or custard cups and refrigerate. Makes 6 servings.

APPLE-RAISIN CRISP

5 cups peeled, sliced tart apples
   (5–6 apples)
1 8¾-ounce can crushed pineapple,
   drained
¼ cup raisins
2 tablespoons lemon juice
½ cup granulated sugar
2 tablespoons melted butter or
   margarine

¼ teaspoon salt
1 teaspoon cinnamon
3 tablespoons butter or margarine,
   softened
⅓ cup granulated sugar
1 tablespoon flour
1 cup 40% bran flakes
vanilla ice cream

Preheat oven to 375°F. In large bowl, combine apples, pineapple, raisins, lemon juice, ½ cup sugar, melted butter, salt and cinnamon; pour into 1½-quart shallow baking dish. Cream 3 tablespoons butter; blend in ⅓ cup sugar and flour. Add bran flakes and mix well; spread over apple mixture. Bake, covered, 15 minutes; remove cover and bake 15 minutes longer or until apples are tender. Serve warm. Nice with vanilla ice cream. Makes 6 to 8 servings.

TUESDAY
Baked Pork Chops
Baked Potatoes
Waxed Beans
Cucumber-and-
Cottage-Cheese Salad
Baked Nectar Pudding*
Tea   Coffee

WEDNESDAY
Easy Beef Cobbler*
Orange and Red-Onion
Salad
Cranberry Chiffon*
Coffee

THURSDAY
Broiled Flounder
with Tartar Sauce
Mixed Vegetables
Chinese-Cabbage Salad
Apple-Raisin Crisp*
Coffee

MEAT-CRESTED TOMATOES

6 large, firm, ripe red tomatoes
salt
1½ pounds boned lamb and pork, ground together
½ cup shredded natural Cheddar cheese
½ cup chopped fresh parsley
1 teaspoon seasoned pepper
½ teaspoon ground allspice
2 eggs, beaten
butter or margarine
hot cooked spaghetti

About 1½ hours before serving: Cut thin slice from stem end of each tomato. Scoop out most of pulp and juice from tomatoes, being careful not to damage outside skin (save pulp and juice for stewed tomatoes or tomato sauce).

Sprinkle inside of each tomato with salt; let stand, right side up, until time to fill. Preheat oven to 350°F.

In large bowl, combine ground lamb and pork, cheese, parsley, seasoned pepper, allspice, 2 teaspoons salt and beaten eggs. In large skillet over medium heat, in 1 tablespoon hot butter, sauté meat until it loses all its red color; drain off fat.

Heap some of meat mixture in center of each tomato. Arrange tomatoes in shallow 10″ by 6″ by 2″ baking dish. Bake 15 to 20 minutes or until meat is piping hot and tomato skins wrinkled.

Serve on bed of hot spaghetti which has been seasoned to taste and tossed with 2 tablespoons melted butter, if desired. Or serve on hot buttered toast slices or split buttered toasted English muffins. Makes 6 servings.

MEAT-CRESTED TOMATOES

CARROTS VICHY

¼ cup butter or margarine
¾ cup boiling water
2 teaspoons salt
¼ teaspoon nutmeg
⅛ teaspoon pepper
1 tablespoon sugar
5 cups diagonally sliced carrots, ¼-inch thick
1 tablespoon lemon juice
½ teaspoon monosodium glutamate
¼ cup chopped parsley

About 20 minutes before serving: In saucepan, add butter to boiling water. Add salt, nutmeg, pepper, sugar and carrots. Simmer, covered, 8 to 10 minutes or until tender-crisp. Stir in lemon juice, monosodium glutamate and parsley. Makes 6 servings.

JELLIED MARSALA FRUIT CUP

2 envelopes unflavored gelatin
½ cup lemon juice
¼ cup currant jelly
½ cup granulated sugar
1½ cups Marsala wine
few drops red food color
1 cup cubed, pared fresh pears or apples
1 cup halved, seedless green grapes
slightly sweetened whipped cream or whipped topping

Early in day: In saucepan, sprinkle gelatin on water to soften; add lemon juice, jelly, sugar. Stir over low heat until melted and clear; add wine and food color. Refrigerate until mixture begins to set; then stir in fruit. Turn into 5-cup mold. Refrigerate about 4 hours or until firm.

To serve: Quickly dip mold in and out of hot water up to ½ inch of top. Invert serving plate on top; invert both. Gently shake until dessert slips out. Lift off mold. If desired, garnish outside of dessert with little bunches of green grapes. Serve with or without whipped cream. Makes 6 to 8 servings.

FRIDAY
*Meat-Crested Tomatoes**
Buttered Spaghetti
*Carrots Vichy**
Seeded Rolls
Jellied
*Marsala Fruit Cup**
Demitasse

SATURDAY
Tomato Soup
Ginger Chicken*
Custard Corn Pudding*
Pumpkin Loaves*
Coffee-Peach Cream*
Milk   Tea

GINGER CHICKEN

1½ tablespoons flour	¼ cup shortening
2 teaspoons salt	1 16-ounce jar refrigerated fruit
1½ teaspoons granulated sugar	salad
1 teaspoon ginger	about ½ cup orange juice
1 3-pound broiler-fryer, cut-up	

About 1 hour before serving: Combine flour, next 3 ingredients; coat chicken. (Reserve leftover flour.) In large skillet over medium heat, melt shortening; fry chicken until golden.

Into measuring cup, drain liquid from fruit; add enough orange juice to make 1 cup. Pour over chicken. (Reserve fruit.) Simmer, covered, 45 minutes or until fork-tender.

In cup, blend leftover flour with 3 tablespoons water; stir into skillet. Cook, stirring, until thickened. Add fruit; heat. Makes 4 servings.

CUSTARD CORN PUDDING

About 1½ hours before serving: Preheat oven to 325°F. Combine 2 cups chopped cooked whole-kernel corn; 2 eggs, slightly beaten; 1 teaspoon sugar; 1½ tablespoons butter or margarine, melted; 2 cups scalded milk; 1¾ teaspoons salt and ¼ teaspoon pepper. Pour into greased 1½-quart casserole. Set in pan of warm water. Bake, uncovered, 1 hour 15 minutes. Makes 4 to 6 servings.

PUMPKIN LOAVES

2 cups granulated sugar	½ teaspoon double-acting baking
1 cup salad oil	powder
3 eggs	1 teaspoon baking soda
2 cups canned pumpkin	1 teaspoon ground cloves
3 cups regular all-purpose flour	1 teaspoon cinnamon
½ teaspoon salt	1 teaspoon nutmeg

Early in day: Grease three 7½″ by 3½″ by 2¼″ loaf pans. Preheat oven to 325°F.

In bowl, with electric mixer at medium speed, beat sugar with oil until blended; add eggs, one at a time, beating well after each addition. Continue beating until light and fluffy; beat in pumpkin.

Onto piece of waxed paper, sift together flour and next 6 ingredients. With mixer at low speed, beat flour mixture into pumpkin mixture.

Divide batter among pans; bake one hour or until cake tester, inserted in center, comes out clean. Cool in pans, on racks, 10 minutes; remove from pans; finish cooling on racks. Freezer-wrap, freeze 2 of loaves; to serve, thaw, unwrapped, at room temperature 30 minutes. Makes 3 loaves.

COFFEE-PEACH CREAM

1 envelope unflavored gelatin	½ cup heavy or whipping cream,
⅓ cup granulated sugar	whipped
⅛ teaspoon salt	¼ teaspoon almond extract
1 cup coffee	1 10-ounce package frozen peaches,
1 teaspoon lemon juice	thawed

Early in day: In double-boiler top, soften gelatin in ½ cup cold water. Set over boiling water; stir until dissolved. Stir in sugar, next 3 ingredients. Refrigerate. Stir gelatin frequently until consistency of unbeaten egg white. Fold into cream with extract. Spoon into sherbet glasses; chill. Serve topped with peaches. Makes 4 servings.

AUTUMN

Autumn, signaled by the falling leaves, spells an end to the long, lazy days of summer. School, the first frost, football games and holiday parties call for a different approach to menu planning. Meals are less casual now, and heartier.

Fortunately, autumn is also the season of mellow fruitfulness, of the bountiful harvest for which thanksgiving is rightfully due. Now is the time when roadside stands and supermarket bins are piled high with Hubbard and acorn squash, pumpkins, yams, cranberries, creamy white cauliflower, broccoli, cabbage, Brussels sprouts, artichokes, rutabaga, royal-purple eggplant and many kinds of apples—crisp, juicy Jonathans, striped Northern Spies, Grimes Goldens, McIntoshes, Delicious and bright-red Baldwins. For extra measure, there's cider too, fresh and full-bodied.

The menus in this section make full use of this bounty, in dishes such as Baked Stuffed Yams, Dinner-in-an Eggplant, Acorn Squash Halves and Sour-Cream Pumpkin Pie. There's emphasis on meals that will stick to the ribs as the cold days come on, as well as on those that save time and work. Among these are skillet meals, and dishes that can be baked together in the oven, freeing you for other activities—or simply to watch for a moment, in wonder, as the leaves turn the world to gold.

4 pounds beef top round steak,
   about 2 inches thick
instant meat tenderizer
seasoned pepper
½ teaspoon oregano
2 tablespoons olive oil
1 garlic clove, minced
¼ cup butter or margarine

3 large green peppers, thinly sliced
1½ cups chopped celery
1 10-ounce jar colossal stuffed
   olives, drained, halved
2 tablespoons bottled capers
2 14½-ounce cans sliced baby
   tomatoes, drained

About 1 hour before serving: Preheat oven to 400°F. Lightly score steak in diamond pattern, on both sides. Apply tenderizer as label directs; then sprinkle both sides with seasoned pepper and oregano. Combine oil and garlic; pour over meat in shallow roasting pan. Roast 20 minutes; turn; roast 20 minutes or until of desired doneness.

   Meanwhile, in large skillet, in hot butter, sauté peppers and celery 10 minutes or until golden; add olives, capers and tomatoes; simmer 15 minutes. Slice steak diagonally, across grain, into thin slices; arrange on heated platter with the sauce. Makes 8 servings.

CHOCOLATE-BERRY ICE-CREAM CAKE

Up to 3 days ahead: Arrange 9 packaged chocolate wafers around sides of buttered 9-inch springform pan. Slightly soften 3 pints of strawberry and 2½ pints of vanilla ice cream. Spoon alternate layers into pan to hold cookies in place. Stand 8 more wafers on edge, in circle on top; freeze.

   About 15 minutes before dessert time: Remove cake from freezer; carefully remove cake-pan rim. Garnish with 10 strawberries, halved. Makes 10 to 12 servings. Freeze any leftovers.

———◆———

CREAMED ONIONS IN ACORN-SQUASH HALVES

About 1 hour before serving: Preheat oven to 375°F. Split 4 acorn squash in half lengthwise; remove seeds and stringy portion. Brush cut surface of each half with melted butter; sprinkle each with ¼ teaspoon seasoned salt. Arrange squash halves, cut side down, on large cookie sheet. Bake 30 minutes; turn cut side up; brush with more melted butter; bake about 30 minutes or until tender.

   About 20 minutes before squash are done, cook two 8-ounce packages frozen small onions with cream sauce as label directs, adding ½ teaspoon each marjoram leaves and thyme leaves. Fill squash halves with creamed onions; sprinkle with paprika. Makes 8 servings.

———◆———

SWEET-SOUR GREEN BEANS

Place 1 pound green beans, cut crosswise into 1-inch lengths, in large skillet or saucepan with tight cover. Add 2 tablespoons bacon fat, 1 cup boiling water and ½ teaspoon salt. Heat quickly, covered, until beans steam; turn down heat and cook 15 to 20 minutes or until tender-crisp. Do not drain. Mix 1 teaspoon cornstarch with 3 tablespoons sugar, 3 tablespoons vinegar, 1 tablespoon soy sauce, ¼ cup cold water, ¼ cup sweet pickle relish; pour over beans; cook, stirring, until slightly thickened and clear. Makes 4 servings.

NEW ENGLAND HAM-AND-NOODLE BAKE

WEDNESDAY

*New England
Ham-and-Noodle Bake**

*Cauliflower
with Green Grapes**

*Spinach-and-Red-Onion
Salad
with Italian Dressing*

Chocolate Pudding

Tea   Coffee

2 cups medium noodles
1 tablespoon salad oil
2 cups cut-up cooked ham
½ cup chopped onions
1 10¾-ounce can condensed

Cheddar-cheese soup
½ cup milk
1 7¾-ounce can oysters, drained
chopped chives (optional)

About 45 minutes before serving: Preheat oven to 375°F. Cook noodles as label directs; drain. Meanwhile, in large skillet in salad oil, sauté ham and onions until golden; add undiluted cheese soup, milk and oysters; cook 2 or 3 minutes, stirring constantly.

In 1½-quart casserole, stir noodles with soup mixture. Bake 20 minutes or until bubbly. Sprinkle with chopped chives. Makes 4 servings.

CAULIFLOWER WITH GREEN GRAPES

Break off each floweret in 1 large head cauliflower, then slice lengthwise into slices ¼-inch thick. In skillet, in 1½ cups boiling water with 1 tablespoon salt, simmer cauliflower, covered, 5 minutes or until tender. Drain. Fold in 2 tablespoons butter or margarine, 1 cup seedless grapes and ½ cup slivered toasted almonds. Makes 4 to 6 servings.

———◆———

VEGETABLE TIP: Scrub and dry yams of the same size; bake in 350°F. oven 45 to 50 minutes or until tender when tested with fork. Immediately cut slice from top of each. With spoon, scoop out yams (do not break skins); mash well. Beat in enough hot milk to make yams creamy. Add butter; season to taste. Pile back into shells.

BAKED LEMON-CAKE PUDDINGS

THURSDAY

Roast Chicken

Stuffed Baked Yams*

Lima Beans

Baked Lemon-Cake Puddings*

Tea   Coffee

1 cup granulated sugar
¼ cup all-purpose flour
2 tablespoons salad oil
⅛ teaspoon salt

2 tablespoons grated lemon peel
⅓ cup lemon juice
1½ cups skim milk, scalded
3 eggs, separated

About 1 hour before serving: Preheat oven to 325°F. Combine sugar, flour, salad oil and salt. Add lemon peel and juice. Slowly stir scalded milk into beaten egg yolks; stir these into lemon mixture until smooth. Beat egg whites stiff but not dry; fold into lemon-egg mixture. Pour into eight 5-ounce custard cups.

Set custard cups in shallow pan; pour boiling water into pan to depth of 1 inch. Bake 40 minutes or until cakelike topping is done. Cool slightly. Makes 8 servings.

———◆———

LIME-SAUCED FLOUNDER ROLLS

FRIDAY

Tomato Juice

*Lime-Sauced Flounder
Rolls**

Hot Fluffy Rice

Mixed-Greens Salad

*Butter-Pecan
Ice Cream*

Tea   Coffee

About 40 minutes before serving: Preheat oven to 375°F. Sprinkle one 16-ounce package thawed frozen flounder fillets with salt, pepper and lime juice; roll up and place in greased 10″ by 6″ by 2″ baking dish. Sprinkle ¼ cup minced onion over top of fish. In small saucepan, over medium heat, melt 2 tablespoons butter or margarine; stir in 2 tablespoons flour and gradually blend in 1 cup milk. Continue cooking over medium heat, stirring constantly, until thickened. Stir in ½ teaspoon salt, ⅛ teaspoon pepper, 2 teaspoons lime juice and 2 teaspoons chopped pimiento. Pour sauce over fish; bake 20 to 30 minutes until fish flakes with fork. Makes 3 or 4 servings.

APPETIZER PIZZAS

APPETIZER PIZZAS

1 10½-ounce can pizza sauce
1 tablespoon grated Parmesan
  cheese
¼ teaspoon garlic powder
2 8-ounce cans refrigerated
  buttermilk biscuits

½ pound Mozzarella cheese,
  shredded
1 4-ounce can sliced mushrooms,
  drained
pitted ripe olives, halved, for
  garnish

Preheat oven to 450°F. In medium pan, heat pizza sauce with Parmesan cheese and garlic powder.

Roll each biscuit from one package into oval about 4 inches long. On well-greased, large cookie sheet arrange biscuits side by side in 2 long rows touching each other; press biscuit edges carefully together with fingers to form wide strip.

Spread half of pizza sauce over biscuits, leaving about ½-inch rim around edges. Sprinkle with half Mozzarella and half mushroom slices. Bake 12 minutes; garnish with olives; continue baking 2 minutes or until crust is browned. With broad spatula, remove pizza to serving platter. Pull apart to serve.

While first pizza is baking, make second pizza with remaining ingredients. Serve hot. Makes 8 to 10 servings or 20 nibblers.

HAM-AND-BEAN CHOWDER

¼ cup butter or margarine
1 cup diced cooked ham
¼ cup chopped celery
¼ cup chopped onion

2 11½-ounce cans condensed
  bean-with-bacon soup
1 tablespoon chopped parsley

In 3-quart saucepan, in butter, lightly brown ham; push to one side. Add celery and onion; cook until tender. Stir in undiluted soup, 2 soup cans water and parsley. Bring just to boiling point, stirring occasionally. Makes 4 main-dish servings.

RELISH TIP: In large bowl or punch bowl, place an inverted soup plate; pile cracked ice on top (this makes room for water as ice starts to melt). Poke carrot, celery and cucumber sticks into ice. Scatter cherry tomatoes, radish roses, cauliflowerettes and stuffed olives or pitted black olives in between.

SATURDAY
Appetizer Pizzas*
Ham-and-Bean Chowder*
Vegetable Relishes*
Fruit Tray
Demitasse

RATATOUILLE

SUNDAY

*Rotisseried
Leg of Lamb*

Ratatouille*
*(Eggplant, Zucchini, Tomatoes,
Green Peppers)*

Mashed Potatoes

Lime Meringue Pie*

Milk   Tea

3 tablespoons olive oil	1 unpared small eggplant, diced
2 medium onions, sliced	2 small zucchini, in ½-inch slices
1 garlic clove, minced	1 bay leaf
2 peeled tomatoes, diced	3 bacon slices
1 large green pepper, cut into	2 teaspoons salt
½-inch strips	⅛ teaspoon pepper

About 40 minutes before serving: In Dutch oven, in hot oil, sauté onions with garlic until tender. Add tomatoes, green pepper, eggplant, zucchini, and bay leaf; sauté, over medium heat, stirring occasionally, 15 minutes.

Meanwhile fry bacon crisp. Crumble bacon; add to vegetables with salt and pepper. Cover; simmer 15 minutes; uncover; simmer 10 minutes. Remove bay leaf. *Serve at once.* Makes 6 servings.

LIME MERINGUE PIE

1 baked 9-inch pie shell	¼ cup lime juice
granulated sugar	3 egg yolks, slightly beaten
¼ cup cornstarch	green food color
salt	3 egg whites
grated peel 1 lime or lemon	½ teaspoon vanilla extract

Early in day: In double boiler, combine ½ cup sugar, cornstarch, ⅛ teaspoon salt; slowly stir in 1¼ cups warm water, peel, juice, then egg yolks. Cook, stirring, until smooth and thick enough to mound when dropped from spoon. Remove from heat; add 1 or 2 drops of green food color; cool slightly.

Preheat oven to 425°F. Spoon filling into pie shell. In small bowl, with electric mixer at high speed, beat egg whites with ½ teaspoon salt and vanilla until frothy throughout (don't allow them to stiffen). Add ¼ cup sugar, a little at a time, beating until stiff peaks form.

Heap meringue on center of pie filling; spread so it touches inner edge of crust all around. Bake 4 minutes or until golden brown. Cool; refrigerate. Makes 6 to 8 servings.

PINEAPPLE-BEAN SUPPER

MONDAY

Pineapple-Bean Supper*

*Lettuce Wedges
with
Chiffonade Dressing**

Hot Garlic Bread

Fresh Applesauce*

Peanut-Butter Cookies

Milk   Coffee

6 slices bacon, diced	1 13½-ounce can pineapple chunks,
1 medium onion, chopped	drained
1 pound frankfurters, cut in chunks	2 tablespoons vinegar
1 17-ounce can butter beans	1 teaspoon prepared mustard
1 16-ounce can barbecue beans	½ teaspoon salt

About 30 minutes before serving: In large skillet over high heat, fry bacon until almost crisp; drain off fat. Add onion and frankfurters; simmer 5 minutes. Add butter beans and remaining ingredients; heat 10 minutes, stirring occasionally. Makes 6 generous servings.

SALAD TIP: Into ½ cup French dressing, stir 2 teaspoons each minced pimiento and parsley and ½ hard-cooked egg, chopped.

FRESH APPLESAUCE

Pare, core and quarter 2 pounds cooking apples (about 8 apples). Simmer, covered, with ½ cup water 15 to 20 minutes or until fork-tender. Stir in ½ cup sugar. Beat smooth with spoon. Makes 6 servings.

ORANGE BARBECUED LAMB

1 tablespoon flour	¼ teaspoon Worcestershire
½ cup catchup	½ teaspoon salt
1 teaspoon grated orange peel	dash pepper
¾ cup orange juice	⅛ teaspoon barbecue spice
¼ cup salad oil	2 cups cubed cooked lamb
¼ cup molasses	

In small saucepan, blend flour with 2 tablespoons water. Add catchup, orange peel, orange juice, salad oil, molasses, Worcestershire, salt, pepper and spice. Bring to boil; cook over low heat, stirring, until mixture thickens. Add lamb; heat through. Makes 4 servings.

SALAD TIP: Use half shredded green and half shredded red cabbage; toss with your favorite coleslaw dressing.

SALAD TIP: Toss drained canned kidney beans (white and red) and whole green beans with Italian dressing and seasoned pepper. Refrigerate.

CHERRY PINWHEELS

1 16-ounce can sour pitted cherries	¼ cup butter or margarine
2 tablespoons flour	1 tablespoon cornstarch
granulated sugar	1 tablespoon cinnamon drops
1 8-ounce can refrigerated crescent dinner rolls	vanilla ice cream (optional)

Preheat oven to 450°F. Drain cherries; reserve ¾ cup liquid; dry cherries on paper towels; coat with flour and 2 tablespoons sugar.

Unroll crescent-roll dough but do not separate; spread each roll lightly with butter; top with cherries. Roll up from short end; cut each into 3 crosswise slices; place, cut side down and touching each other, in jelly-roll pan; bake 15 minutes or until golden.

In small saucepan, stir cornstarch with 1 tablespoon sugar and bit of cherry liquid; stir in rest of liquid and cinnamon drops. Simmer over low heat, stirring, until clear and thickened. Serve warm, topped with the hot cherry sauce and ice cream. Makes 6 servings.

LUNCHEON MEAT MOZZARELLA

1 12-ounce can luncheon meat	1 12-ounce can or jar spaghetti sauce
1 egg, beaten	4 slices Mozzarella cheese
⅓ cup dried bread crumbs	oregano leaves
3 tablespoons butter or margarine	

About 30 minutes before serving: Slice luncheon meat into 4 lengthwise slices; dip into egg, then into bread crumbs.

Preheat oven to 400°F. In large skillet, in hot butter, sauté meat until golden on both sides.

Into 8″ by 8″ by 2″ baking dish, pour half of spaghetti sauce; add meat slices; top with cheese slices; pour on rest of sauce. Sprinkle with oregano. Bake 15 minutes or until bubbly. Makes 4 servings.

ACCOMPANIMENT TIP: Sauté ⅓ cup chopped blanched almonds in ¼ cup butter until golden; toss with ½ pound cooked spaghetti and 2 teaspoons poppy seed.

TUESDAY
Orange-Barbecued Lamb*
Hot Rice
Julienne Carrots
Red-and-Green Coleslaw*
Banana Cake
Tea   Coffee

WEDNESDAY
Grilled Cheeseburgers
Potato Chips
Bean Salad*
Cherry Pinwheels*
Tea   Coffee

THURSDAY
Luncheon Meat
Mozzarella*
Hot Crunchy Spaghetti*
Slivered Zucchini
Romaine-and-Chicory
Salad
Lime Gelatin
with Peach Slices
Milk   Tea

BEVERAGE TIP: Heat pineapple juice with dash of nutmeg. Serve in mugs.

FISH-AND-SHRIMP CACCIATORE

2 tablespoons butter or margarine
1 garlic clove, minced
1 tablespoon chopped parsley
1 medium onion, sliced
½ cup white wine
1 8-ounce can tomato sauce
½ pound halibut, cubed

½ pound flounder fillets, cut into 2-inch pieces
1 pound boned pike slices, cut into 2-inch pieces
½ pound shrimp, shelled, deveined
1 teaspoon salt
¼ teaspoon pepper

In medium skillet over low heat, in butter, sauté garlic, parsley and onion 5 minutes or until onion is soft *but not* brown.

In large saucepan, heat wine; add tomato sauce, onion mixture, fish and shrimp, ½ cup water, salt, pepper. Simmer, covered, 10 minutes or until fish is tender. Remove to platter. Boil sauce to reduce it slightly; strain; pour over fish. Makes 4 servings.

FRESH APPLE PIE

⅔ to ¾ cup granulated sugar (or half granulated and half brown sugar)
1 to 2 tablespoons flour (if fruit is very juicy)
⅛ teaspoon salt
½ teaspoon grated lemon peel
1 to 2 teaspoons lemon juice

¼ teaspoon nutmeg
½ teaspoon cinnamon
6 to 7 cups thinly sliced, pared, cored cooking apples (2 pounds)
pastry for two-crust pie or 1 package piecrust mix
1 tablespoon butter or margarine

Combine sugar with flour, salt, peel, lemon juice, nutmeg and cinnamon (amount of sugar depends on tartness of apples). Preheat oven to 425°F.

Place half of apples in pastry-lined pie plate; sprinkle with half of sugar mixture. Top with rest of apples, heaping them in center, then with rest of sugar mixture; dot with butter. Adjust top crust on apples.

Bake 40 to 50 minutes or until filling is tender and crust nicely browned. Makes 6 to 8 servings.

———◆———

MEAT TIP: During roasting, brush loin of pork with juice from spiced apple rings mixed with a little corn syrup.

There should be enough pork left from roast for Monday's Sweet-Sour Roast Pork, page 122.

ORANGE MERINGUE SOUFFLÉS

¾ cup orange marmalade
1 tablespoon lemon juice
3 egg whites, at room temperature
⅛ teaspoon salt

3 tablespoons granulated sugar
½ teaspoon cornstarch
about ¼ cup slivered blanched almonds

About 30 minutes before serving: Preheat oven to 350°F. Melt orange marmalade over low heat; stir in lemon juice.

Beat egg whites with salt until foamy; gradually beat in sugar, mixed with cornstarch, until meringue is stiff but not dry. Carefully fold in marmalade mixture. Divide among six 5-ounce soufflé dishes. Top each with some slivered almonds.

Bake about 15 minutes or until golden; then serve immediately (soufflés fall if they stand). Makes 6 servings.

FRIDAY
Spiced Pineapple Juice*
Fish-and-Shrimp Cacciatore*
Broccoli Parmesan
Parkerhouse Rolls
Fresh Apple Pie*
Tea Coffee

SATURDAY
Roast Loin of Pork*
Spiced Apple Rings
Mashed Potatoes
Hot Sauerkraut
Orange Meringue Soufflés*
Tea Coffee

FRUIT-COCKTAIL UPSIDE-DOWN CAKE

SUNDAY

Steaks
Smothered in Onions
Frozen Potato Puffs
Green Beans and Celery
Tossed Green Salad
Fruit-Cocktail
Upside-Down Cake*
Tea   Coffee

1¼ cups sifted regular all-
    purpose flour
2 teaspoons double-acting baking
    powder
¼ teaspoon salt
3 tablespoons butter or margarine
½ cup packed brown sugar

1 16-ounce can fruit cocktail
⅓ cup shortening, softened
½ cup granulated sugar
1 egg
1 teaspoon vanilla extract
whipped cream

About 1½ hours before serving: Preheat oven to 350°F. Sift flour, baking powder, salt. In 8″ by 8″ by 2″ cake pan over low heat on burner, melt butter; remove from heat; sprinkle with brown sugar.

Drain fruit, reserving ½ cup syrup. Arrange fruit on sugar mixture.

In large bowl with electric mixer at medium speed, mix shortening with sugar, then with egg and vanilla, until *very light and fluffy*—about 4 minutes. At low speed, beat in alternately, *just until smooth,* flour mixture in thirds and syrup in halves. Spread batter carefully over fruit.

Bake cake 1 hour or until cake tester inserted in center comes out clean. Remove from oven; cool on rack 10 minutes. With spatula, loosen cake from pan. Invert serving plate onto pan; turn over; remove pan.

Serve cake warm with whipped cream. Makes 6 to 8 servings.

SWEET-SOUR ROAST PORK

MONDAY

Sweet-Sour Roast Pork*
Rice
Chow Mein Noodles
Snow Peas
Vanilla Ice Cream
Macaroons
Hot Tea

3 tablespoons butter or margarine
¼ cup green pepper, cut into
    strips
¼ cup coarsely chopped onion
1 tablespoon cornstarch
1 8½-ounce can crushed pine-

apple, undrained (1 cup)
2 tablespoons vinegar
1 tablespoon soy sauce
4 ½-inch-thick slices cooked
    roast pork, trimmed of fat

Preheat broiler if manufacturer directs. In medium skillet over low heat, melt butter. Sauté green pepper and onion about 5 minutes; stir in corn-starch and pineapple. Heat, stirring, until thickened. Add vinegar and soy sauce and pour over pork in shallow open pan. Broil about 5 minutes or until bubbly. Makes 4 servings.

VEGETABLE TIP: Pare eggplant; cut into ¼-inch crosswise slices. Sprinkle with salt and pepper. Dip into beaten egg, then into cracker crumbs. In skillet, in deep hot salad oil, quickly fry eggplant until golden brown on both sides—6 to 8 minutes.

GLAZED PEARS AND APPLES

TUESDAY

Broiled Chicken
Fried Eggplant*
Stewed Tomatoes
Glazed Pears
and Apples*
Tea   Coffee

¾ cup granulated sugar
¼ cup butter or margarine
2 cups boiling water
2 ripe apples

2 ripe pears
¼ cup lemon juice
⅓ cup apricot jam
¼ cup sherry

Early in day: Preheat oven to 350°F. Simmer sugar, butter and boiling water together 5 minutes. Meanwhile, pare apples and pears; place in 3-quart casserole; pour lemon juice and sugar syrup over fruit.

Cover; bake 45 minutes or until tender; cover; refrigerate.

To serve: Arrange pears and apples in serving dish. Add apricot jam to sherry; brush generously over fruit. Makes 4 servings.

RED CABBAGE ROYALE

APPETIZER TIP: Chill a can or two of condensed consommé. To serve, spoon jellied consommé into dishes. Top each with a thin lemon slice, a dollop of sour cream and chives or sliced stuffed olives.

MEAT TIP: Split a knackwurst almost through, lengthwise; open and spread generously with prepared mustard, then with pickle relish. Broil 5 minutes; place well-drained pineapple slice on top and broil 5 minutes more. Serve on split hamburger bun.

BAKED POTATOES À LA MODE

6 medium baking potatoes	3 tablespoons grated Parmesan
salad oil	cheese
2 3-ounce packages cream cheese	2 tablespoons milk

About 1 hour before serving: Preheat oven to 450°F. Wash, then dry, potatoes; brush with salad oil. Place on cookie sheet; bake 45 minutes or until fork-tender.

Meanwhile, in small bowl, blend cheeses with milk; refrigerate. When potatoes are tender, prick each with fork to let out steam; cut slit in each; press open; fill with cheese topping. Makes 6 servings.

RED CABBAGE ROYALE

1 medium head red cabbage	2 tablespoons cider vinegar
1½ cups apple cider	¼ cup butter or margarine
2 teaspoons salt	¾ cup seedless green grapes
1 small onion, minced	

Wash cabbage; reserve several outer leaves for garnish. With sharp knife, slice remaining cabbage into fine shreds; set aside. In large skillet over medium-high heat, bring cider, salt and onion to boil. Add vinegar, shredded cabbage; cook 10 to 15 minutes, stirring now and then with fork, until most of liquid is reduced and cabbage is tender. Stir in butter, grapes; remove from heat. Line sides of 1-quart serving dish with uncooked cabbage leaves; heap cooked cabbage-grape mixture in center. Makes 6 servings.

DESSERT TIP: Fold 1 cup cooked rice into packaged vanilla-pudding-and-pie-filling mix, made as label directs; add light or dark raisins or snipped, pitted dates or prunes to taste. Serve with sprinkle of cinnamon-sugar, and cream, whipped cream, vanilla ice cream, or maple or maple-blended syrup.

WEDNESDAY
Jellied Consommé*
Knackwurst and Pineapple*
Baked Potatoes
à la Mode*
Red Cabbage Royale*
Easy Rice Pudding*
Apple Cider

ROAST-BEEF-HASH LOAF

About 1 hour before serving: Preheat oven to 375°F. In large bowl, mix two 15-ounce cans roast-beef hash; 1 large stalk celery, chopped; 1 small onion, chopped; ¼ cup each sweet pickle relish and catchup; 1 egg, beaten; ½ teaspoon seasoned pepper and ½ cup packaged dried bread crumbs. Pack mixture into 9″ by 5″ by 3″ loaf pan. Bake 45 minutes.

Meanwhile, into one 10¾-ounce can condensed Cheddar-cheese soup, stir ¼ to ⅓ cup milk. Heat slowly, stirring often. Turn hash onto platter; top with 6 tomato slices; spoon on sauce; pass rest. Makes 6 servings.

PUFFY OMELET WITH CREOLE SAUCE

About 45 minutes before serving: In medium pan, in 2 tablespoons salad oil, sauté ¾ cup coarsely chopped green pepper, ¾ cup chopped celery and ¼ cup chopped onion until golden, about 5 minutes. Add 4 medium tomatoes, peeled and coarsely chopped, ½ teaspoon each oregano and salt. Simmer, covered, 10 minutes; keep this Creole Sauce warm.

Preheat oven to 350°F. In large bowl, with electric mixer at high speed, beat 8 egg whites until foamy; add ½ teaspoon cream of tartar, beating until stiff but not dry. In small bowl, with mixer at medium speed, beat 8 egg yolks with ½ cup cold water and ½ teaspoon salt until very light and fluffy; carefully fold yolk mixture into beaten whites.

In 10-inch ovenproof skillet, heat 2 tablespoons butter. Add half of egg mixture; cook over low heat 3 minutes or until puffy and golden on underside when lifted with spatula. Bake 10 minutes or until light brown and until center springs back when lightly pressed.

With spatula, loosen omelet; make cut partway through its center in line with handle. Spoon on half of sauce. With spatula, fold omelet in half; turn onto warmed platter. Use rest of egg mixture for second omelet; fill with remaining sauce. Makes 4 servings.

SPICY STUFFED SQUASH

4 extra-large acorn squash	¼ teaspoon pepper
salad oil	⅛ teaspoon cayenne
2 cups chopped onions	1½ teaspoons oregano
2 pounds ground beef chuck	2 garlic cloves, minced
1 medium green pepper, seeded, diced	1 8-ounce can tomato sauce
seasoned salt	¼ cup chopped stuffed olives
	3 eggs, beaten

About 2 hours before serving: Slice tops from squash and reserve; remove seeds. Plunge squash into boiling salted water; boil 10 to 15 minutes or until almost tender when pierced with fork. Remove from water; drain.

In skillet, in 3 tablespoons hot oil, sauté onions until golden; add chuck; brown. Add green pepper, 2 teaspoons seasoned salt, pepper, cayenne, oregano and garlic. Sauté a few minutes, then add tomato sauce and olives; simmer, covered, 15 minutes. Cool slightly. Stir in eggs.

Preheat oven to 350°F. Cut thin slice from bottom of each squash so it stands upright; sprinkle insides with seasoned salt. Stuff with meat mixture; cover with squash tops; arrange in greased shallow pan. Bake 1 hour. Let stand 15 minutes before cutting in half. Makes 8 servings.

ONE-APIECE STUFFED SQUASH: The filling above makes enough to fill 8 to 12 individual small squash. Prepare as above; bake 30 minutes.

SUNDAY

*Stuffed Chicken Paprika**

*Buttered Turnips**

*Green Beans
with Almonds*

Hot Crescent Rolls

*Tart Cran-Apple Pie**

Tea   Coffee

STUFFED CHICKEN PAPRIKA

1 7-ounce package herb-and-spice rice mix
½ cup snipped celery leaves
½ teaspoon seasoned pepper
1 tablespoon instant minced onion

1 4- or 5-pound roasting chicken
2 tablespoons butter or margarine
½ teaspoon salt
½ to 1 teaspoon paprika

About 2¼ hours before serving: Cook rice mix as label directs but omit butter if called for. To cooked rice add celery leaves, seasoned pepper and onion; toss well. Use to stuff chicken; close openings with toothpicks or skewers; tie securely.

In large Dutch oven, heat butter; sauté chicken until brown. Sprinkle with salt. Add ½ cup water; cover tightly and simmer for 1½ to 1¾ hours or until tender. Remove toothpicks and strings; sprinkle with paprika. Makes 6 to 8 servings.

VEGETABLE TIP: Buy firm, heavy white turnips. Pare; cut in ¼-inch slices or ½-inch cubes. Cook in ½-inch boiling salted water 9 to 12 minutes or until fork-tender; drain. Season with salt, pepper and butter or margarine.

TART CRAN-APPLE PIE

¾ cup granulated sugar
3 tablespoons cornstarch
¼ teaspoon salt
¾ cup light corn syrup
1½ cups washed cranberries
2 tablespoons butter or margarine

1½ teaspoons grated orange peel
1½ cups chopped, pared, cored, cooking apples
flaky pastry for two-crust 9-inch pie or 1 package piecrust mix

In saucepan, mix sugar, cornstarch, salt; gradually add corn syrup, ¼ cup water. Cook, stirring, until mixture thickens slightly and boils. Add cranberries; cook until skins break. Add butter, orange peel; cool. Preheat oven to 425°F. Add apples to cranberry mixture; pour into lined 9-inch pie plate. Adjust top crust. Bake 40 to 50 minutes. Makes 6 to 8 servings.

MONDAY

*Mexican Casserole**

*Green Salad**
with
Creamy Onion Dressing

*Spanish Cream**

Milk   Coffee

MEXICAN CASSEROLE

1 tablespoon butter or margarine
1 12-ounce can chopped ham, diced
1 20-ounce can tomatoes
½ cup diced green pepper
¼ teaspoon seasoned salt
¼ teaspoon seasoned pepper
½ teaspoon paprika

1 8-ounce package spaghetti twists
1 10-ounce package frozen peas
1 3-ounce can sliced mushrooms, drained
1 4-ounce package shredded Cheddar cheese (1 cup)

About 45 minutes before serving: Preheat oven to 375°F. In large skillet, in butter, sauté diced ham until light brown. Add tomatoes, green pepper, seasoned salt and pepper, and paprika. Simmer 15 minutes, using spoon to break tomatoes into small pieces, and stir occasionally. Meanwhile, cook spaghetti twists and peas as labels direct; drain. Add with mushrooms and cheese to ham mixture; toss. Pour into greased 2½-quart casserole. Bake, covered, 30 minutes or until hot. Makes 6 servings.

SALAD TIP: To salad greens, add bottled bacon bits, packaged croutons, chopped hard-cooked eggs, sliced olives, or cut-up anchovy fillets.

APPLE DESSERT CROWNS

SPANISH CREAM

1 envelope unflavored gelatin	3 eggs, separated
½ cup granulated sugar	3 cups milk
¼ teaspoon salt	1 teaspoon vanilla extract

Early in day: In double-boiler top, mix gelatin, ¼ cup sugar, salt. Stir in egg yolks; slowly stir in milk. Cook over boiling water, stirring until mixture coats spoon. Chill until mixture mounds when dropped from spoon; stir in vanilla. Beat egg whites until they form moist peaks, then gradually add ¼ cup sugar, beating until stiff. Fold in gelatin mixture. Leave in bowl; chill until set. If desired, serve with drained canned fruit or whipped cream. Makes 6 generous servings.

———◆———

MEAT TIP: Brown ½-inch-thick pork chops in skillet; drain. Season; pour on some tomato juice; top with sliced onions. Cook, covered, about 30 minutes, adding juice if needed.

APPLE DESSERT CROWNS

4 red Delicious apples	8 walnut halves
1 large seedless orange, sectioned	4 iceberg-lettuce wedges
¼ cup seedless raisins	8 wedges provolone cheese
lemon juice	sour cream or yogurt

Wash, core, but do not pare apples. Cut ½-inch slice from top of each; also cut slice from bottom so apple stands upright. With melon baller, scoop balls from top slices and insides of apples, leaving ⅛-inch shells. Toss balls with orange sections, raisins; cover; refrigerate.

Cut sawtooth edge around top of each apple; also, for easy eating, make slits from bottom of each V nearly to base. Brush inside shell and edge generously with lemon juice. Fill shells with fruit mixture. Garnish with walnuts, lettuce and cheese. Serve with sour cream or yogurt. Makes 4 servings.

TUESDAY
*Savory Pork Chops**
Baked Potatoes
Buttered Cauliflower
Cracker Basket
*Apple Dessert Crowns**
Tea   Coffee

menus for Autumn / 127

ROLLED CARAWAY-SEED TOAST

VEAL PARMIGIANA

salad oil	salt
4 6-ounce frozen breaded veal	pepper
steakettes	4 slices packaged pizza cheese
2 10¼-ounce cans Marinara sauce	

Preheat oven to 400°F. In medium skillet, in hot salad oil, sauté steakettes on both sides until golden brown; drain on paper towel. Meanwhile, heat Marinara sauce; season to taste with salt and pepper.

Arrange steakettes in 8″ by 8″ by 2″ baking dish; top with sauce and cheese; bake 12 to 15 minutes. Makes 4 servings.

ROLLED CARAWAY-SEED TOAST

Preheat oven to 425°F. Trim crusts from 24 thin slices white bread (about 1½ pounds bread); lightly flatten out slices with rolling pin. With ¼ cup butter or margarine, melted, brush tops of bread and sprinkle generously with caraway seed. Roll up each slice, securing with toothpick; place on greased cookie sheet. Bake 10 minutes or until golden. Remove picks; serve hot. Makes 12 servings.

CREAMY BEEF-ONION STEW

2½ pounds lean beef chuck, cut into 1½-inch cubes	2 teaspoons salt
1 onion, stuck with 4 cloves	¼ teaspoon pepper
2 bay leaves	1½ pounds tiny white onions
1 large carrot, coarsely chopped	1½ tablespoons cornstarch
	1 cup light cream or milk

About 2½ hours before serving: In large saucepan, combine meat, 2 cups hot water, onion, bay leaves, carrot, salt and pepper. Simmer, covered, 2 hours or until meat is almost fork-tender. About 1½ to 2 cups liquid should remain; skim off any surface fat.

Discard bay leaves and cloves. Add tiny onions; simmer, covered, 10 to 15 minutes or until onions are tender, stirring occasionally.

In small bowl, stir cornstarch with cream or milk until smooth; gradually stir into meat mixture. Cook, stirring occasionally, until gravy is thickened. If desired, garnish with parsley. Makes 8 servings.

APPLE SNOW

1 quart apple juice	2 teaspoons grated lemon peel
¼ cup granulated sugar	8 lemon twists
2 tablespoons lemon juice	

Early in day: In medium bowl, combine apple juice, sugar, lemon juice and peel; stir until sugar is dissolved.

Pour into ice-cube trays (kept just for such use); freeze.

At serving time: With side of tablespoon, scrape off spoonfuls of frozen mixture; pile in sherbet glasses; serve at once with twists of lemon. Makes 8 servings.

HOMESTEAD CHOWDER

Pour boiling water over one 2½-ounce jar sliced dried beef, cut into small pieces; drain. In large saucepan, in 2 tablespoons butter or margarine, sauté beef with ¼ cup chopped onion until onion is barely tender.

WEDNESDAY
Veal Parmigiana*
Buttered Noodles
Sliced Carrots
Green Salad
Rolled Caraway-Seed Toast*
Chocolate Cake
Tea   Coffee

THURSDAY
Creamy Beef-Onion Stew*
Mashed Potatoes
Broccoli
Apple Snow*
Tea   Coffee

Add one 10½-ounce can each condensed cream-of-celery and cream-of-mushroom soup; stir until smooth. Add 1 soup can water, ½ soup can milk, one 8-ounce can succotash and one 8-ounce can stewed tomatoes, quartered. Heat, stirring occasionally. Makes 4 servings.

SANDWICH TIP: Cover half of bread slices with cheese slices or cheese spread. Spread with prepared mustard. Top with bread slices. Brush outsides with melted butter or margarine. Toast in broiler or skillet.

MARINATED SHRIMP CANAPÉS

MARINATED SHRIMP CANAPÉS

Several hours before serving: Pour ½ cup Italian dressing over 1 pound cooked, cleaned medium shrimp; cover; refrigerate.

Just before serving: Drain shrimp well. Run tines of fork down length of a cucumber all the way round; cut into ⅛-inch slices. On as many garlic toast rounds as you have shrimp, place slice of cucumber; sprinkle with salt and pepper. Top with a shrimp and dot of sour cream (about ⅓ cup sour cream in all). Garnish with parsley. Makes 30 appetizers.

FRUITED POT ROAST

3 tablespoons shortening	1 teaspoon seasoned pepper
1 4- to 5-pound beef rump	2 tablespoons brown sugar
2 medium onions, sliced	2 cups apple cider
¼ teaspoon ground cloves	1½ cups dried apricots
2 teaspoons salt	1½ cups prunes

About 3 hours before serving: In Dutch oven, in hot shortening, brown rump roast well. Add onions, cloves, salt, seasoned pepper, brown sugar and 1 cup cider. Bring to boil; simmer, covered, 2 hours. Meanwhile, soak apricots and prunes in water to cover.

After roast has cooked 2 hours, add drained fruits and 1 cup cider. Simmer, covered, 30 minutes or until beef is fork-tender and apricots and prunes are cooked. If desired, thicken gravy. Makes 10 servings.

PUMPKIN CHIFFON DESSERT

2 envelopes unflavored gelatin	1½ cups milk
1½ cups packed light brown sugar	2 16-ounce cans pumpkin
salt	2 teaspoons lemon juice
1 teaspoon cinnamon	⅔ cup granulated sugar
¾ teaspoon nutmeg	whipped topping for garnish
½ teaspoon ginger	pecan halves for garnish
6 eggs, separated	

Several hours before serving: In medium saucepan, combine gelatin, brown sugar, 1 teaspoon salt and spices. In medium bowl, stir egg yolks and milk until smooth; stir into gelatin. Cook over medium heat, stirring constantly, until mixture begins to boil; quickly stir in pumpkin and lemon juice; refrigerate until cooled mixture begins to mound when dropped from spoon.

In large bowl, with electric mixer at high speed, beat egg whites with ¼ teaspoon salt until frothy. Slowly add sugar, beating until stiff peaks form. Fold in pumpkin mixture. Spoon into serving dishes.

Just before serving: Garnish with whipped topping and nuts. Makes 12 generous servings.

FRIDAY
Homestead Chowder*
*Grilled
Cheese Sandwiches**
*Carrot and Celery
Sticks*
Canned Apricots
Milk   Coffee

SATURDAY
Tomato Juice
*Marinated Shrimp
Canapés**
Fruited Pot Roast*
Parslied Potatoes
Green Salad
Pumpkin Chiffon Dessert*
Tea   Coffee

1 pound boned lamb shoulder, cubed
instant meat tenderizer
butter or margarine
2 tablespoons Worcestershire
1 small onion, minced
1 13½-ounce can onions, drained
2 1- to 1½-pound eggplants
lemon juice
seasoned salt
seasoned pepper
oregano leaves
1 16-ounce can whole tomatoes
½ teaspoon basil
1 small head chicory, washed

About 1 hour before serving: Sprinkle lamb with meat tenderizer as label directs. In large skillet, in 3 tablespoons hot butter, brown meat well; add Worcestershire, minced onion. Cover; simmer 50 minutes or until meat is tender. Add drained onions last 10 minutes.

Meanwhile, cut lengthwise slice, ¾-inch thick, from top of each eggplant; also slice a little skin from underside so each stands level. Then, ¼-inch in from top edge, cut deeply around each to free pulp. Cut pulp into strips, ½-inch wide; with teaspoon, scoop out remaining pulp, leaving ¼-inch-thick shell. Preheat oven to 375°F.

Sprinkle inside of each eggplant shell with 1 tablespoon lemon juice, ½ teaspoon seasoned salt, ¼ teaspoon seasoned pepper and ⅛ teaspoon oregano; brush each with 2 tablespoons melted butter. Place shells in well-buttered 12″ by 8″ by 2″ baking dish; cover; bake 30 to 35 minutes or until tender.

About 20 minutes before lamb is done, in saucepan stir tomatoes, basil, eggplant pulp; cover; cook over medium heat 15 minutes.

Remove eggplant shells to platter; garnish with chicory. Fill each with lamb-and-tomato mixture. Cut in half. Makes 4 servings.

RAISIN PILAF

Preheat oven to 375°F. Grease 1½-quart casserole. In saucepan, in ¼ cup butter or margarine, sauté 1 small onion, sliced; ¼ cup slivered almonds; ¼ cup raisins, until golden. Add 1 cup uncooked regular white rice; mix well. Add 2 cups hot chicken broth. Place in casserole. Cover; bake 30 minutes or until liquid is absorbed. Makes 4 servings.

ANGEL DELIGHT

About 20 minutes before serving: Preheat broiler if manufacturer directs.

Mix 2 tablespoons each soft butter and light brown sugar. Lightly spread 4 angel-food-cake wedges with 1½ teaspoons butter mixture. Place wedges on cookie sheet; broil 2 minutes. Makes 4 servings.

GOURMET FRANKS

1 tablespoon butter or margarine
1 pound frankfurters (8 to 10), cut in chunks
½ cup chopped onions
1 4-ounce can mushroom slices, drained
2 teaspoons flour
½ cup chicken broth

In medium skillet over medium heat, in butter, sauté frankfurters until golden; push to one side of skillet. Add onions and mushrooms; cook until tender, 3 or 4 minutes. Sprinkle flour over mixture. Gradually stir in chicken broth and simmer, stirring until slightly thickened. Makes 4 servings.

DINNER-IN-AN-EGGPLANT

APPLE-ONION SALAD

¼ cup salad oil
3 tablespoons lemon juice
1 teaspoon granulated sugar
1 teaspoon salt
½ teaspoon garlic powder

½ teaspoon dry mustard
1 medium head lettuce
½ medium onion, sliced paper-thin
2 medium apples, cored and sliced
   into rings

In salad bowl, combine oil, juice, sugar, salt, garlic and mustard. Break lettuce into salad bowl; add onion. Halve apple rings; add to mixture. Toss salad. Makes 6 servings.

TUESDAY
Broiled Ham Steaks
Mashed Sweet Potatoes
Brussels Sprouts
*Apple-Onion Salad**
Lemon Meringue Pie
Tea   Coffee

*Broiled Hamburgers
on Buns*

Succotash

*Orange-and-Avocado
Salad**

Black Raspberry Gelatin

Spice Cookies   Tea

ORANGE-AND-AVOCADO SALAD

Peel and section 4 large oranges. Slice 2 peeled pitted avocados into same bowl; toss. Cover; refrigerate.

In jar with cover, combine 3 tablespoons each orange juice, canned pineapple juice and salad oil with 2 tablespoons lemon juice, ½ teaspoon salt and 2 teaspoons granulated sugar. Shake well. Makes about ¾ cup dressing.

To serve: Drain orange sections and avocados; place in large salad bowl. Add 1 quart bite-size salad greens. Toss with dressing. Makes 6 to 8 servings.

CHICKEN LIVERS HAWAIIAN

¼ cup butter or margarine	1 tablespoon cornstarch
½ cup chopped onions	2½ tablespoons light-brown sugar
1 cup chopped celery	1 teaspoon salt
½ green pepper, slivered	⅛ teaspoon pepper
1½ pounds chicken livers	2 tablespoons cider vinegar
2 cups fresh pineapple chunks	

About 30 minutes before serving: In large skillet, in hot butter, sauté onions, celery and green pepper 5 minutes. Add chicken livers; cook 10 minutes or until lightly browned; add pineapple. Combine cornstarch, brown sugar, salt, pepper and vinegar; stir in ¾ cup water. Add to livers; cook, stirring until thickened. Makes 4 servings.

THURSDAY

*Chicken Livers
Hawaiian**

Hot Rice

Peas and Mushrooms

Breadsticks

Apple Brown Betty*

Tea   Coffee

APPLE BROWN BETTY

⅓ cup butter or margarine, melted	½ teaspoon nutmeg
2 cups fresh bread crumbs	¼ teaspoon cinnamon
6 cups sliced, pared, cored apples	1 tablespoon grated lemon peel
½ cup granulated or brown sugar	2 tablespoons lemon juice

Preheat oven to 375°F. Toss butter with crumbs; arrange one third of this mixture in greased 1½-quart casserole. Cover with half of apples and half of combined sugar, nutmeg, cinnamon and lemon peel. Cover with one third of crumbs, rest of apples and rest of sugar mixture. Spoon on combined lemon juice and ¼ cup water. Top with rest of crumbs. Cover; bake 30 minutes. Uncover; bake 30 minutes longer or until apples are done. Makes 6 servings.

MOTHER'S OATMEAL BREAD

FRIDAY

*Scrambled Eggs
with Canadian Bacon*

*Mother's
Oatmeal Bread**

Tossed Salad

*Cherry-Vanilla
Ice Cream*

Tea   Coffee

Early in day: In large bowl, add 2 cups boiling water to 1 cup uncooked rolled oats; let stand ½ hour.

Sprinkle 1 envelope active dry yeast into ¼ cup warm water; stir to dissolve. To rolled oats, add ½ cup light molasses, 2 teaspoons salt, 1 tablespoon butter or margarine and dissolved yeast; mix well.

Gradually beat in 6 cups sifted regular all-purpose flour until dough leaves sides of bowl. Cover bowl with clean towel; let rise in warm place (80°F. to 85°F.) until doubled in bulk—about 1 hour.

Beat dough again; divide into 2 greased 9″ by 5″ by 3″ loaf pans. Cover with towel; let rise until doubled—about 45 minutes.

Preheat oven to 350°F. Bake loaves 50 minutes or until they sound hollow when tapped. Remove from pans; cool, on side, on racks; store, covered. Makes 2 loaves.

PEPPER-CABBAGE RELISH   DILLED CUCUMBERS

DILLED CUCUMBERS

Up to 1 week before serving: Slice 2 pared cucumbers very thinly. In saucepan, combine 1 cup white vinegar, 1 cup granulated sugar, ½ cup water, 2 teaspoons each salt and snipped fresh dill; bring to boil. Pour over cucumber slices in 1-quart jar; tightly cover; refrigerate. Makes 1 quart.

PEPPER-CABBAGE RELISH

¾ cup white vinegar
2 teaspoons salt
⅓ cup granulated sugar
1 tablespoon mustard seed
6 cups shredded green cabbage

1 cup diced green pepper
2 4-ounce cans pimientos, cut into
   ¾-inch cubes
1 red onion, thinly sliced

About 3 hours before serving: In medium saucepan, combine vinegar with ¾ cup water, salt, sugar and mustard seed. Bring this marinade to boil, then simmer 5 minutes; cool.

   In large bowl, combine cabbage, green pepper, pimientos, onion; pour on marinade; toss. Refrigerate, covered, 2 hours, tossing occasionally. Makes 6 to 8 servings.

SOUR-CREAM PUMPKIN PIE

1 9-inch unbaked pie shell, with
   high fluted edge, chilled
1 cup granulated sugar
¼ teaspoon salt
1 teaspoon cinnamon
½ teaspoon ginger

¼ teaspoon nutmeg
¼ teaspoon ground cloves
1½ cups canned pumpkin
3 eggs, separated
1 cup sour cream

Preheat oven to 450°F. In large bowl, combine sugar and next 6 ingredients. Beat egg yolks well; stir into pumpkin mixture along with sour cream. Beat egg whites until soft peaks form; fold into pumpkin mixture; pour into chilled pie shell. Bake 10 minutes; lower oven heat to 350°F.; bake 1½ hours longer or until table knife, inserted in center, comes out clean. Cool on rack. Makes 6 to 8 servings.

SATURDAY
Roast Turkey
Mashed Potatoes
French-Style
Green Beans
*Dilled Cucumbers**
*Pepper-Cabbage Relish**
Corn Crisps
Sour-Cream
*Pumpkin Pie**
Tea   Coffee

TURKEY-DIVAN SANDWICHES

1 10-ounce package frozen asparagus spears	¼ pound process sharp Cheddar cheese, shredded (1 cup)
1 tablespoon butter or margarine	4 buttered toast slices
2 tablespoons flour	4 large cooked turkey slices
1 cup milk	1 4-ounce can sliced mushrooms

Cook asparagus as label directs; drain. In small saucepan, melt butter; stir in flour, then milk; cook, stirring constantly, until thickened. Stir in cheese until melted. Place toast on cookie sheet. Top with asparagus spears, then with turkey slices and drained mushrooms. Spoon on cheese sauce. Broil 3 to 5 minutes or until golden. Makes 4 servings.

MACARONI-MEAT BAKE

MONDAY

Macaroni-Meat Bake*

Mashed Parsnips*

Green Salad

Doughnut Basket

Hot Spiced Cider*

1 8-ounce package elbow macaroni	dash salt
1 12-ounce can luncheon meat, cubed	1 10¾-ounce can condensed Cheddar-cheese soup
½ cup diced green pepper	1 cup milk
¼ teaspoon seasoned pepper	butter or margarine

Cook macaroni as label directs; drain. Meanwhile, preheat oven to 375°F.

In large bowl, combine macaroni, meat, green pepper, seasoned pepper, salt and undiluted cheese soup mixed with milk. Turn into 2-quart casserole. Dot with butter. Bake 60 minutes or until bubbly. Makes 6 servings.

VEGETABLE TIP: Buy smooth, firm, well-shaped small to medium parsnips. Wash; pare; halve; cut into quarters or slices. Cook in ½ inch boiling salted water 10 to 15 minutes. Mash well; season with salt, pepper and butter or margarine.

HOT SPICED CIDER

In saucepan, combine 2 quarts apple cider, ⅔ cup brown sugar, ¼ teaspoon salt, 6 whole cloves and 4 cinnamon sticks. Bring to boil; simmer 5 minutes; strain. Makes 8 servings.

FLANK STEAK JARDINIÈRE

TUESDAY

Orange-Grapefruit Juice

Flank Steak Jardinière*

Mashed Potatoes

Lettuce-and-Tomato Salad with Italian Dressing

Cheese and Fruit*

Coffee

1 10¾-ounce can beef gravy	instant meat tenderizer
½ teaspoon Worcestershire	¼ teaspoon garlic powder
1 cup cooked mixed vegetables, drained	¼ teaspoon pepper
1½- to 2-pound beef flank steak	1 tablespoon salad oil

Preheat broiler if manufacturer directs. Simmer gravy with Worcestershire and drained vegetables a few minutes; keep warm. With sharp knife, score steak in diamond pattern on both sides; sprinkle with tenderizer as label directs, then with garlic powder and pepper; brush both sides with salad oil.

Place steak on greased broiler; broil about 4 minutes on each side for "rare." Arrange on heated platter, then cut diagonally, across grain, into very thin slices. Pass with vegetable gravy. Makes 4 servings.

DESSERT TIP: Place crock of Cheddar cheese with port wine in center of serving tray. Surround with variety of crackers, then with outer ring of pared and cored apple wedges dipped in lemon or orange juice.

FRUITED LAMB RIBLETS

4 pounds lamb riblets
salt and pepper
1 teaspoon cinnamon
¾ cup packed brown sugar
½ teaspoon nutmeg

1 cup grapefruit juice
1 12-ounce package pitted prunes, chopped
½ cup chopped dried apricots

About 1¼ hours before serving: Preheat oven to 350°F. Trim excess fat from lamb. Place lamb on rack in shallow roasting pan. Sprinkle with salt and pepper. Bake for 30 minutes.

Meanwhile, in medium saucepan, combine 1½ teaspoons salt, cinnamon, brown sugar, nutmeg, grapefruit juice, prunes and apricots. Cover and cook over medium heat 15 minutes or until prunes and apricots are tender; stir occasionally. Spoon some of sauce over lamb and bake lamb 30 to 40 minutes more or until tender, basting occasionally with more sauce. Makes 6 to 8 servings.

CINNAMON-APPLE CAKE

¾ cup butter or margarine
1¼ cups granulated sugar
3 eggs
2 cups sifted regular all-purpose flour
1 teaspoon double-acting baking

powder
1 tablespoon granulated sugar
½ teaspoon cinnamon
1 cooking apple, pared, cored, sliced

Grease and flour 9-inch springform pan. Preheat oven to 350°F. Cream butter with 1¼ cups sugar until light and fluffy; add eggs, one at a time, beating well after each addition.

Sift flour and baking powder; fold into egg mixture; spread in pan.

In small bowl, combine 1 tablespoon sugar and cinnamon; in it dip apple slices until well coated; arrange slices, spoke fashion, in circle · around outer edge of cake batter. Sprinkle any remaining cinnamon-sugar mixture on center of cake.

Bake 45 minutes or until cake tester, inserted in center, comes out clean. Cool in pan, on rack, 10 minutes; remove side of pan and finish cooling. Makes 10 wedges.

───◆───

LEMONY BAKED PORK CHOPS

6 center pork loin chops
1 teaspoon seasoned salt
¼ teaspoon seasoned pepper

1 lemon, cut into 6 slices
⅓ cup catchup
dash Tabasco

Sprinkle pork chops with seasoned salt and seasoned pepper.

Preheat oven to 375°F. In large skillet over high heat, brown chops well on both sides. Remove to 12″ by 8″ by 2″ baking dish; place lemon slice on each. In small dish, combine catchup, Tabasco and ⅓ cup water. Pour over chops. Bake 50 minutes or until fork-tender. Makes 6 servings.

TWO-RICE SALAD

Early in day: Prepare 2 cups cooked wild rice, and 2 cups cooked white rice. Refrigerate. Just before serving, in medium bowl, toss all rice with ½ cup French dressing, ¼ cup diced pimiento and 2 tablespoons chopped parsley. Serve on lettuce leaves, if you like. Makes 6 servings.

TWO-RICE SALAD

WEDNESDAY
Fruited Lamb Riblets*
Buttered Noodles
Cinnamon-Apple Cake*
Milk   Coffee

THURSDAY
Lemony
Baked Pork Chops*
Two-Rice Salad*
Broccoli
Banana Cream Pie
Tea   Coffee

PANTRY TUNA SCALLOP

FRIDAY

*Pantry Tuna Scallop**

Avocado-Grapefruit Salad

Canned Peaches

Milk   Coffee

1 package scalloped potato mix
1 cup thinly sliced onions
3 tablespoons butter or margarine
3 tablespoons flour
½ teaspoon salt
⅛ teaspoon pepper
1¼ cups milk
2 6½- or 7-ounce cans tuna, drained
½ cup mayonnaise or cooked salad dressing
½ cup shredded process Cheddar cheese
½ teaspoon Tabasco
1 teaspoon prepared mustard
paprika

About 1 hour before serving: In 2-quart casserole, prepare and bake potatoes as label directs but add onions; after 15 to 25 minutes stir with fork.

Meanwhile, in saucepan over low heat, melt butter; blend in flour, salt and pepper. Gradually stir in milk; cook, stirring, until thickened and smooth; fold in tuna.

Last 15 minutes, pour tuna mixture over partially cooked potatoes. Spread with combined mayonnaise, cheese, Tabasco and mustard. Bake, uncovered, 15 minutes, or until hot and bubbly. *Let cool 10 minutes;* sprinkle with paprika. Makes 4 to 6 servings.

FRANK-AND-BURGER LOAF

SATURDAY

*Frank-and-Burger Loaf**

*Tomato-Olive Aspic on Chicory**

Cheesecake

Milk   Coffee

1 loaf Italian bread (20 inches long and 4 inches wide)
½ cup evaporated milk
1 egg
1 pound ground beef round
1 tablespoon minced onion
2 tablespoons chopped green pepper
1 tablespoon chopped pimiento
1¼ teaspoons salt
⅛ teaspoon pepper
⅛ teaspoon monosodium glutamate
3 frankfurters
6 sweet gherkins

About 1 hour and 45 minutes before serving: Cut thin slice from top of bread. Carefully scoop out enough crumbs from center to make 2 cups, loosely packed. Set bread shell and top aside. Preheat oven to 375°F.

In large bowl, combine crumbs, milk and egg; let stand 10 minutes. Add beef and next 6 ingredients; mix well.

Spread half of meat mixture evenly over bottom of bread shell; arrange franks, end to end, lengthwise along center, with sweet gherkins beside them, also end to end.

Top with rest of meat mixture, filling shell. Replace bread top; secure with toothpicks. Place on cookie sheet; cover loosely with foil; bake 1 hour and 30 minutes. To serve, remove toothpicks and cut loaf into 1-inch-thick slices. Makes 5 to 6 servings.

ROUND FRANK-BURGER LOAF: Use ½-pound round loaf of Italian bread. Prepare filling as above. Spread half of beef mixture evenly on bottom of bread shell. Cut 2 frankfurters crosswise into 3 equal sections each and arrange, end to end, in circle in shell; then lay 3 or 4 sweet gherkins, end to end, as inner circle. Complete filling and covering shell. Bake at 375°F. 2 hours, removing foil for last 25 minutes. To serve, remove toothpicks; cut into 6 wedge servings.

SALAD TIP: Place stuffed-olive slices in bottom of mold; cover with some tomato aspic mixture; refrigerate until firm. Fill with rest of aspic; refrigerate until firm. Unmold on bed of chicory.

BLUE-CHEESE DIP

1 cup sour cream
1/3 cup milk
1/4 pound natural blue cheese,
 crumbled

3 dashes Tabasco
1/2 teaspoon Worcestershire
shredded-wheat crackers or
 potato-flavored snack-crackers

In small bowl, blend sour cream with milk; beat in blue cheese, Tabasco and Worcestershire. Cover; refrigerate.

To serve: Surround dip bowl with crackers. Makes 1 1/3 cups.

BRAISED ROLLED-BEEF ROAST WITH SOY GRAVY

2 tablespoons salad oil
1 garlic clove, halved
1 4- to 5-pound beef rolled rump
1 teaspoon celery salt
1/4 teaspoon pepper

soy sauce
1 tablespoon vinegar
1 tablespoon honey
1/2 teaspoon ginger
2 tablespoons cornstarch

About 3 1/2 hours before serving: In Dutch oven or other large, heavy kettle over medium heat, in salad oil, cook garlic until golden; discard garlic; brown roast on all sides. Sprinkle with celery salt and pepper.

In cup, combine 3/4 cup water, 2 tablespoons soy sauce, vinegar, honey and ginger; pour over meat. Simmer, covered, 3 hours or until meat is tender; turn 2 or 3 times; add more water, if necessary, during cooking.

Transfer meat to warm platter; remove strings; keep warm. Skim fat from pan juices. In cup, mix cornstarch with 2 tablespoons soy sauce until smooth; stir into juices. Cook, stirring, until thickened. Pass with meat. Makes 6 servings, plus enough meat for meat pie, below.

THUMBPRINT COOKIES

Preheat oven to 375°F. Mix 1/2 cup butter, softened, 1/2 teaspoon salt, 1 teaspoon vanilla extract, 1/2 cup packed brown sugar until fluffy. Blend in 1 1/2 cups sifted regular all-purpose flour, 2 tablespoons milk, 1/4 cup semi-sweet-chocolate pieces, chopped. Shape into 1" balls; place on ungreased cookie sheets; with thumb, make depression in each. Bake 10 to 12 minutes. Roll in sifted confectioners' sugar; cool. Meanwhile, over hot, *not boiling*, water, stir 3/4 cup semi-sweet chocolate pieces with 1 table-spoon shortening until smooth. Cool slightly; add 2 tablespoons light corn syrup, 1 tablespoon water and 1 teaspoon vanilla extract. Fill center of each cookie. Makes 36 cookies.

CHILEAN MEAT PIE

1 medium onion
2 cups cut-up cooked pot roast
10 stuffed or pitted ripe olives
2 hard-cooked eggs
1 teaspoon oregano
salt

1/8 teaspoon cayenne
1/4 cup canned condensed bouillon
 or consommé
1 17-ounce can cream-style corn
2 eggs, well beaten
1/8 teaspoon pepper

In food grinder, finely grind onion, meat, olives, hard-cooked eggs.

Preheat oven to 375°F. Combine meat, oregano, 1/2 teaspoon salt, cayenne, undiluted bouillon. To corn, add eggs, 1/4 teaspoon salt, pepper. Line bottom and sides of greased 9" pie plate with meat mixture; top with corn mixture. Bake 45 minutes. Increase oven heat to 400°F.; bake 15 minutes. Remove; cool 10 minutes. Makes 6 servings.

HAM-AND-CHEESE PANCAKE SANDWICHES

1 cup packaged pancake mix	¾ cup diced cooked ham
1 egg	½ cup shredded Cheddar cheese
1 tablespoon salad oil	2 teaspoons chopped parsley
1¼ cups milk	2 10-ounce packages frozen mixed
1 teaspoon prepared mustard	vegetables in onion sauce

In medium bowl, combine pancake mix with egg, salad oil, milk, mustard, ham, cheese and parsley.

On hot, greased griddle, drop 2 measuring tablespoonfuls of batter, spreading with back of spoon into round about 4 inches in diameter. Cook, over low heat, until pancake is golden brown on both sides. Repeat until batter is used (makes 12 pancakes); keep warm.

Meanwhile, cook frozen mixed vegetables as package label directs.

For each serving, spoon some of hot vegetables between and on top of pair of pancakes. Makes 6 servings.

BEAN-AND-SAUSAGE STUFFING

Place 1 pound sausage links in skillet with ¼ cup cold water. Simmer, covered, 5 minutes. Drain off water; pan-fry sausages slowly until golden. Drain sausages on paper towels; slice into ¼-inch slices. In medium skillet, in ½ cup butter or margarine, sauté 1½ cups finely chopped celery and ¼ cup finely chopped onion until soft. In large bowl, combine 1 7-ounce package herb-seasoned stuffing croutons with 1 cup hot water. Add sausages, sautéed vegetables, one 15-ounce can kidney beans, drained, and 2 teaspoons chili powder; mix well. Makes about 6 cups stuffing for a 6-pound capon.

CHICKEN SOUP WITH CROUTONS

Early in day: In large kettle, combine bones left from poultry; 2 quarts cold water; 1 carrot, pared, sliced; 1 onion, sliced; 1 stalk celery, sliced; 2 sprigs parsley; 1 bay leaf; 3 peppercorns; 2 teaspoons salt and ⅛ teaspoon pepper. Simmer, covered, 2 hours. Strain; season to taste. Cool quickly; refrigerate. Serve hot topped with croutons. Makes 1½ quarts.

GERMAN SKILLET DINNER

1 tablespoon butter or margarine	1 pound ground beef chuck
1 16-ounce can sauerkraut, undrained	1¼ teaspoons salt
	¼ teaspoon pepper
⅔ cup uncooked regular white rice	1 8-ounce can tomato sauce
1 medium onion, chopped	

In large skillet, heat butter; spread sauerkraut over butter; sprinkle with rice and onion. Top with chuck, salt, pepper and tomato sauce. Cook, covered, over low heat, 25 to 30 minutes. Makes 4 servings.

LEMON DESSERT SAUCE

In saucepan, mix ½ cup granulated sugar, 1 tablespoon cornstarch, dash salt; gradually stir in 1 cup boiling water. Boil, stirring constantly, 5 minutes or until thickened. Add 2 tablespoons butter or margarine, 1 teaspoon grated lemon peel and 3 tablespoons lemon juice. Makes enough for 5 servings.

CHICKEN SOUP WITH CROUTONS

TUESDAY
Ham-and-Cheese
Pancake Sandwiches*

Lettuce Wedges
with Sliced Tomatoes

Chocolate-Chip
Ice Cream

Hot Chocolate   Tea

WEDNESDAY
Roast Capon

Bean-and-Sausage
Stuffing*

Pineapple-Glazed Yams

Cauliflower

Vanilla Pudding

Tea   Coffee

THURSDAY
Chicken Soup
with Croutons*

German Skillet Dinner*

Lima Beans

Pumpernickel Bread

Warm Gingerbread Squares

Lemon Dessert Sauce*

Tea   Coffee

CHEESE-BAKED HADDOCK

2 16-ounce packages frozen haddock or cod fillets, partially thawed	¼ teaspoon pepper
	½ teaspoon dry mustard
¼ cup butter or margarine	2 cups milk
¼ cup all-purpose flour	¼ pound shredded Cheddar cheese
1 teaspoon salt	

About 35 minutes before serving: Preheat oven to 350°F. Place fish in greased 12″ by 8″ by 2″ baking dish. In saucepan, melt butter; stir in flour, salt, pepper and mustard. Cook, stirring constantly, over medium heat for 1 minute. Gradually add milk; cook, stirring, until thickened. Add cheese; stir until melted; pour over fish. Bake, uncovered, 25 to 30 minutes or until fish flakes easily with fork. Makes 6 servings.

VEGETABLE TIP: Cook little new potatoes in jackets; peel. Toss with melted butter, lemon juice, chives, salt and pepper to taste.

BAKED HUBBARD-SQUASH SQUARES

Preheat oven to 375°F. Scrub outside of 2½-pound piece of Hubbard squash. With long sharp knife, cut squash into serving pieces about 4″ by 2″. With spoon, remove seeds and stringy portion. Brush with some of 3 tablespoons butter or margarine, melted; sprinkle with salt and pepper.

Arrange squash pieces, side by side with cut sides down, in greased baking pan. Bake, uncovered, 30 minutes. Turn cut sides up; brush with more melted butter; sprinkle with salt and pepper. Bake 30 minutes or until tender, brushing often with melted butter. When squash is done, mash, in each shell, with fork. Makes 4 to 6 servings.

BEET-AND-HORSERADISH RELISH

1 16-ounce can diced beets	⅛ teaspoon pepper
1 tablespoon sugar	½ cup vinegar
1 tablespoon minced onion	½ cup horseradish
2 teaspoons salt	

Drain beets; reserve liquid. Combine beets with sugar, onion, salt, pepper, vinegar, horseradish. Add enough beet liquid to cover. Refrigerate. Makes 6 servings.

ROCKY ROAD BROWNIES

1 package brownie mix with nuts	3 tablespoons hot water
2 tablespoons butter	1 cup confectioners' sugar
2 envelopes (2 ounces) no-melt unsweetened chocolate	2 cups miniature marshmallows

Early in day: Make brownies as package label directs.

Meanwhile, in medium saucepan over low heat, stir butter, chocolate and water until blended; remove from heat; stir in sugar until smooth.

On removing brownies from oven, immediately cover with miniature marshmallows, then drizzle with chocolate icing. Let stand in pan until cool; cut into 12 to 16 squares.

———◆———

VEGETABLE TIP: To 3 cups hot, unseasoned, mashed rutabagas, add 1 teaspoon salt, ⅛ teaspoon pepper, 2 tablespoons butter or margarine, ⅔ cup shredded process Cheddar cheese, 1 tablespoon minced onion, and ½ teaspoon bottled thick meat sauce. Mix well. Makes 4 servings.

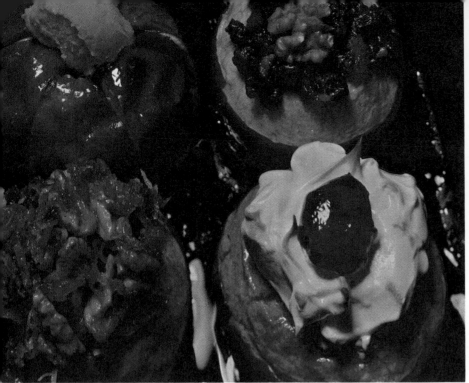

BAKED APPLES

CARROT-RAISIN SALAD

3 cups grated carrots
½ cup dark raisins
½ cup mayonnaise

1 teaspoon lemon juice
⅛ teaspoon salt
lettuce cups

Early in day: In medium bowl, combine carrots, raisins, mayonnaise, lemon juice and salt. Mix well with fork. Cover. Refrigerate.

Serve in lettuce cups. Makes 4 servings.

BAKED APPLES

Preheat oven to 350°F. Core 6 medium red cooking apples. Starting at stem end, pare one-third of way down. Arrange in 10″ by 6″ by 2″ baking dish, pared-end up; pour 1 cup light corn syrup over apples.

Bake ½ to 1 hour or until apples are easily pierced with fork, spooning syrup from pan over them frequently. (Time varies with apples.) When apples are tender, remove from oven.

Serve slightly warm as is or with cream or ice cream. Makes 6 servings.
Mincemeat Apples: Prepare Baked Apples as above. Top each with 1 tablespoon prepared mincemeat, a walnut half.
Orange-Glazed Apples: Top each Baked Apple with 1 tablespoon orange marmalade.
"Porcupine" Apples: Stick slivered, blanched almonds into pared part of each Baked Apple; over each, spoon vanilla pudding (prepared as label directs, chilled and beaten with fork).
Praline Apples: Melt 3 tablespoons butter or margarine, then toss with ¼ cup flaked coconut, ¼ cup brown sugar and ¼ cup broken walnuts. Use to top Baked Apples.
Snow-Peaked Apples: Top each warm Baked Apple with swirl of meringue, then coconut, if desired. Bake at 375°F. until toasted, about 5 minutes, then top with bit of currant jelly.
Apple Petals: Core unpared apples; cut each into sixths, halfway down. Bake as above. Serve topped with spoonful of cheese spread.

SATURDAY
Roast Veal
Browned Potatoes
*Mashed Rutabagas**
*Carrot-Raisin Salad**
*Baked Apples**
Tea   Coffee

HAM-BURGER ROLL-UPS

SUNDAY
Ham-Burger Roll-Ups*
Scalloped Potatoes*
Tossed Salad
Butterscotch Cream Pie
Tea   Coffee

1 cup fresh bread crumbs
½ cup milk
1½ pounds ground beef round
2 teaspoons instant minced onion
1½ teaspoons Worcestershire
2 teaspoons seasoned salt
¼ teaspoon seasoned pepper
6 slices boiled ham, ⅛-inch thick
whole cloves
3 tablespoons butter or margarine

⅔ cup packed light brown sugar
½ cup orange juice
2 teaspoons prepared mustard
1 17-ounce can apricot halves, drained
1 8-ounce can cling-peach slices, drained
½ cup drained canned pineapple chunks
½ cup green grapes (optional)

About 1 hour and 10 minutes before serving: In medium bowl, soak crumbs in milk a few minutes; combine with beef, minced onion, Worcestershire, seasoned salt and pepper. Preheat oven to 350°F.

Spread some of meat mixture on each ham slice; roll up, jelly-roll fashion; place, seam-side down, side by side, in oblong baking dish and stud each with 3 whole cloves.

In small saucepan, into butter, stir brown sugar and orange juice; cook until sugar is melted; stir in mustard. Pour over ham rolls; bake 45 minutes, basting occasionally.

Add apricots, peaches, pineapple chunks and grapes; bake 10 minutes longer. Makes 6 servings.

SCALLOPED POTATOES

4 cups thinly sliced, pared potatoes
⅔ cup minced onions
2 tablespoons flour
1 teaspoon salt

⅛ teaspoon pepper
2 tablespoons butter or margarine
1½ cups milk, scalded
paprika

Preheat oven to 375°F. In greased 2-quart casserole, arrange layer of potatoes; cover with some of onions; sprinkle with some of combined flour, salt and pepper; dot with some of butter. Repeat process, ending with butter. Pour milk over all; sprinkle with paprika. Cover; bake 45 minutes; uncover; bake 15 minutes more, or until tender. Makes 4 servings.

SWISS SCRAMBLED EGGS

MONDAY
Swiss Scrambled Eggs*
Crisp Bacon
Hashed-Brown Potatoes
Toasted Bran Muffins
Chocolate
Whipped Dessert*
Milk   Tea

2 tablespoons butter or margarine
8 eggs
⅓ cup half-and-half or light cream
1 teaspoon salt

cayenne
¾ cup shredded Swiss cheese
parsley and toast points, for garnish

In 8-inch skillet, melt butter. In medium bowl, beat eggs lightly with half-and-half, salt and dash cayenne. Fold in ½ cup of the cheese.

Pour mixture into hot skillet; cook over medium heat 2 minutes, stirring gently several times until eggs are moist and slightly underdone.

Sprinkle remaining ¼ cup cheese over eggs and cook until eggs are set. Garnish with parsley, toast points and a very light sprinkle of cayenne. Makes 4 servings.

DESSERT TIP: Top whipped dessert, made from mix, with toasted flaked coconut, crushed peanut brittle, sliced bananas or crushed chocolate wafers.

CLOVE-STUDDED ONIONS

TUESDAY
Tomato Juice
*Creamed Dried Beef
on Cabbage**
Buttered French Bread
Angel-Food Cake
Tea   Coffee

WEDNESDAY
*Browned Rice-and-Pork
Casserole**
Clove-Studded Onions*
*Celery and Cucumber
Sticks*
Hot Biscuits
Applesauce à la Mode*
Milk   Tea

THURSDAY
Moravian Goulash*
Buttered Noodles
*Pickled Red Beets
on Lettuce*
Green Beans
*Orange-Pineapple
Gelatin*
Tea   Coffee

CREAMED DRIED BEEF ON CABBAGE

¼ cup butter or margarine
6 cups finely shredded cabbage,
  packed
¾ teaspoon salt
2 tablespoons flour
1¼ cups milk

1 3-ounce can sliced mushrooms,
  drained
1 2½-ounce jar sliced dried beef,
  cut into ½-inch strips
1 8½-ounce can peas, drained
⅛ teaspoon pepper

About 30 minutes before serving: In large skillet, in 2 tablespoons butter, sauté cabbage and salt until tender-crisp—3 to 5 minutes.

In medium saucepan over medium heat, melt 2 tablespoons butter. Stir in flour until smooth; slowly add milk, stirring constantly.

Add mushrooms, dried beef, peas and pepper, stirring often until hot. Arrange cabbage in thin layer on heated platter; pour beef mixture on top. Makes 4 servings.

BROWNED RICE-AND-PORK CASSEROLE

4 loin pork chops ¾-inch thick
seasoned salt
½ cup uncooked regular white rice
1 10¾-ounce can beef gravy
1 teaspoon salt

dash pepper
4 medium onions
2 large carrots, cut on angle into
  1-inch slices

About 1½ hours before serving: Preheat oven to 350°F. Trim excess fat from chops; heat fat in skillet. Sprinkle chops with seasoned salt. In hot fat, brown chops well on both sides; remove to 2-quart casserole. Add rice to drippings in skillet; cook, stirring until browned; stir in gravy, ¼ cup water, salt, pepper. Arrange onions and carrots on top of chops; pour on gravy mixture. Bake, uncovered, 1 hour or until tender. Makes 4 servings.

CLOVE-STUDDED ONIONS

About 45 minutes before serving: Peel 16 small yellow onions, leaving a little of bottom to help hold shape during cooking. Stud each onion top with 3 cloves. In medium saucepan, dissolve 4 chicken-bouillon cubes in 2 cups water; add onions, 4 to 8 cloves and 1 teaspoon seasoned salt. Simmer 20 to 25 minutes until tender, stirring occasionally; drain. Remove cloves. Makes 4 servings.

DESSERT TIP: Toast a plain- or raisin-poundcake slice. Spread sides with butter or margarine, softened; sprinkle with cinnamon. Spoon on canned applesauce; sprinkle with cinnamon. Place big scoop of vanilla ice cream at side.

MORAVIAN GOULASH

¼ cup butter or margarine
3 cups thinly sliced onions
4 teaspoons paprika
2½ pounds beef chuck, cut into
  1½-inch cubes

2½ teaspoons salt
1 8-ounce can tomatoes
1 cup dill pickles (cut into bite-size
  chunks)

In large skillet, in hot butter, sauté onions until golden; stir in paprika. Add beef; sprinkle with salt and brown well. Add tomatoes; cover; simmer over low heat 30 minutes. Add 3 cups water; simmer 1 hour longer or until meat is tender. Add pickles; cook 5 minutes. Makes 8 servings.

FISH TIP: Combine 1 garlic clove, minced, with ¼ cup salad oil, 3 tablespoons lemon juice, ½ teaspoon each thyme leaves and salt. Let fish stand in this marinade 30 minutes in refrigerator, turning occasionally. Preheat broiler if manufacturer directs. Broil fish about 3 minutes on each side or until it flakes easily with fork.

SCALLOPED TOMATOES

butter or margarine	1 teaspoon salt
¼ cup minced onion	¼ teaspoon pepper
2¼ cups fresh bread crumbs	dash cayenne
½ teaspoon sugar	1 29-ounce can tomatoes

Preheat oven to 375°F. In small saucepan, in 3 tablespoons butter, sauté onion until tender. Add 2 cups of the bread crumbs, sugar, salt, pepper, cayenne. In greased 1½-quart casserole, arrange layer of tomatoes; top with layer of onion-bread mixture; repeat until all is used, ending with tomatoes on top. Combine ¼ cup bread crumbs with 1 tablespoon butter, melted; sprinkle over tomatoes. Bake, uncovered, 45 minutes. Makes 5 or 6 servings.

LEMON-BERRY PINWHEEL

Split spice-cake layer in half horizontally; cut each half into 8 wedges. "Frost" tops of all 16 wedges with raspberry jam. Arrange 8 wedges in pinwheel pattern in 11-inch pie plate or round platter. Spoon half of filling from 16½- or 18-ounce can ready-to-use lemon pudding on these slices. Arrange remaining frosted wedges on top; spoon remaining pudding between wedges and in center. Refrigerate. Makes 8 servings.

LEMON-BERRY PINWHEEL

FRIDAY
*Broiled Cod Steaks**
*Scalloped Tomatoes**
Sautéed Mushrooms
*Lemon-Berry Pinwheel**
Tea   Coffee

SAVORY PINEAPPLE CHICKEN

2 teaspoons rosemary leaves, crushed	10 tiny white onions
1 tablespoon salt	1 teaspoon ginger
½ teaspoon black pepper	1¼ cups canned unsweetened pineapple juice
2 3-pound broiler-fryers, cut-up	paprika

About 1 hour and 15 minutes before serving: Preheat oven to 400°F. Mix rosemary, salt, pepper; rub into chicken. Arrange chicken, skin-side up, in 13″ by 9″ by 2″ baking dish. Scatter onions over chicken; sprinkle with ginger, pour on pineapple juice, sprinkle with paprika.

Bake, uncovered, 40 minutes or until fork-tender. Makes 6 servings.

VEGETABLE TIP: Toss cooked sliced carrots in melted butter or margarine to which a pinch of rosemary has been added.

SUGARY RAISIN BISCUITS

1 8-ounce package refrigerated buttermilk biscuits	3 tablespoons raisins
2 tablespoons butter or margarine, melted	2 tablespoons granulated sugar
	¼ teaspoon cinnamon

About 15 minutes before serving: Preheat oven to 450°F. Brush biscuit tops generously with some of melted butter. Combine raisins, sugar and cinnamon; sprinkle over biscuits. Fold biscuits in half, pinching dough to seal edges securely. Place on cookie sheet; brush with remaining butter. Bake 8 to 10 minutes until browned. Makes 10 biscuits.

SATURDAY
Savory
*Pineapple Chicken**
*Carrots Rosemary**
Buttered Kernel Corn
Lettuce Wedges
with
Parmesan Dressing
Sugary
*Raisin Biscuits**
Strawberry Ice Cream
Tea   Milk

menus for Autumn / 145

FLANK STEAK WITH STUFFING

butter or margarine
1 medium onion, chopped
1 4-ounce can mushroom stems
   and pieces, drained
¼ cup chopped parsley
1½ cups fresh bread crumbs
1 teaspoon poultry seasoning

½ teaspoon salt
dash pepper
1 egg, slightly beaten
1 2-pound beef flank steak
1 10½-ounce can condensed
   consommé

About 2 hours before serving: In skillet, in 2 tablespoons butter, sauté onion and mushrooms until golden.

In bowl, combine parsley, crumbs, poultry seasoning, salt, pepper and egg; mix in onion and mushrooms.

Remove fat from steak; with sharp knife, score steak on both sides. Place mushroom mixture lengthwise down center of steak. Bring both long sides just together; fasten with string, tied at 1-inch intervals.

In large skillet, in 2 tablespoons butter, brown steak well on all sides; add undiluted consommé; simmer, covered, 1½ hours or until steak is fork-tender. Remove meat to heated platter; remove string; cut meat into 1-inch slices. Thicken pan juices, if desired. Makes 4 servings.

DESSERT TIP: For an interesting compote, add a little port wine and brown sugar to cooked dried prunes.

———◆———

ONION-AND-APPLE DINNER LOAF

About 45 minutes before serving: Preheat oven to 425°F. Lay 12-ounce can luncheon meat on broad side; cut almost, but not all the way, through into 6 slices; place in 9-inch pie plate. Thinly slice 1 onion; tuck slices between meat slices. Then spoon bit of apple butter (or applesauce) between slices, using about ¼ cup in all. Pour a 16-ounce can barbecue beans around meat; brush onion with bit of melted butter or margarine. Bake about 30 to 35 minutes. Then spoon beans from one side of luncheon meat to other side; arrange 5 spiced apples in space. Makes 6 servings.

SALAD TIP: Into orange-flavor gelatin, at slightly syrupy stage, fold grated carrots. Refrigerate until firm. To serve, unmold on bed of lettuce; top with mayonnaise.

RICE CUSTARD PUDDING

½ cup uncooked regular white rice
3 eggs
⅓ cup granulated sugar
2 teaspoons vanilla extract
½ cup light or dark raisins

1½ teaspoons grated lemon peel
3½ cups milk
1 teaspoon nutmeg
2 tablespoons butter or margarine

Preheat oven to 300°F. Cook rice as label directs. Into 2-quart casserole, break eggs; beat slightly with fork. Stir in sugar, vanilla, raisins, lemon peel. Stir milk into rice; stir into egg mixture; sprinkle with nutmeg; dot with butter. Set casserole in baking pan; fill pan with hot water to 1 inch from top of casserole. Bake, uncovered, 1 hour 25 minutes, stirring once after half an hour. Custard is done when knife inserted in center comes out clean. Remove casserole from baking pan; cool. Makes 6 to 8 servings.

EASY SEAFOOD PLATTER

EASY SEAFOOD PLATTER

1 12-ounce package frozen thin-cut
   French fries
2 6-ounce packages frozen deviled
   crabs
1 6-ounce package frozen breaded
   fried shrimp
1 8-ounce package frozen fish sticks
1 8-ounce package frozen fish cakes

1 7-ounce package frozen precooked breaded sea scallops
1 cup mayonnaise
2 to 3 teaspoons curry
2 tablespoons milk
tomato and lemon wedges for
   garnish

Preheat oven to 425°F. Bake potatoes and crabs 5 minutes. Add remaining fish; bake 15 minutes more or until hot. Mix mayonnaise, curry, milk;
serve with fish, garnished with tomato and lemon. Makes 8 servings.

TUESDAY
*Easy Seafood Platter**
Cabbage Salad
Frozen
Apple Turnovers
Milk   Coffee

HORSERADISH-SEASONED BEEF

¼ cup flour	1 tablespoon Worcestershire
1 tablespoon salt	1 teaspoon curry
¼ teaspoon pepper	1 teaspoon molasses
2 pounds beef round steak, cut in 1½-inch cubes	½ teaspoon ginger
	1 cup sour cream
2 tablespoons salad oil	2 tablespoons horseradish
2 medium onions, sliced	

About 3 hours before serving: In plastic bag, mix flour, salt and pepper; shake meat in this mixture. Preheat oven to 350°F. In Dutch oven over medium heat, in hot oil, brown meat well on all sides. Add onions, Worcestershire, curry, molasses, ginger and 1 cup water; stir.

Cover; bake 2½ hours or until meat is fork-tender. Remove from oven; let stand few minutes to cool slightly. Mix sour cream with horseradish; stir into meat. Caution: If too hot, sour cream will curdle. Makes 6 servings.

YELLOW SQUASH AU GRATIN

In skillet, melt ¼ cup butter or margarine. Add 4 cups thinly sliced yellow squash; 1 onion, sliced; .1 teaspoon salt; dash pepper and 2 peeled tomatoes, sliced. Cook, covered, 10 minutes or until squash is tender. Top with ½ cup shredded process Cheddar cheese. Makes 4 servings.

——————◆——————

SPAGHETTI WITH QUICK SALAMI SAUCE

3 tablespoons butter or margarine	salami, diced
1 cup chopped onions	1 tablespoon granulated sugar
1 4-ounce can mushroom stems and pieces, drained	1 tablespoon Worcestershire
	1 teaspoon salt
2 tablespoons flour	dash pepper
1½ cups tomato juice	1 16-ounce package spaghetti
1 8-ounce package sliced hard	

In large skillet over medium heat, in melted butter, cook onions and mushrooms until tender. Stir in flour until blended.

Stir in tomato juice, salami, 1 cup water, sugar, Worcestershire, salt and pepper. Simmer 30 minutes; stir occasionally. Meanwhile, cook spaghetti as label directs; serve with sauce. Makes 4 servings.

HEAVENLY ORANGE WHIP

4 to 5 medium oranges	¾ cup granulated sugar
4 egg yolks	⅛ teaspoon salt
2½ cups orange juice	3 tablespoons lemon juice
2 envelopes unflavored gelatin	2 cups heavy cream, whipped

Early in day: Grate one orange; reserve peel and remove sections. Peel and section remaining oranges. Cut sections in half to make 1½ cups; set aside. (Use extra orange sections in Saturday's pudding, page 149.)

In medium saucepan, with wire whisk or egg beater, beat egg yolks slightly, then beat in 1 cup orange juice until well blended. Stir in gelatin, sugar and salt. Cook mixture over medium heat, stirring constantly, until just boiling; remove from heat. Stir in reserved orange peel, remaining 1½ cups orange juice and lemon juice. Refrigerate mixture, stirring occasionally, until it mounds when dropped from spoon. Fold in reserved orange sections and whipped cream. Pour into 8- to 10-cup mold. Refrigerate until set. Unmold. Makes 10 to 12 servings.

WEDNESDAY

Horseradish-Seasoned Beef*

Buttered Rice

Yellow Squash au Gratin*

Chicory-and-Pear Salad

Ice Cream with Maple Sauce

Coffee

THURSDAY

Spaghetti with Quick Salami Sauce*

Garlic Buttered French Bread

Escarole Salad

Heavenly Orange Whip*

Tea   Coffee

BAKED FLOUNDER

About 30 minutes before serving: Preheat oven to 500°F. Grease foil-lined roasting pan. With sharp knife, make 5 parallel diagonal slashes, about ½ inch deep, along top and bottom sides of one 3-pound cleaned flounder. Sprinkle with 1 teaspoon salt; lay in pan.

In small bowl, combine 2 quartered green onions, 3 tablespoons soy sauce, 2 tablespoons cooking sherry, ⅛ teaspoon ginger and ½ cup canned chicken broth; pour over fish. Cover; bake 20 to 25 minutes or until fish flakes easily with fork, basting occasionally.

About 15 minutes before fish is done, in small bowl, combine ½ pound pork, cut in julienne strips; 2 tablespoons soy sauce; 1 teaspoon cornstarch and ⅛ teaspoon ginger. In small saucepan or skillet, heat 2 tablespoons salad oil until *very hot;* add pork mixture; stir-fry (quickly stir and toss) until pork loses its red color; set aside.

In large saucepan or skillet, heat 2 tablespoons salad oil until very hot; add 1 medium green pepper, cut in julienne strips; one 5-ounce can bamboo shoots, cut in julienne strips; and ¼ teaspoon salt; stir-fry 2 minutes. Add stir-fried pork; toss until hot.

Remove flounder to platter; discard green onions; pour some sauce over fish. Arrange pork-and-green-pepper mixture on top. Serve with remaining sauce. Makes 4 to 6 servings.

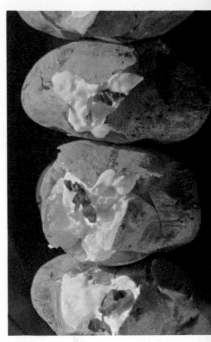

TANGY BAKED POTATOES

FRUIT-STUFFED PORK CHOPS

4 pork loin chops, 1¼ inches thick	¼ teaspoon ginger
½ cup seedless raisins	salt
½ cup chopped celery	pepper
½ cup chopped green pepper	2 teaspoons paprika
2 tablespoons finely chopped onion	1½ cups cider or apple juice
1 cup chopped apple	

About 1 hour and 30 minutes before serving: Preheat oven to 425°F. Trim excess fat from chops. Along fat side of each chop, cut pocket, almost to bone.

Combine raisins, celery, green pepper, onion, apple and ginger. Fill each pocket with about 1 tablespoon stuffing. Place chops in 10″ by 6″ by 2″ baking dish; cover with any remaining stuffing. Sprinkle each chop with ¼ teaspoon salt, ⅛ teaspoon pepper and ¼ teaspoon paprika; pour on cider. Bake, covered, 30 minutes.

Turn chops; sprinkle lightly with salt, pepper and paprika. Cover; bake 30 minutes longer; uncover; bake 15 minutes more or until fork-tender. Makes 4 servings.

TANGY BAKED POTATOES

Preheat oven to 425°F. Wash, then dry, 4 small baking potatoes. Bake 45 to 60 minutes or until fork-tender.

Meanwhile, combine ½ cup plain yogurt or sieved soft-curd cottage cheese with ¼ teaspoon each garlic and celery salt. (If using cottage cheese, moisten with 1 tablespoon milk before adding seasonings.)

Top each split potato with some yogurt mixture. Makes 4 servings.

DESSERT TIP: Make up package of coconut-cream pudding-and-pie-filling mix; cool. Spoon into dishes. Sprinkle with nutmeg and garnish with orange sections.

FRIDAY
Tomato Soup
*Baked Flounder**
Coleslaw
*Hot
Baking-Powder Biscuits*
Assorted Cupcakes
Milk   Tea

SATURDAY
*Fruit-Stuffed
Pork Chops**
Lightly Buttered Peas
*Tangy Baked Potatoes**
*Coconut Cream
Pudding**
Coffee   Milk

CHEESE-TOPPED BEET MOLD

SUNDAY

*Fresh Ham
with Applesauce*

Sweet Potatoes

*Cheese-Topped
Beet Mold**

Rye Bread

Coffee Angel Ring*

Milk   Tea

3 3-ounce packages cream cheese
  with chives, softened
seasoned salt
⅛ teaspoon pepper
3 tablespoons milk

2 16-ounce cans diced beets
1 6-ounce package lemon-flavor
  gelatin
salad greens

Early in day: In small bowl, blend cheese, ¾ teaspoon seasoned salt, pepper and milk; refrigerate. Meanwhile, drain beets; measure juice; add water, if necessary, to make 1½ cups. Heat to boiling; pour over lemon gelatin to dissolve. Stir in 2 cups cold water; add ¼ teaspoon seasoned salt. Refrigerate until syrupy (about 1 hour).

Rinse 8- or 9-inch square pan with cold water. Fold drained beets into syrupy beet mixture; pour into pan; refrigerate until completely set (4 or 5 hours). Spread cheese mixture on top. Refrigerate 30 minutes. Serve on greens on platter. Makes 12 servings.

COFFEE ANGEL RING

Early in day: Prepare 1 package angel-food-cake mix as label directs but stir 3 tablespoons instant coffee into dry mixture; cool cake.

In medium bowl, combine one 16-ounce box confectioners' sugar, 2 tablespoons instant coffee, 1 egg or 2 egg yolks, 1 tablespoon butter and 3 tablespoons milk. With electric mixer at medium speed, beat 5 minutes or until smooth and easy to spread. Frost cake; sprinkle with one 4-ounce can diced, roasted almonds (about 1 cup). Makes 10 to 12 servings.

POTATO-TOPPED MEAT LOAF

MONDAY

*Potato-Topped
Meat Loaf**

Okra Medley*

Green Salad

*Apricots
in Orange Gelatin*

Tea   Coffee

1¼ pounds ground beef chuck
½ pound ground pork
1½ teaspoons salt
¼ teaspoon black pepper
¾ cup fine dry bread crumbs
1 egg, beaten
½ cup milk

½ of 5½-ounce package instant
  whipped potatoes
6 tomato slices
1 4-ounce package shredded sharp
  Cheddar cheese (1 cup)
parsley for garnish

Preheat oven to 350°F. In medium bowl, combine ground chuck, pork, salt, pepper, bread crumbs, egg, milk. Spread evenly in 10″ by 6″ by 2″ baking dish. Bake 40 minutes. Drain off excess fat.

Meanwhile, make up one half package of whipped potatoes as label directs for 5 servings. Spread over baked meat. Arrange 6 tomato slices on top of potatoes; sprinkle with cheese. Bake 10 to 15 minutes to melt cheese. Garnish with parsley. Makes 6 servings.

OKRA MEDLEY

1½ cups sliced summer squash
1½ cups okra, cut in ½-inch slices
1 cup thinly slivered, pared carrots
1¼ teaspoons salt

1 bunch green onions
dash pepper
3 tablespoons butter or margarine

If squash is large, cut in half lengthwise; then slice. Cook squash, okra and carrots with salt in 1 inch boiling water, covered, about 7 minutes. Meanwhile, cut green onions (tops and all) into 1-inch pieces. Add to okra; cook 3 to 5 minutes or until all vegetables are just tender-crisp. Season with pepper, butter, and more salt if needed. Makes 4 servings.

TUESDAY

Curried Chicken*
on Rice
Mixed Greens Salad
Sesame Sticks
Coconut Cake*
Milk   Tea

1 2½- to 3-pound broiler-fryer, cut up
¼ cup flour
½ teaspoon salt
dash pepper
2 tablespoons shortening

1 10½-ounce can condensed cream-of-chicken soup
1 teaspoon curry
¼ cup toasted slivered almonds
hot fluffy rice

About 50 minutes before serving: Wash, then dry, chicken. Combine flour, salt and pepper; use to coat chicken. In large skillet over medium heat, in hot shortening, brown chicken on both sides.

In medium bowl, combine undiluted soup, ¾ cup water and curry; pour over chicken. Simmer, covered, 40 minutes or until chicken is tender; stir often. Sprinkle with almonds. Serve over rice. Makes 4 servings.

DESSERT TIP: Combine ⅓ cup honey; ¼ cup butter or margarine, melted; 1 cup flaked coconut. Spread over top of hot 9″ by 9″ by 2″ white cake; broil *slowly* until golden, about 5 minutes.

———◆———

PEAR WALDORF SALAD

2 cups diced, pared pears or 1 cup each diced pears and unpared apples
2 tablespoons lemon juice
1 teaspoon sugar
½ cup mayonnaise

1 cup thinly sliced celery
½ cup broken walnuts or flaked coconut
lettuce
French dressing

Toss fruits with lemon juice, sugar, 1 tablespoon mayonnaise. Just before serving, add celery, walnuts, rest of mayonnaise; toss. Serve on lettuce; top with French dressing. Makes 4 servings.

WEDNESDAY

Hot Pork Sandwiches
with Gravy
Brussels Sprouts
and Onions
Pear Waldorf Salad*
Boston Cream Pie*
Tea   Coffee

DESSERT TIP: Bake 1 package yellow-cake mix as label directs but use two 9-inch pie plates. Split one layer horizontally; place wider half on plate. Spread with vanilla pudding. Frost top layer with chocolate frosting; set on bottom layer. Cut into wedges. Freeze second layer for cake, page 154.

———◆———

APPETIZER TIP: Try shredded cheese mixed with snipped parsley, garlic salt, and a little lemon juice; or soften cream cheese with a little milk and season with horseradish and garlic salt. Serve with crackers.

KIELBASA LENTIL SOUP

1 1-pound package lentils, washed
2 16-ounce cans tomatoes
2 bay leaves
1 tablespoon salt
¼ teaspoon pepper

1½ pounds kielbasa
8 bacon slices, cut-up
1 cup chopped carrots
1 cup chopped celery
1 medium onion, sliced

THURSDAY

Cheese Spreads*
Assorted Crackers
Kielbasa Lentil Soup*
Broiled
Grapefruit Halves
Coffee

About 1 hour before serving: In large saucepan, in 5 cups water, heat lentils, tomatoes, bay leaves, salt and pepper to boiling. Reduce heat. Add kielbasa. Cover and simmer 15 minutes.

Meanwhile, in large skillet over high heat, fry bacon until slightly limp. Spoon all but 1 tablespoon fat from skillet. Add carrots, celery, and onion. Cook over medium heat 15 minutes, stirring occasionally; add to lentils. Cook 30 minutes. Slice kielbasa. Makes 8 servings.

QUICHE LORRAINE

1 9-inch unbaked pie shell, well chilled
1 tablespoon butter or margarine, softened
12 bacon slices
4 eggs
2 cups heavy or whipping cream
¾ teaspoon salt
dash nutmeg
dash sugar
dash cayenne
⅛ teaspoon pepper
¼ pound natural Swiss cheese, shredded (1 cup)

Preheat oven to 425°F. Rub surface of unbaked pie shell with butter. Fry bacon until crisp; crumble into small pieces. Combine eggs, cream, salt, nutmeg, sugar, cayenne, pepper; beat just long enough to mix thoroughly. Sprinkle pie shell with bacon and cheese; pour in cream mixture. Bake 15 minutes. Reduce oven heat to 300°F.; bake 40 minutes or until table knife inserted in center comes out clean. Makes 6 servings.

MARBLE ANGEL-FOOD CAKE

Early in day: Sift 2 tablespoons flour mixture from 1 package angel-food-cake mix with 3 tablespoons cocoa. Use balance of flour mixture with egg-white mixture to prepare angel-food batter as label directs. Place half of batter in second bowl; gently fold in cocoa mixture until blended.

Alternately spoon white and dark batters into 10-inch tube pan; with rubber spatula, cut through mixture several times, swirling light and dark batters for marbleized effect. Bake and cool as label directs.

Cut cake into 3 even layers; fill and top with Mocha Filling and Topping (below); refrigerate. Serve cut into large wedges. Makes 12 servings.

MOCHA FILLING AND TOPPING

Cream 1 cup butter or margarine with 1⅔ cups sifted confectioners' sugar until blended. Add dash salt, 1 teaspoon vanilla extract, 2 egg yolks; beat thoroughly. Add 2 squares unsweetened chocolate, melted; ⅓ cup water; 2 teaspoons instant coffee; beat well. Fold in 2 egg whites, stiffly beaten. Makes 2¾ cups.

APPETIZER TIP: Fill celery stalks with this mixture: Into one 3-ounce package cream cheese, softened, stir 4 stuffed olives, chopped; 10 blanched almonds, minced; and 1 tablespoon mayonnaise.

VEAL ROMAN STYLE

1 pound very thin veal cutlets, ¼-inch thick
½ teaspoon salt
¼ teaspoon pepper
½ teaspoon ground sage
8 paper-thin slices cooked ham
butter or margarine

With mallet, flatten veal until 1/16-inch to ⅛-inch thick; cut into 8 pieces. Sprinkle both sides with salt, pepper, sage. On each piece of veal, lay slice of ham; fasten with toothpicks. In skillet, in 3 tablespoons butter, sauté veal, a few pieces at a time, 2 minutes on each side or until golden; transfer to heated platter, ham side up. To pan, add 2 tablespoons water; stir to loosen browned bits; stir in 2 tablespoons butter just until melted; pour over veal. Makes 4 servings.

SALAD TIP: Into ½ cup bottled or homemade French dressing, stir 2 teaspoons finely cut anchovies. Serve tossed with greens.

FRIDAY
*Quiche Lorraine**
Green Beans
Pineapple-Orange-and-Date Salad
*Marble Angel-Food Cake**
*with Mocha Filling and Topping**
Tea   Coffee

SATURDAY
*Stuffed Celery**
*Veal Roman Style**
Italian Bread
*Tossed Greens with Anchovy Dressing**
Spumoni
Demitasse

SUNDAY

*Lamb Chops Bravo**

*Hot Mandarin Rice**

Buttered Carrots

Cottage-Cheese-and-Cucumber Salad

Cherry Strudel

Milk   *Coffee*

Preheat broiler if manufacturer directs.

    Trim most of fat from eight 2-inch-thick lamb loin chops. With paring knife, score fat edge of each chop. Rub with garlic, sprinkle with salt and pepper. Place chops on broiler pan. Broil 12 minutes per side for "medium," or 15 minutes per side for "well done," brushing several times with melted currant-jelly (about ½ cup).

    When chops are done, brush again with jelly. Makes 8 servings.

ACCOMPANIMENT TIP: Toss hot rice with drained canned Mandarin-orange sections.

SAUCY FRANK DINNER

MONDAY

*Saucy Frank Dinner**

Coleslaw

Chocolate Pudding

Tea   *Coffee*

1 tablespoon butter or margarine	1 teaspoon granulated sugar
½ cup chopped onions	dash Tabasco
1 10¾-ounce can condensed tomato soup	1 pound frankfurters, quartered
1 8-ounce can tomato sauce	½ pound bow-tie noodles
1 tablespoon Worcestershire	chopped parsley for garnish

About 45 minutes before serving: In large saucepan melt butter; sauté onions until tender; stir in undiluted tomato soup, tomato sauce, ½ cup water, Worcestershire, sugar, Tabasco. Add frankfurters; simmer 10 minutes; stir once or twice.

    Meanwhile cook noodles as label directs; drain; arrange on platter. Place franks in center; sprinkle with parsley. Makes 4 servings.

CASHEW VEAL ON RICE WITH PEAS AND ZUCCHINI

TUESDAY

*Cashew Veal on Rice with Peas and Zucchini**

Hearts of Romaine with Oil and Vinegar

*Broiled-Fruit Cake**

Tea   *Coffee*

1 6-ounce package curried rice	1 1-pound package frozen breaded veal steaks
¾ pound zucchini (about 3), sliced ¼-inch thick	seasoned pepper
salt	1 large lime, sliced
1 10-ounce package frozen peas	about 12 cashew nuts
3 tablespoons butter or margarine	paprika for garnish

About 40 minutes before serving: Cook rice as label directs.

    Cook zucchini, covered, in ¼-inch boiling salted water, until tender-crisp, about 10 minutes. Cook peas as label directs.

    In skillet over medium heat, in butter, sauté half of frozen veal steaks until brown on both sides. Remove; brown rest of veal.

    Arrange curried rice down center of long oval platter. Sprinkle steaks with pepper; arrange on rice, with lime slice on each; sprinkle with cashews. Arrange zucchini down one side, peas down other; sprinkle with paprika. Makes 5 to 6 servings.

BROILED-FRUIT CAKE

1 9-inch yellow-cake layer	2 tablespoons light brown sugar
⅓ cup strawberry jelly	⅛ teaspoon cinnamon
1 30-ounce can apricot halves	2 tablespoons butter or margarine
1 8-ounce can sliced cling peaches	

Preheat broiler if manufacturer directs. Set cake layer on cookie sheet; spread with jelly; top with well-drained apricots and peaches. Combine brown sugar, cinnamon and butter, and dot over fruit. Broil until fruit starts to brown. Remove to platter. Makes 8 servings.

HOT TOMATO BOUILLON

WEDNESDAY

Hot Tomato Bouillon*

*Minute Steak
Sandwiches*

Fresh Mushroom Salad*

Potato Chips

Peach Raspberry Treat*

Tea   Coffee

In large saucepan, combine two 10¾-ounce cans condensed tomato soup and two 10½-ounce cans condensed beef bouillon, undiluted; 4½ cups tomato juice; 2 teaspoons granulated sugar and 1 to 2 teaspoons Worcestershire; heat to boiling. Serve hot. Makes 8 servings.

SALAD TIP: In large bowl, combine 1½ pounds thinly sliced mushrooms and ¼ cup chopped green onions; toss lightly with ⅓ cup Italian dressing; refrigerate ½ hour. Arrange leaves from 3 Belgian endives in salad bowl; place marinated mushrooms in center. Makes 6 servings.

PEACH-RASPBERRY TREAT

1 30-ounce can cling-peach halves	2 10-ounce packages frozen raspberries, thawed
⅓ cup sweet or cream sherry	4 teaspoons cornstarch
1½ to 2 pints vanilla ice cream	1 teaspoon lemon juice

Day before or 2 hours ahead: Drain peaches; place in medium bowl with sherry; cover; refrigerate overnight or several hours. With ice-cream scoop, make as many ice-cream balls as peach halves. Place balls on cookie sheet; freezer-wrap; freeze.

Drain syrup from thawed raspberries into medium saucepan; heat to boiling. Combine cornstarch with ¼ cup water; stir into raspberry syrup. Cook, stirring, until thickened; gently stir in raspberries and lemon juice. Cover; refrigerate.

To serve: Place ice-cream ball in center of each peach in serving dish. Spoon over sauce. Makes 6 to 8 servings.

THURSDAY

*Sausage-Macaroni
Skillet**

*Tossed Greens
with
Artichokes and Pimento*

*Tangerines, Nuts
and Cheese Bowl*

Tea   Coffee

SAUSAGE-MACARONI SKILLET

1 pound pork-sausage meat	1 tablespoon granulated sugar
1 medium onion, chopped	½ teaspoon salt
1 green pepper, chopped	¼ teaspoon pepper
1 16-ounce can tomatoes	1 cup sour cream
1 cup uncooked elbow macaroni	¼ cup milk

In large skillet over high heat, brown sausage, breaking it into small pieces, with onion and green pepper; spoon off all fat. Stir in tomatoes, macaroni, sugar, salt and pepper. Cover and simmer, stirring occasionally, for 20 minutes. Remove from heat; stir in sour cream and milk. Makes 4 servings.

FRIDAY

Crab Newburg*
in Patty Shells

Buttered Broccoli

*Chinese-Cabbage
Salad*

Lemon Sherbet

Chocolate Cookies

Tea   Coffee

CRAB NEWBURG

6 tablespoons butter or margarine	1 teaspoon salt
2 tablespoons flour	3 tablespoons sherry
3 cups cut-up, cooked or canned crab	3 egg yolks
⅛ teaspoon nutmeg	2 cups light cream
dash paprika	6 patty shells

In double-boiler top, over low heat, melt butter; stir in flour, crab, nutmeg, paprika, salt, sherry. Beat yolks slightly; add cream; mix well. Slowly stir yolks into crab; cook over hot water, stirring, until just thickened. Spoon into patty shells. Makes 6 servings.

CHILI-MEATBALL-AND-VEGETABLE SOUP

CHILI-MEATBALL-AND-VEGETABLE SOUP

1 pound ground beef chuck
¼ cup bread crumbs
¼ cup tomato juice
2 tablespoons minced onion
4 to 5 teaspoons chili powder
salt and pepper
2 tablespoons shortening

2 10½-ounce cans condensed beef
  broth
1 16-ounce can tomatoes
1 10-ounce package frozen mixed
  vegetables
1 medium onion, sliced
½ cup packaged precooked rice

About 45 minutes before serving: Combine beef, crumbs, tomato juice, minced onion, chili powder, 1½ teaspoons salt and ¼ teaspoon pepper. Shape into 16 one-inch balls. In skillet, in hot shortening, brown meatballs. Drain; set aside.

In large kettle, combine undiluted broth with 2 soup cans water, tomatoes, vegetables, onion, rice and 1 teaspoon salt. Cover; heat to boiling; reduce heat; add meatballs; simmer 10 minutes. Makes 8 servings.

CREAM PUFFS

½ cup butter or margarine
1 cup boiling water
½ teaspoon salt

1 cup sifted regular all-purpose
  flour
4 eggs, unbeaten

Preheat oven to 400°F. In saucepan over high heat, melt butter with boiling water, stirring occasionally. Turn heat low; add salt and flour at once; stir vigorously until mixture leaves sides of pan in smooth ball. Immediately remove from heat; add eggs, one at a time, beating until smooth after each addition. Then beat until mixture has satinlike sheen. Drop by tablespoons, 3 inches apart, on greased cookie sheet, shaping each into mound that points up in center. Bake 50 minutes or until golden; cool on rack.

To serve: Slice off tops; fill with ice cream or sweetened whipped cream flavored with vanilla. Replace tops; sprinkle with confectioners' sugar; top with Hot Butterscotch Sauce (recipe follows). Makes 8 puffs.

HOT BUTTERSCOTCH SAUCE

In saucepan, combine 2 cups packed brown sugar; ½ cup light cream; ¼ cup light corn syrup; ¼ cup butter. Bring to boil; cook stirring, 5 minutes, or until thickened. Makes 2 cups.

SATURDAY

*Chili-Meatball-
and-Vegetable Soup**

French Bread

Green Salad

Cream Puffs*

Hot Butterscotch Sauce*

Tea   Coffee

SUNDAY
*Fruit-Glazed Ham**
*Nutted Yam Balls**
Buttered Broccoli
Brownie Pudding Cake
Tea   Coffee

MONDAY
*Burgers Italiano
on Hero Rolls**
Buttered Peas
*Carrot and Celery
Sticks*
Cheese and Crackers
Tea   Coffee

TUESDAY
Tomato Juice
*Welsh Rabbit**
Cauliflower
Green Salad
Raspberry Gelatin
Lemon Snaps
Milk   Coffee

FRUIT-GLAZED HAM

Day before: Remove gelatin from one 5-pound canned ham; place ham in pan; with fork, pierce deeply several times. Into small bowl, drain juice from one 17-ounce can purple plums; refrigerate plums. Combine juice, 1 cup packed light brown sugar, 2 teaspoons grated orange peel, ¾ cup orange juice, 1 teaspoon dry mustard, ¼ teaspoon ground cloves; pour over ham. Cover; refrigerate 24 hours, turning ham occasionally in marinade.

About 2 hours before serving: Preheat oven to 325°F. Remove ham; place on rack in shallow pan; bake 1½ hours, basting with marinade. Remove from oven; make ⅛-inch-thick slashes in top; sprinkle with ½ cup packed light brown sugar; pour on rest of marinade. Bake 30 minutes or until meat thermometer reaches 160°F. Garnish with reserved plums. Makes 20 servings. (Save some ham for stuffing, page 160.)

NUTTED YAM BALLS

Drain, then mash, two 17-ounce cans yams; add ½ teaspoon salt, ⅛ teaspoon pepper, ¼ cup miniature marshmallows and 1 tablespoon butter or margarine, melted. Form into 10 balls. Preheat oven to 350°F. Heat ⅓ cup honey with 1 tablespoon butter. With 2 forks, roll each yam ball, first in honey mixture, then in 1½ cups chopped pecans; place in baking dish. Spoon 2 tablespoons melted butter over yams; bake 15 minutes. Makes 10 servings.

———◆———

BURGERS ITALIANO ON HERO ROLLS

1½ pounds ground beef chuck	2 teaspoons grated Parmesan cheese
1 egg, beaten	¼ cup pizza-flavored catchup
1 teaspoon seasoned salt	6 thin slices Mozzarella cheese
⅛ teaspoon seasoned pepper	6 hero rolls, split
⅓ cup diced onion	

About 30 minutes before serving: Preheat broiler if manufacturer directs. In medium bowl, mix chuck, egg, seasoned salt, seasoned pepper, onion and Parmesan. Shape into 6 rectangular patties; broil 6 minutes; turn; broil 2 minutes. Top each patty with 2 teaspoons catchup and slice of Mozzarella; broil until bubbly. Serve in rolls. Makes 6.

———◆———

WELSH RABBIT

Melt 1 tablespoon butter or margarine in double boiler. Slowly stir in 1 pound shredded process Cheddar cheese (4 cups). As cheese melts, stir in all but 1 tablespoon of ¾ cup light beer, a little at a time, over a period of about ½ hour. Combine dash cayenne, 1 tablespoon dry mustard, ½ teaspoon Worcestershire, ¼ teaspoon salt, 1 tablespoon beer; add 1 egg, unbeaten; stir quickly with spoon. Add to cheese mixture. Serve over crackers or toast. Makes 4 or 5 servings.

———◆———

TUNA RING WITH BLUE-CHEESE SAUCE

About 1½ hours before serving: Preheat oven to 375°F. In large bowl, combine two 6½- or 7-ounce cans tuna, drained, flaked; with ½ cup minced onion; one 10-ounce package frozen mixed vegetables, thawed; ½ cup shredded Cheddar cheese; ¼ cup chopped parsley; ½ teaspoon

TUNA RING WITH BLUE-CHEESE SAUCE

salt; ¼ teaspoon seasoned pepper and 1 teaspoon celery salt. Add all but 2 tablespoons of 1 egg, beaten.

In medium bowl, place 4 cups packaged biscuit mix; stir in 1¼ cups milk until a soft dough; beat 20 strokes.

On floured pastry cloth, knead dough 6 times until smooth. With lightly floured, stockinette-covered rolling pin, roll dough into rectangle 18″ by 13″. Spread with tuna mixture; roll up lengthwise. Arrange in ring on greased cookie sheet. With kitchen shears, make 13 cuts almost, but not all the way, through ring; twist slices slightly; brush with reserved egg. Bake 35 to 40 minutes or until golden.

About 15 minutes before serving: In medium saucepan, place 1 cup sour cream; crumble in 2 to 4 ounces Danish blue cheese. Cook over low heat, stirring occasionally, until blended. Serve with Tuna Ring; garnish with parsley. Makes 6 servings.

WEDNESDAY
Cran-Apple Juice
Tuna Ring
with
*Blue-Cheese Sauce**
Tomato-Cucumber-and-Romaine Salad
Hot Peaches
with Soft Ice Cream
Tea   Coffee

AVOCADO-DELIGHT SALAD

About 10 minutes before serving: Cut 4 ripe avocados lengthwise in halves; remove pits, then brush lightly with lemon juice. Fill each half with 6 melon balls; arrange on salad plate, garnished with greens. Pass salad dressing. Makes 8 servings.

HAM-AND-CORN-BREAD STUFFING

¼ cup butter or margarine	½ cup finely chopped onion
1 cup finely chopped celery	1 8-ounce package corn-bread
½ cup finely chopped green	stuffing
pepper	1 cup diced cooked ham

In skillet, in hot butter, sauté celery, green pepper and onion until soft. In bowl, combine corn-bread stuffing, ½ cup hot water, vegetables and ham. Makes about 7 cups stuffing for an 8- to 10-pound bird.

SNAPPY GINGER PIE

1½ cups graham-cracker crumbs	granulated sugar
¼ cup butter or margarine, melted	2 eggs, slightly beaten
1 8-ounce plus 1 3-ounce package	½ cup diced crystallized ginger
cream cheese, softened	1 pint sour cream

Early in day: In 9-inch pie plate, thoroughly mix graham-cracker crumbs and melted butter. Press mixture to cover bottom and sides of pie plate. Preheat oven to 350°F.

In large bowl, combine all cream cheese, ½ cup sugar and eggs; with electric mixer at medium speed, beat until smooth; fold in ⅓ cup of the ginger. Pour into prepared pie shell. Bake 30 minutes.

Meanwhile, in small bowl, combine sour cream and ¼ cup sugar. With electric mixer at medium speed, beat until sugar is dissolved. Remove pie from oven and spread with sour-cream mixture; garnish top with remaining ginger. Turn oven off. Return pie to oven for 10 minutes to set sour cream. Refrigerate until pie is firm (about 5 hours) or until serving time. Makes 10 to 12 servings.

———◆———

SARDINE PIZZA

1 15¾-ounce package cheese	1 4-ounce package shredded
pizza mix	Mozzarella cheese (1 cup)
2 3¾- or 4-ounce cans sardines	

About 35 minutes before serving: Preheat oven to 425°F. Prepare pizza crust as label directs. Cover crust with pizza sauce; top with drained sardines, split; sprinkle with cheese. Bake 20 to 25 minutes, or until crust browns and cheese melts. Makes 4 to 6 servings.

APPLE TAPIOCA

About 35 minutes before serving: Preheat oven to 375°F. Pare 3 large apples; cut into eighths; arrange slices in even rows in 9″ by 9″ by 2″ baking dish. Dot with 2 tablespoons butter or margarine and sprinkle with 1 teaspoon mace.

In saucepan, combine ⅓ cup quick-cooking tapioca, 1 cup packed light-brown sugar, 2 tablespoons lemon juice, ¾ teaspoon salt and 2¼ cups water; heat to boiling, stirring constantly. Pour over apple slices. Bake 20 minutes. Serve hot or warm with light cream. Makes 6 servings.

AVOCADO-DELIGHT SALAD

DELMONICO TURKEY SANDWICHES

3 tablespoons butter or margarine
3 tablespoons flour
¾ teaspoon salt
¼ teaspoon prepared mustard
dash cayenne
2 cups milk
2 cups shredded process sharp

Cheddar cheese
4 toast slices
8 medium slices cooked turkey
dash paprika
4 crisp bacon slices
2 sliced medium tomatoes

Preheat oven to 450°F. In medium saucepan over low heat, melt butter. Add flour, salt, mustard, cayenne; stir until blended. Slowly add milk; cook, stirring constantly, until smooth and thickened. Remove from heat. Stir in cheese until melted. Arrange toast in 9″ by 9″ by 2″ baking dish; top with turkey slices; pour cheese sauce over turkey. Sprinkle with paprika. Bake 10 minutes. Garnish with bacon and tomato slices. Makes 4 servings.

FIVE-FRUIT SHERBET

5 ripe bananas
grated peel 2 oranges
1 cup orange juice
½ cup lemon juice

2 cups granulated sugar
3 cups bottled cranberry-apple
  juice
3 egg whites

Several days ahead: Peel and slice bananas; then mash sliced bananas with fork or in blender. Stir in orange peel, orange and lemon juices, sugar and cranberry-apple juice. Turn into 15½″ by 10½″ by 2½″ roasting pan and freeze until mushy.

Beat egg whites until stiff. Turn mixture into large bowl; with electric mixer at low speed, beat well; gently fold in beaten egg whites. Return to pan; refreeze until mushy; then beat again and refreeze, covered with foil.

To serve: Let frozen sherbet sit at room temperature about 15 minutes; spoon into sherbet glasses. Makes 14 to 16 servings. (Store leftovers, covered, in freezer.)

SATURDAY
*Delmonico
Turkey Sandwiches**
Buttered Asparagus
Five-Fruit Sherbet*
Tea   Coffee

butter or margarine	inch thick
¾ pound chicken livers	pickle sticks
½ pound mushrooms	carrot sticks
salt	¼ cup flour
pepper	1 cup chopped onions
8 thin slices boneless beef top round	2 teaspoons canned tomato paste
(4 to 6 ounces each)	1¼ cups canned condensed beef
4 to 6 ounces boiled ham, ⅛-	bouillon

About 3 hours before serving: In medium skillet, in 2 tablespoons hot butter, sauté chicken livers with mushrooms until livers are browned and mushrooms tender. Sprinkle with ½ teaspoon salt and ¼ teaspoon pepper. Chop mixture fine, almost to a paste.

Sprinkle beef slices with 1½ teaspoons salt and ¼ teaspoon pepper; spread some of liver mixture on each slice. Cut ham into 1-inch crosswise strips; arrange strips on beef slices crosswise, alternating them with pickle or carrot sticks; roll up and secure with toothpicks; roll in flour. In Dutch oven, in ¼ cup hot butter, brown well. Add onions; sauté a few minutes longer; add tomato paste, undiluted beef bouillon; simmer, covered, 1½ hours or until tender.

Remove toothpicks and arrange beef birds on heated platter. Pour gravy over all. Makes 8 servings.

CHEESE STRATA

12 day-old bread slices	½ teaspoon prepared mustard
8 ounces process Cheddar cheese,	1 tablespoon minced onion
thinly sliced	1 teaspoon salt
4 eggs	⅛ teaspoon pepper
2½ cups milk	

About 2 hours before serving: Remove crusts* from bread. Arrange 6 bread slices in greased 12" by 8" by 2" baking dish; cover with cheese slices, then rest of bread. Beat eggs; blend in milk and rest of ingredients; pour over bread. Refrigerate for 1 hour.

About 1 hour ahead: Preheat oven to 325°F. Bake strata, uncovered, 50 minutes or until puffy and brown. *Serve at once.* Makes 6 servings.

* Dry crusts in 250°F. oven for later use as bread crumbs for toppings, etc.

SPECIAL-DAY WAFFLES

2 cups regular all-purpose flour	2 cups buttermilk
3 teaspoons double-acting	4 eggs, well beaten
baking powder	1 cup butter or margarine, melted,
1 teaspoon baking soda	or salad oil
1 teaspoon salt	

Preheat waffle iron as manufacturer directs. Sift flour, baking powder, soda, salt. Combine buttermilk, eggs; add to flour mixture. With hand beater, or mixer at high speed, beat until smooth; stir in butter.

When waffle iron is ready, pour batter into center until it spreads to about 1" from edges. Bring cover down gently. Cook as manufacturer directs. *Do not raise cover during baking.*

When waffle is done, lift cover; loosen waffle with fork; serve at once. Reheat iron before pouring in next waffle. Makes 6 to 8 servings.

POPOVERS

POULTRY TIP: After chicken is fried, pour drippings from skillet. Return ¼ cup drippings to skillet; add 3 to 4 tablespoons flour; stir over low heat, loosening brown bits until smooth. When flour is slightly browned, stir in 2½ cups milk; cook, stirring until thickened. Add a little bottled sauce for gravy and 1 tablespoon chopped parsley. Serve with chicken.

POPOVERS

3 eggs
1 cup milk
3 tablespoons butter or
  margarine, melted

1 cup sifted regular all-purpose
  flour
½ teaspoon salt

1 hour before serving: Preheat oven to 375°F. Grease nine 6-ounce custard cups. In large bowl, with electric mixer at low speed, beat eggs with milk and butter. Then gradually beat in flour, by heaping tablespoonfuls, until well blended; beat in salt. Pour batter into cups.

Place cups in shallow pan or on cookie sheet and bake 40 minutes; quickly cut slit in side of each popover to let out steam. Bake 10 minutes longer. Remove popovers from cups and serve hot, or cool on racks to reheat later. Makes 9 popovers.

To reheat popovers: Preheat oven to 350°F. Wrap popovers in foil and heat 15 minutes.

PRIZE PRUNE PIE

WEDNESDAY

*Fried Chicken
with Cream Gravy**

*Popovers**

Carrots and Peas

Tomato Aspic

*Prize Prune Pie**

Tea   Coffee

1 9-inch unbaked pie shell
2¾ cups cooked pitted prunes
1 egg
⅓ cup granulated sugar
⅛ teaspoon salt
1 tablespoon lemon juice

½ cup prune juice
½ cup packed brown sugar
¼ cup butter or margarine
⅓ cup regular all-purpose
  flour
¼ teaspoon cinnamon

Preheat oven to 425°F. In pie shell, arrange prunes. Beat egg with sugar, salt, lemon juice and prune juice; pour over prunes.

Meanwhile, with fork, blend together brown sugar, butter, flour and cinnamon. Sprinkle mixture over pie. Bake 40 minutes. Cool on rack. Makes 8 servings.

HAM STEAK À LA GRAPEFRUIT

THURSDAY

*Ham Steak
à la Grapefruit**

Mashed Potatoes

Brussels Sprouts

*French Endive
with French Dressing**

*Orange-Nut Bread**

Milk   Coffee

1 cup fresh or reconstituted
  grapefruit juice
⅓ cup granulated sugar
4 teaspoons cornstarch

1¼ pounds fully cooked ham steak,
  about ¾-inch thick
light brown sugar
1 peeled and sectioned grapefruit

About 30 minutes before serving: Preheat broiler if manufacturer directs. In medium saucepan, combine grapefruit juice with sugar; bring to boil; stir in cornstarch mixed smooth with 2 tablespoons water; stir constantly until a thickened sauce.

With pointed knife, slash fat edge of ham slice in several places. Place on broiler rack; sprinkle lightly with brown sugar; spoon some of sauce over ham. Broil ham about 5 minutes or until edges brown; turn; repeat; broil a few minutes longer. Arrange grapefruit sections on ham; broil until fruit is heated through.

Place ham on heated platter; pass rest of grapefruit sauce in gravy boat. Makes 4 servings.

SALAD TIP: In jar, combine ¾ teaspoon salt, dash pepper and paprika, ¼ teaspoon sugar, ¼ cup lemon juice, ¾ cup salad oil, 1 garlic clove. Shake well. Refrigerate. Shake before using. Makes 1 cup dressing.

ORANGE-NUT BREAD

3 tablespoons butter or margarine, softened
¾ cup granulated sugar
2 eggs
2¼ cups sifted regular all-purpose flour
1 teaspoon salt

3 teaspoons double-acting baking powder
1 cup milk
½ cup grated orange peel
1 cup coarsely chopped walnuts
10 walnut halves

Day ahead: Preheat oven to 350°F. In large bowl, with electric mixer at medium speed, beat butter with sugar until creamy. Beat in eggs, one at a time. Beat in, alternately, flour sifted with salt and baking powder, and milk, until smooth. Fold in peel, chopped nuts. Pour into greased, floured 9″ by 5″ by 3″ loaf pan; top with walnut halves. Bake 1 hour or until done. Cool in pan 5 minutes; remove; cool on rack. Makes 6 servings.

LINGUINI WITH WHITE CLAM SAUCE

1 pound linguini
½ cup butter or margarine
1 cup chopped onions
3 to 5 small garlic cloves, minced
½ cup chopped parsley

1 teaspoon salt
1 teaspoon basil
dash black pepper
2 10½-ounce cans minced clams
1 8-ounce bottle clam juice

About 15 minutes before serving: Cook linguini as label directs. Meanwhile, in large skillet, in hot butter, sauté onions, garlic, parsley, salt, basil and pepper until onion is tender. Add clams and juice. Boil 1 minute.

Serve linguini topped with clam sauce. Makes 6 servings.

CHOCOLATE-POUNDCAKE RING

2¾ cups sifted cake flour
¾ teaspoon cream of tartar
½ teaspoon baking soda
1½ teaspoons salt
1¾ cups granulated sugar
1 cup shortening
⅔ cup milk

1 teaspoon vanilla extract
3 whole eggs
1 egg yolk
4 squares unsweetened chocolate, melted
½ cup semisweet chocolate pieces
2 tablespoons light corn syrup

Early in day: Grease cast-aluminum bundt cake pan, 10″ by 4″. Preheat oven to 350°F.

Into large bowl, sift flour, cream of tartar, baking soda, salt, sugar. Add shortening, milk, extract; with electric mixer at low speed, beat until well blended. Beat in eggs and egg yolk, along with melted unsweetened chocolate; beat until blended.

Turn into cake pan; bake 1 hour and 10 minutes or until cake tester, inserted in center of cake, comes out clean. Cool in pan 10 minutes; remove from pan to rack; cool.

In double-boiler top, over hot, *not boiling,* water, melt semisweet chocolate pieces. Remove from heat; stir in corn syrup and 1 tablespoon water until smooth. Drizzle over cake. Makes 10 to 12 servings.

CHOCOLATE-POUNDCAKE RING

FRIDAY
*Linguini with White Clam Sauce**
Breadsticks
Green Salad
*Chocolate-Poundcake Ring**
Demitasse

SATURDAY

*Traditional Cassoulet**

Hard Rolls

*Tossed Salad
with Mushrooms**

*Orange
Baked Alaskas**

Tea   Coffee

TRADITIONAL CASSOULET

3 cups packaged dried pea or navy beans
2 teaspoons salt
1/2 pound salt pork, cut into 5 slices
1 garlic clove
4 parsley sprigs, 1 stalk celery, diced, 2 bay leaves, 1/2 teaspoon whole thyme, all tied in double-cheesecloth bag
2 tablespoons salad oil
2 pounds lean pork, cut into 1 1/2-inch chunks
1 pound lean lamb, cut into 1 1/2-inch chunks
1 cup white wine or canned chicken broth
1 8-ounce can tomato sauce
5 large carrots, pared, halved crosswise
2 medium onions, peeled
1 cup sliced celery
4 whole cloves
1 kielbasa sausage
1/2 cup chopped green onions

Early in day: In large kettle, boil beans with 2 quarts water and salt, 2 minutes. Remove from heat; let stand 1 hour; add salt pork, garlic, bag of seasonings; simmer, covered, 40 minutes, skimming if necessary.

Meanwhile, in large skillet, in hot oil, sauté pork and lamb, a few chunks at time, until golden. Add to beans with wine, tomato sauce, carrots, onions, celery, cloves, sausage and all but 1 tablespoon green onions. Simmer, covered, 40 minutes. Discard bag of seasonings. Cut sausage into 1/2-inch slices. Transfer, with bean mixture, to 4- to 6-quart casserole; cover; refrigerate.

About 2 1/2 hours before serving: Preheat oven to 350°F. Bake cassoulet, covered, 2 to 2 1/2 hours or until bubbly. Garnish each serving with green onions. Makes 8 to 10 servings.

TOSSED SALAD WITH MUSHROOMS

About 30 minutes before serving: In covered jar, combine 2/3 cup salad oil, 1/2 cup tarragon vinegar, 2 tablespoons granulated sugar, 2 teaspoons garlic salt and 1/4 teaspoon pepper; refrigerate this salad dressing.

Around sides of large salad bowl, arrange leaves from 1 head romaine with ends pointing up. In mixing bowl, sprinkle 1/4 pound mushrooms, sliced, with 1/4 cup lemon juice; then drain off juice and discard. Add 2 quarts chicory and escarole, cut in bite-size pieces, and 2 to 3 heads endive, leaves separated. Shake salad dressing; toss with greens and mushrooms; place in salad bowl. Makes 8 to 10 servings.

ORANGE BAKED ALASKAS

Day or two before serving: Slice top from each of 8 large navel oranges, about one-third of the way down. With sharp knife, cut all sections from inside; reserve for breakfast. Cut thin slice from bottom of each orange so it sits level. With sharp knife, cut sawtooth pattern around top of each orange shell.

Divide 3 pints vanilla ice cream among orange shells, pressing it down so it fills sawtooth edge; set in shallow pan; freeze.

With electric mixer at high speed, beat 4 egg whites in medium bowl until they form peaks. Add 1/2 cup granulated sugar gradually, continuing to beat until stiff peaks form; fold in 1/2 teaspoon orange extract.

Spoon meringue onto ice cream in each shell, sealing it well to shell. Sprinkle with flaked coconut; freeze.

About 15 minutes before serving: Preheat oven to 500°F. Set pan of oranges in oven; bake 2 or 3 minutes or until coconut and meringue are just tinged with brown. Serve immediately. Makes 8 servings.

WINTER

In the winter dark, a kitchen's lighted windows are a beacon, promising warmth and the welcome smells of freshly baked bread, beans bubbling in a pot, a roast in the oven. By now, in most sections of the country, fresh vegetables, except for the root variety, are scarce and costly. But winter fruit offers new variety: oranges and grapefruit, like globes of imprisoned sunlight; casabas and Christmas melons; Bosc, Comice and Anjou pears; many kinds of grapes; tart cooking apples and sugar-sweet figs and dates.

Now, too, frozen and packaged foods, a convenience at any time, really come into their own, bringing to the winter table the tastes and textures of all the seasons. The menus in this section use these and other ingredients in many different ways, to freshen appetites and make your reputation as a cook.

Among memorable main dishes are Chicken in Orange Gravy, Celery-Stuffed Flank Steak, Tuna Loaf with Cucumber Sauce and Family Pot Roast. As usual, both guest and family meals are planned with an eye to economy. But in this special season for entertaining, there is an occasional royal exception, like Standing Rib Roast Supreme, complemented by a rich but delicate dessert.

Although some of these more elaborate meals require extra preparation, much of it is the do-ahead kind that leaves you free to enjoy your guests. And in winter, as at any other season, good food and good friends are well met.

CHICKEN DELHI

SUNDAY
*Chicken Delhi**
*Sambals**
Buttered Rice
Green Beans
Fresh Pineapple
Spears
Tea

1½ teaspoons ginger
⅛ teaspoon ground coriander
⅛ teaspoon pepper
2 3-pound broiler-fryers
¼ cup butter or margarine, melted
1 cup grated onion

1 tablespoon turmeric
1½ teaspoons salt
½ pint yogurt
½ pint light cream
1 small onion, thinly sliced

About 2¼ hours before serving: Preheat oven to 350°F. Combine ginger, coriander, pepper; rub into chickens. Place chickens in shallow open roasting pan.

Combine butter with grated onion, turmeric, salt, yogurt, cream; pour some over chickens. Roast chickens 1 hour, basting often with rest of yogurt mixture.

Top chickens with onion rings; roast 1 hour longer or until tender. Skim off fat from gravy; pour some gravy over chickens; pass rest. Makes 8 servings.

ACCOMPANIMENT TIP: Sambals, or side boys as they are often called, might include banana slices, freshly grated coconut, chutney, toasted slivered almonds, chopped green pepper, chopped hard-cooked egg and raisins, to be passed with the Chicken Delhi.

———◆———

TUNA-POTATO PATTIES

MONDAY
Apricot Nectar
*Tuna-Potato Patties**
Buttered
Mixed Vegetables
Coleslaw
Orange-Frosted
Yellow Cake
Milk   Tea

1 6½- or 7-ounce can tuna, drained
1 tablespoon lemon juice
1 4-serving package instant mashed
  potatoes
1 teaspoon dried parsley flakes
1 tablespoon instant minced onion
1 egg, beaten

1 teaspoon seasoned salt
¼ teaspoon seasoned pepper
¼ cup flour
3 tablespoons salad oil
1 8-ounce can tomato sauce with
  cheese

About 20 minutes before serving: In medium bowl, flake tuna; sprinkle with lemon juice. Prepare potatoes as label directs but omit salt; add to tuna, with parsley flakes, onion, egg, seasoned salt and pepper; mix well. With floured hands, gently shape into 8 patties; coat with flour.

In medium skillet, in hot salad oil, sauté patties until brown on both sides. Heat tomato sauce. Serve with patties. Makes 4 servings.

———◆———

QUICK BEEF CHOWDER

TUESDAY
*Quick Beef Chowder**
Toasted English Muffins
Waldorf Salad
Chocolate Ice Milk
Oatmeal Cookies
Tea   Coffee

2 tablespoons salad oil
1 medium onion, chopped
1 green pepper, diced
2 24-ounce cans beef stew
1 30-ounce can Italian tomatoes
1 10½-ounce can condensed cream-
  of-celery soup

1 12-ounce can whole-kernel corn,
  undrained
1 tablespoon chopped parsley
½ teaspoon salt
½ teaspoon marjoram
¼ teaspoon onion salt
1 bay leaf

About 30 minutes before serving: In Dutch oven, in hot salad oil, sauté onion and green pepper until golden; stir in beef stew, tomatoes, undiluted celery soup, corn, parsley, salt, marjoram, onion salt, bay leaf. Heat, covered, 15 minutes or until hot, stirring occasionally.

Serve at once in soup bowls. Nice with toasted split English muffins. Makes 6 main-dish servings.

MEAT TIP: In small bowl, beat ¼ cup butter until creamy. Add 1 tablespoon finely chopped parsley, a dash of salt and pepper and a few drops of lemon juice. Refrigerate until firm. Cut into small pieces. Serve on broiled steak.

OLD-FASHIONED HERB BREAD

1 13¾-ounce package hot-roll mix	1 egg, beaten
½ teaspoon marjoram leaves	1 tablespoon sesame seed
½ teaspoon dill weed	

About 2½ hours before serving: Prepare hot-roll mix as label directs but add marjoram and dill weed to flour mixture. Let rise in warm place (80° to 85°F.) one hour or until double in bulk; punch down.

On greased cookie sheet, shape dough into round loaf about 4 inches in diameter. With scissors, cut 2-inch gashes in loaf, dividing circle into 5 "petals." Gently separate "petals." Let rise again in warm place until double in bulk.

Preheat oven to 375°F. Brush dough with egg; sprinkle with sesame seed. Bake 40 minutes or until bread sounds hollow when tapped gently. Cool 10 minutes on rack before serving. Or cool completely, then wrap and store at room temperature to serve next day. Makes 1 loaf.

———◆———

DANISH CHEESEROLE

1 cup uncooked elbow macaroni	¾ cup milk
1 pound ground beef round	1 canned pimiento, minced
1 whole egg	1 tablespoon butter or margarine, melted
5 bread slices, crusts removed	
salt	3 or 4 ounces Danish blue cheese, crumbled
¼ teaspoon pepper	
3 eggs, separated	1 cup shredded Cheddar cheese

About 1½ hours before serving: Cook macaroni; drain. Preheat oven to 350°F.

Mix beef; whole egg; 2 bread slices, crumbled; 1 teaspoon salt; pepper. Press into bottom of 10-inch fluted pie plate, 1½-inches deep.

In large bowl, beat egg yolks slightly; stir in milk; 3 bread slices, crumbled; pimiento; ½ teaspoon salt; melted butter; cheeses and macaroni. Beat egg whites stiff; fold in. Pour mixture onto meat in pie plate. Bake 50 to 60 minutes or until top is lightly browned. Makes 8 servings.

———◆———

LEMON SCAMPI

2 pounds thawed frozen or fresh jumbo shrimp	juice 1 medium lemon
	½ teaspoon salt
½ cup butter or margarine	⅛ teaspoon pepper
2 garlic cloves, minced	chopped parsley for garnish

Peel shrimp; leave tail shells on; devein. Preheat broiler if manufacturer directs.

In small skillet over medium heat, melt butter. Add garlic and lemon juice; simmer 3 minutes, stirring often.

Arrange shrimp on heatproof platter or broiler pan; pour on garlic butter. Sprinkle with salt and pepper. Broil, turning once, 5 to 7 minutes.

To serve, pour pan juices over shrimp and sprinkle with parsley. Makes 4 servings.

LEMON NESTS

VEAL À LA FORESTIÈRE

1½ pounds *thin* veal cutlets
1 garlic clove, cut
flour
¼ cup butter or margarine
½ pound mushrooms, thinly sliced

½ teaspoon salt
dash black pepper
⅓ cup dry vermouth
1 teaspoon lemon juice

About 45 minutes before serving: Flatten veal to ¼-inch thickness. Cut into 2-inch pieces; rub with garlic; sprinkle with flour.

In large skillet, in hot butter, sauté veal, a few pieces at a time until golden brown. Return to skillet; top with mushrooms; sprinkle with salt, pepper, vermouth.

Cook, covered, over low heat, 20 minutes or until fork-tender, adding water if necessary. Sprinkle with lemon juice. Makes 4 to 6 servings.

LEMON NESTS

1 3¼-ounce package regular lemon-pudding-and-pie-filling mix
2 tablespoons coarsely grated lemon peel
⅛ teaspoon cream of tartar

6 tablespoons granulated sugar
1 2-ounce package whipped topping mix
thin lemon slices for garnish

Early in day: Make pudding as label directs but add lemon peel. Remove from heat; cover surface with waxed paper; refrigerate.

Preheat oven to 225°F. With electric mixer at high speed, beat egg whites left from pudding with cream of tartar until foamy. At high speed, gradually add sugar, beating until meringue forms stiff peaks. Quickly spread on bottom and up sides of six 6-ounce custard cups; bake 45 minutes; remove from oven; cool on rack.

When pudding is cold, remove paper. Beat pudding with egg beater. Make whipped topping as label directs; refrigerate ⅓ cup; fold rest into pudding; refrigerate.

1½ hours before serving: Fill each meringue nest with pudding; top with some of reserved topping and a lemon twist. Makes 6 servings.

SATURDAY
*Veal à la Forestière**
Baked Potatoes
Glazed Carrots
Jellied Lime Salad
*Lemon Nests**
Tea   Coffee

menus for Winter / 171

VENETIAN CALVES' LIVER

SUNDAY

*Venetian Calves' Liver**

*Country Potatoes**

Italian Green Beans and Mushrooms

Hard Rolls

*Frozen Taffy Pie**

Tea   Coffee

1½ tablespoons butter or margarine

1 medium or ½ large sweet or Spanish onion, sliced

1 pound calves' liver, cut in 1-inch squares

1 teaspoon basil

½ teaspoon salt

⅛ teaspoon pepper

4 lemon wedges for garnish

About 10 minutes before serving: In large skillet over low heat, in melted butter, sauté onion slices, separated into rings, about 3 minutes or until tender. Add liver, basil, salt and pepper; sauté, turning frequently, until liver is browned; add ¼ cup water; bring to boil.

Serve topped with lemon wedges. Makes 4 servings.

VEGETABLE TIP: Slice or dice 6 cold, peeled, cooked potatoes. In skillet, in 3 tablespoons melted butter or margarine, sauté, without stirring, until golden on underside. Turn; brown on other side. Sprinkle with ¾ teaspoon salt and ⅛ teaspoon pepper. Makes 4 to 6 servings.

FROZEN TAFFY PIE

Early in day: In bowl, combine ¼ cup butter or margarine, melted, and 2 cups flaked coconut; press mixture to bottom and sides of 9-inch pie plate. Refrigerate until firm.

Into saucepan, pour 1 cup milk; sprinkle with 1 envelope unflavored gelatin; let gelatin soften, then place over low heat and stir constantly until dissolved. Remove from heat; stir in ½ cup milk and ⅓ cup molasses. Chill until mixture mounds slightly when dropped from spoon.

Whip 1 cup heavy or whipping cream until stiff; fold into gelatin mixture; turn into coconut crust; freeze.

About 15 minutes before serving: Sprinkle frozen pie with shaved unsweetened chocolate. For easier slicing, let stand at room temperature 15 minutes. Makes 8 servings.

—◆—

LUCANIAN EGGS AU GRATIN

MONDAY

*Lucanian Eggs au Gratin**

Tossed Greens with Cherry Tomatoes and Green-Pepper Chunks

Salt Sticks

*Apple Fritters**

Tea   Coffee

2 tablespoons butter or margarine

1 medium onion, chopped

2 15-ounce cans macaroni and cheese

6 hard-cooked eggs

¼ teaspoon salt

dash pepper

½ cup grated Parmesan cheese

About 40 minutes before serving: In small skillet, melt butter; sauté onion until golden. In bowl, mix together sautéed onion and macaroni and cheese. Preheat oven to 375°F.

In 1½-quart casserole, place half of macaroni mixture. Halve hard-cooked eggs lengthwise; lay 6 halves on top of macaroni; sprinkle with half of salt, pepper and cheese. Repeat. Bake 30 minutes or until hot and bubbly. Makes 6 servings.

APPLE FRITTERS

About 20 minutes before serving: Pare and core 3 large green apples; slice into ¼-inch-thick rings. In medium bowl, mix 1 cup biscuit mix with 1 egg. Gradually beat in ½ cup milk to make thick batter. Dip apple rings into batter; drain slightly. In large skillet, in 2 inches hot salad oil, fry rings 2 minutes on each side or until golden brown. Drain on paper towels. Sprinkle with cinnamon sugar. Makes 4 to 6 servings.

SPINACH SPECIAL

About 15 minutes before serving: Wash one 16-ounce bag spinach. Place in large kettle with 1½ teaspoons salt. Simmer, covered, 6 minutes; drain. Stir in 1 pared and coarsely grated carrot, 1 pared and grated apple, and ½ teaspoon lemon juice. Simmer, covered, a few minutes or until hot. Makes 4 servings.

CARAMEL-PEACH CRUNCH

½ cup flour
1 cup uncooked rolled oats
¾ cup packed dark brown sugar
1 teaspoon cinnamon
½ teaspoon salt

½ cup butter or margarine, melted
1 29-ounce can cling-peach halves or slices, drained

Preheat oven to 400°F. In bowl, combine flour, oats, sugar, cinnamon, salt; add butter; mix well.

In 9″ pie plate or 10″ by 6″ by 2″ baking dish, arrange peaches; sprinkle on oats mixture. Bake 25 to 30 minutes or until bubbly. Serve warm with vanilla ice cream. Makes 6 servings.

CORN-FLAVOR FOLDOVERS

1½ cups sifted regular all-purpose flour
½ cup cornmeal
1 tablespoon granulated sugar
2 teaspoons double-acting baking powder

2 teaspoons salt
¾ cup sour cream
1 egg, beaten
1 teaspoon thyme leaves
2 tablespoons butter or margarine, melted

About 45 minutes before serving: Into bowl, sift flour with cornmeal, sugar, baking powder and salt. Stir in sour cream, egg and thyme; mix to soft dough.

Preheat oven to 425°F. Place dough on floured pastry cloth; knead 1 to 2 minutes.

Roll into circle ¼-inch thick; cut into 2-inch rounds; brush each with melted butter; fold in half; brush tops with more melted butter.

On cookie sheet, arrange foldovers with edges touching. Bake 15 to 20 minutes or until golden; serve hot. Makes about 2 dozen.

BAKED RUBY PEARS

dash ground cardamom
¼ cup honey
1½ cups cranberry juice
⅛ teaspoon red food color

6 Anjou pears
6 whole cloves
1 small cinnamon stick

Early in day: In medium saucepan, mix cardamom with honey; stir in cranberry juice and food color; simmer 10 minutes. Meanwhile, preheat oven to 350°F. and peel pears, leaving stems intact. (Cut thin slices from bottoms so pears will stand upright when served.) Place pears on sides in 2½-quart casserole; add cloves and cinnamon; pour cranberry sauce over pears. Cover and bake 45 minutes or until tender, basting and turning every 15 minutes. Remove from oven; cool; refrigerate, turning pears occasionally, until well chilled.

To serve: Arrange pears upright in serving dish; remove cloves and cinnamon from syrup and pour some of syrup over pears. Or serve pears in individual dishes. Makes 6 servings.

BAKED RUBY PEARS

TUESDAY
Broiled Hamburgers
Mustard Pickles, Olives
Carrot and Celery Sticks
Poppyseed Noodles
Spinach Special*
Ice-Cream Sundaes
Tea   Coffee

WEDNESDAY
Broiled Ham Steaks
French Fries
Buttered Mixed Vegetables
Caramel-Peach Crunch*
Vanilla Ice Cream
Milk   Coffee

THURSDAY
Baked Chicken
Cauliflower with Cheese Sauce
Mashed Potatoes
Corn-Flavor Foldovers*
Romaine-and-Cucumber Salad
Baked Ruby Pears*
Tea   Coffee

RICE-TUNA PIE

FRIDAY

*Rice-Tuna Pie**

*Carnival
Cabbage Salad**

Broiled Grapefruit

Tea   Coffee

1 cup packaged precooked rice	salt
3 eggs	pepper
1 cup shredded Cheddar cheese	1/4 cup chopped chives
1 6½- or 7-ounce can tuna, drained	1 tomato, sliced
1 cup milk, scalded	

About 1 hour before serving: Preheat oven to 400°F. Cook rice as label directs. Combine with one egg, beaten. With back of spoon, press mixture to bottom and partially up sides of 9-inch pie plate to form shell.

Over rice sprinkle half of cheese and half of tuna; repeat layers.

In small bowl, beat 2 remaining eggs; gradually stir in scalded milk. Add 1/8 teaspoon salt, 1/8 teaspoon pepper and chives; pour into rice shell; bake 20 minutes. Arrange tomato slices on pie; sprinkle with salt and pepper; bake 5 minutes. Makes 6 to 8 servings.

CARNIVAL CABBAGE SALAD

1 envelope onion-salad-dressing mix	1/3 cup mayonnaise
4 cups shredded green cabbage	1 Golden Delicious apple, cored, diced
2 cups shredded red cabbage	

About 1 hour before serving: Prepare salad dressing mix as package label directs.

In bowl, combine green cabbage with 6 tablespoons onion-salad dressing; in bowl, combine red cabbage with 1/4 cup same dressing (chill remaining dressing for later use). Cover bowls; refrigerate 45 minutes.

To serve, toss green and red cabbage, mayonnaise and apple. Makes 6 to 8 servings.

———◆———

SOUP TIP: Float popcorn on soup, or cut process cheese into various shapes with small cookie cutters, or cut into small squares and triangles, and use to top each serving.

HASH-FILLED BAKED ONIONS

SATURDAY

*Cream-of-Mushroom
Soup**

*Hash-Filled
Baked Onions**

Green Beans Amandine

French Rolls

*Raspberry-Swirl
Ice Cream*

*Butter-Flavored
Cookies*

Tea   Coffee

4 large Bermuda onions, peeled	1/4 teaspoon seasoned pepper
1 15- or 15½-ounce can corned-beef hash	1/2 teaspoon Worcestershire
1 tablespoon brown sugar	butter or margarine
1/2 teaspoon dry mustard	1 20½-ounce can pineapple slices, drained
3/4 teaspoon seasoned salt	watercress for garnish

About 2½ hours before serving: In large covered saucepan, in boiling salted water, cook onions until tender, about 30 minutes.

Meanwhile, in medium bowl, mix well hash, sugar, mustard, seasoned salt and pepper and Worcestershire.

Slice top from each onion; with knife, remove centers; chop enough of centers to make 1/2 cup. Preheat oven to 400°F. In medium skillet, in 1 tablespoon butter, cook chopped onion about 5 minutes; combine with hash mixture; spoon into onions.

In greased 12″ by 8″ by 2″ baking dish, arrange 4 pineapple slices; lay stuffed onion on each; top with a half pineapple slice; secure with toothpicks. Brush onions with melted butter; bake 40 minutes or until lightly golden, basting occasionally.

Serve in individual casseroles; garnish with cress. Makes 4 servings.

SUNDAY
Family Pot Roast*
Baked Potatoes
Sautéed Parsnips*
Assorted Breads
Concord Grape Gelatin
with Whipped Topping
Tea   Coffee

FAMILY POT ROAST

4 pounds boneless beef round or rolled rump roast	1 cup sliced onions
salt and pepper	6 peppercorns
3 tablespoons shortening or salad oil	5 whole allspice
1 cup sliced carrots	1 bay leaf
1 cup sliced celery	1/4 teaspoon thyme leaves
	1 tablespoon flour

About 3 hours before serving: Preheat oven to 350°F. Sprinkle beef with 1½ teaspoons salt and 1/4 teaspoon pepper. In Dutch oven or large oven-proof pan, melt shortening; brown beef on all sides. Add carrots and next 6 ingredients; cook several minutes until vegetables are browned.

Add 2 cups water; cover pan and bake 2 hours or until beef is fork-tender, turning occasionally. Place meat on warm platter. Discard spices. Put vegetables and liquid through coarse strainer or food mill; return to pan. Blend flour with 1/4 cup water and stir into vegetable mixture. Cook, stirring, until gravy is thickened. Season to taste. Pass gravy. Makes 12 to 14 servings.

VEGETABLE TIP: Pare and halve lengthwise medium-size parsnips. Cook, covered, in large skillet with a little water until just fork-tender; drain. To parsnips in skillet, add 2 to 3 tablespoons butter, chopped chives, salt and pepper to taste. Heat, turning frequently.

———◆———

FRANKS COUNTRY STYLE

In large skillet, in 3 tablespoons hot oil, brown 8 medium onions, sliced; 4 green peppers, sliced; 1 pound frankfurters, sliced ½-inch thick; ½ teaspoon salt and 1/8 teaspoon pepper. Cover; simmer, stirring often, 25 minutes. Add one 12-ounce can vacuum-packed whole-kernel corn; 2 tomatoes, quartered; 3/4 teaspoon salt. Simmer 5 minutes or until vegetables are fork-tender. Makes 4 servings.

MONDAY
Franks Country Style*
Mashed Potatoes
Buttered Peas
Chocolate-Cream
Bread Pudding*
Tea   Coffee

CHOCOLATE-CREAM BREAD PUDDING

3¾ cups milk	granulated sugar
3 squares unsweetened chocolate	1 tablespoon vanilla extract
½ teaspoon salt	1/4 teaspoon almond extract
2 eggs	5 dry bread slices cut into 1/4″ cubes
2 eggs, separated	

Early in day: Preheat oven to 400°F. In saucepan, heat milk with chocolate and salt, over low heat, until chocolate is melted; beat with hand beater until blended.

In large bowl, slightly beat whole eggs and egg yolks; stir in 3/4 cup sugar. Gradually stir in melted chocolate; add extracts and bread cubes; let stand about 10 minutes.

Turn chocolate mixture into 1½-quart casserole; set in pan filled with hot water to come halfway up side of casserole. Bake 1 hour or until table knife inserted in center comes out clean.

Beat egg whites until foamy. Add 1/4 cup sugar, gradually, while beating, until sugar is well blended. Continue beating until meringue stands in stiff peaks.

Lightly pile meringue in mounds around edge of pudding. Return pudding to oven for 5 to 10 minutes or until golden.

Serve warm or cool. Makes 4 to 6 servings.

APPLE DESSERT PANCAKE WITH SOUR CREAM

SHOULDER LAMB CHOPS WITH AVERY BUTTER

6 lamb shoulder chops, ¾-inch
  thick
¼ cup butter or margarine
1 teaspoon salt
1 teaspoon dry mustard

1 teaspoon paprika
2 teaspoons water
2 tablespoons lemon or orange juice
¼ teaspoon Tabasco

About 20 minutes before serving: Broil chops to desired doneness. Meanwhile, in small pan, melt butter; stir in remaining ingredients. Heat 2 or 3 minutes. Pour over chops. Makes 6 servings.

APPLE DESSERT PANCAKE WITH SOUR CREAM

2 tablespoons butter or margarine
granulated sugar
1 teaspoon ground cinnamon
1½ McIntosh apples, pared, sliced
  ¼-inch thick
3 tablespoons flour

¼ teaspoon double-acting baking
  powder
dash salt
2 eggs, separated
3 tablespoons milk
sour cream

In 10-inch skillet with ovenproof handle, melt butter. Stir in 2 tablespoons sugar and cinnamon. Add apple slices; cook, over low heat, about 5 minutes.

   Meanwhile, preheat oven to 400°F. Combine flour, baking powder, salt, egg yolks and milk. Beat egg whites with 3 tablespoons sugar until they form soft peaks; fold into flour mixture. Spread batter over apple slices. Bake 10 minutes or until golden and puffy. Remove from oven; loosen edges with spatula. Invert flat plate over skillet; invert both; lift off skillet. Cut into wedges; serve with sour cream. Makes 6 servings.

TUESDAY

*Shoulder Lamb Chops
with Avery Butter**

Herbed Rice

Buttered Beets

Big Green Salad

*Apple Dessert Pancake
with Sour Cream**

Tea   Coffee

SPAGHETTI-CHEESE PIE

WEDNESDAY

Minestrone

*Spaghetti-Cheese
Pie**

Italian Green Beans

Escarole Salad

Vanilla Ice Milk

Coffee

1 8-ounce package spaghetti
½ pound sliced bacon
½ cup frozen chopped onions
¼ pound fresh mushrooms, sliced
3 eggs
1 cup milk
¼ teaspoon pepper

1 teaspoon Worcestershire
2 cups packaged shredded Cheddar
cheese
¼ cup buttered fresh bread crumbs
2 tablespoons chopped parsley for
garnish

About 1¼ hours before serving: Cook, then drain spaghetti as label directs. Preheat oven to 350°F.

Meanwhile, in large skillet, sauté bacon; remove from skillet; drain off all but 1 tablespoon drippings; add onions and mushrooms; brown lightly. Break bacon into 1-inch pieces.

Arrange cooked spaghetti in 10-inch pie plate; place mushroom mixture and bacon on top. In medium bowl, beat eggs slightly; beat in milk, pepper, Worcestershire; stir in cheese. Pour over spaghetti. Top with bread crumbs. Bake 25 minutes.

Remove from oven; sprinkle with parsley; let stand 5 minutes before cutting. Makes 6 servings.

————◆————

SAUSAGE AND SWEETS

THURSDAY

*Sausage and Sweets**

*Chinese-Cabbage
Salad*

Hot Butterfly Rolls

*Chocolate Mousse**

Tea   Coffee

1 1-pound package sausage links
1 10½-ounce can condensed
consommé
1 tablespoon cornstarch
2 tablespoons brown sugar
1 teaspoon orange peel

1 tablespoon orange juice
2 medium cooking apples, pared
and sliced ½-inch thick
1 18-ounce can sweet potatoes,
drained
¼ cup chopped pecans (optional)

About 30 minutes before serving: In large skillet, fry sausage as label directs. Meanwhile, in saucepan, blend undiluted consommé with cornstarch, brown sugar, orange peel and orange juice. Heat, stirring occasionally, until slightly thickened. When sausage is browned, pour off drippings. Add soup mixture and apple slices; cook over low heat about 10 minutes, basting with glaze. Add sweet potatoes; cook about 5 minutes longer. Garnish with pecans. Makes 4 servings.

DESSERT TIP: Make up package of regular chocolate-pudding-and-pie-filling mix as label directs but reduce milk to 1½ cups and add one 1-ounce square unsweetened chocolate; place waxed paper directly on pudding; cool. Remove paper; beat in 2 or 3 tablespoons from ½ pint heavy cream. Whip remaining cream; fold in. Refrigerate. Makes 6 servings.

————◆————

BOSTON DINNER CHOWDER

FRIDAY

*Boston Dinner Chowder**

Oyster Crackers

*Hearts of Lettuce
with
Creamy Onion Dressing*

Applesauce

Cinnamon-Sugar Cookies

Tea   Coffee

2 10¼-ounce cans frozen condensed
cream-of-potato soup
1 soup can milk
1 small onion, thinly sliced

1 16-ounce package frozen flounder
or cod fillets, thawed, cut into
1-inch crosswise slices
chopped parsley

About 25 minutes before serving: In large saucepan, over low heat, heat undiluted soup, milk and onion until soup melts. Add fish; cook over medium heat 15 minutes or until hot; sprinkle with parsley. Makes 6 servings.

ROLLED PORK ROAST

ROLLED PORK ROAST

1 6-pound rolled pork loin (about 18 inches long)	¾ cup orange marmalade
salt and pepper	1 tablespoon flour
2½ medium oranges	½ teaspoon dry mustard
whole cloves	1 tablespoon grated orange peel
	watercress for garnish

About 3½ hours before serving: Place loin, fat-side up, on rack in shallow open roasting pan; sprinkle with salt and pepper; roast (see chart, page 220).

Meanwhile, cut unpeeled oranges into ¼-inch-thick slices. Halve slices; insert 3 cloves in peel of each; cover; refrigerate.

When roast is done, remove from oven; increase oven heat to 400°F. Remove string, if any; with sharp knife, make about 12 crosswise slashes, 1½-inches deep, across top of roast. In bowl, mix marmalade, flour, mustard, grated orange peel. Spread roast with some of marmalade mixture; dip orange slices in rest; insert one slice in each slash. Spoon remaining marmalade over oranges.

Return roast to oven for 12 minutes or until glazed. Remove to wooden board; cut in half crosswise; place halves, side by side, on platter. Garnish with cress. Makes 6 to 8 servings. Save leftovers for Monday.

DESSERT TIP: Fill packaged meringue shells with lime sherbet; top with thawed frozen strawberries.

CAFÉ DIABLE

In chafing dish, place 6 pieces lump sugar, 8 cloves; 1-inch piece cinnamon stick; 1-inch strip lemon peel, cut up; 6 tablespoons (3 ounces) cognac. Do not stir. Ignite cognac; stir. In a minute, slowly stir in 1 quart strong coffee; ladle into demitasse cups. Makes 8 servings.

SATURDAY
Rolled Pork Roast*
Buttered Noodles
Mixed-Greens Salad
Lime-Sherbet Meringues*
Café Diable*

DUCKLINGS, HUNTER STYLE

SUNDAY

*Ducklings,
Hunter Style* *

Homemade Mashed Potatoes *

Jellied Orange Salad

Melba Toast

*Apricot Bars
à la Mode* *

Tea   Coffee

2 tablespoons salad oil	1 cup white wine
2 4-pound ducklings, quartered	1 cup canned chicken broth
16 small white onions, peeled	8 mushrooms
1 cup sliced celery	1½ teaspoons cornstarch
1½ teaspoons seasoned salt	parsley for garnish

About 2 hours before serving: In large skillet, in hot oil, brown ducklings on all sides. Drain off all but 4 tablespoons fat.

In Dutch oven, in 2 tablespoons duckling fat, sauté onions 5 minutes; add celery, duckling quarters; sprinkle with seasoned salt; sauté 6 minutes. Add wine and broth; simmer, covered, 1 hour or until tender.

In skillet, in 2 tablespoons duckling fat, sauté mushrooms 5 minutes.

Combine cornstarch with ¼ cup water; stir into gravy in Dutch oven; bring to boil and cook, stirring, until thickened; add mushrooms. Serve garnished with parsley. Makes 8 servings.

HOMEMADE MASHED POTATOES

9 medium potatoes (3¼ pounds), pared, quartered	6 tablespoons butter or margarine
salt	¾ cup hot milk
	dash pepper

In large saucepan, in 1-inch boiling salted water, cook potatoes, covered; boil 20 to 25 minutes or until fork-tender. Drain. Place over low heat 1 or 2 minutes to dry out, shaking pan gently. With potato masher or electric mixer, mash potatoes thoroughly until smooth. Beat in enough butter and milk to make potatoes fluffy. Season to taste. Makes 8 servings.

APRICOT BARS À LA MODE

⅔ cup dried apricots	¼ teaspoon salt
½ cup butter or margarine	2 eggs
¼ cup granulated sugar	1 cup packed light brown sugar
sifted regular all-purpose flour	½ teaspoon vanilla extract
½ teaspoon double-acting baking powder	½ cup chopped walnuts
	vanilla ice cream

MONDAY

Bert's Pork Barbecue *

Mixed Vegetables

Coleslaw

*Baked Apples
with
Foamy Sauce* *

Tea   Coffee

About 1½ hours before serving: Rinse apricots; place in small saucepan; cover with water; simmer 10 minutes; drain. Cool; chop fine. Preheat oven to 350°F. Grease 8″ by 8″ by 2″ baking dish.

In bowl, with electric mixer at medium speed, mix butter, sugar, 1 cup flour until crumbly. Press mixture over bottom of baking dish; bake 25 minutes; remove from oven.

Sift ⅓ cup flour with baking powder and salt. In large bowl, with electric mixer at low speed, beat eggs; gradually beat in brown sugar, baking-powder mixture and vanilla; stir in chopped walnuts and apricots. Spread over layer in baking dish. Bake 30 minutes or until set; cool in pan; cut into 8 bars. Serve, topped with ice cream. Makes 8 servings.

BERT'S PORK BARBECUE

¼ cup vinegar	1 thick lemon slice
2 tablespoons sugar	1 onion, sliced
1 tablespoon prepared mustard	¼ cup butter or margarine
½ teaspoon pepper	2 cups thinly sliced cooked pork
1½ teaspoons salt	½ cup catchup
¼ teaspoon cayenne	2 tablespoons Worcestershire

DUCKLINGS, HUNTER STYLE

In large skillet, mix ½ cup water with vinegar, sugar, mustard, pepper, salt, cayenne, lemon, onion and butter. Bring to boil; add pork; simmer, uncovered, 20 minutes or until pork is thoroughly heated. Add catchup and Worcestershire; bring to boil. Pass sauce in gravy boat. Makes 4 servings (1¾ cups sauce).

DESSERT TIP: Beat 1 egg white with pinch of salt until foamy; slowly add 2 tablespoons brown sugar, beating until stiff. To 1 egg yolk, add 2 tablespoons brown sugar; beat until light-colored; fold into egg-white mixture. Fold in ¼ cup heavy or whipping cream, whipped, and ½ teaspoon vanilla extract. Makes 1½ cups. Serve with baked apples. Or serve over drained canned peaches or apricots. Nice too, spooned onto warm gingerbread or chocolate cake squares.

CELERY-STUFFED FLANK STEAK

About 2 hours before serving: Trim excess fat from one 2-pound flank steak. Score surface of steak in diamond pattern on both sides; sprinkle with 1½ teaspoons instant meat tenderizer as label directs, then with ¼ teaspoon pepper.

In medium bowl, combine 1 cup fresh bread crumbs, ¾ cup chopped celery, 2 tablespoons instant minced onion, 1 tablespoon butter or margarine, melted, ½ teaspoon salt, ¼ teaspoon thyme leaves, ⅛ teaspoon pepper, 2 tablespoons water; spread evenly on one side of steak, leaving 1-inch border. Roll up from long side, jelly-roll fashion; secure with toothpicks or string. Sprinkle lightly all over with all-purpose flour.

In large Dutch oven, in 1 tablespoon hot butter or margarine, sauté steak roll on all sides until brown. Slip rack under steak; add 1 cup boiling water; cover; simmer 1½ hours. Remove to heated platter. *Remove toothpicks or string;* keep warm.

Mix 1 tablespoon cornstarch with ¼ teaspoon ginger and 1 tablespoon cold water; stir into liquid in Dutch oven; cook, stirring, until thickened. Stir in more water, if necessary. Serve as gravy with sliced steak. Makes 6 servings.

DESSERT TIP: Early in day, thaw, then slice, one 12-ounce frozen poundcake, into 2 layers. Spoon 1 pint butter-pecan ice cream onto bottom layer. Cover with top layer. Freeze. Serve with chocolate sauce.

—————◆—————

POACHED EGGS EPICURE

3 English muffins, split	6 eggs
2 4¾-ounce cans chicken spread	chopped chives
½ teaspoon ground thyme	

About 20 minutes before serving: Toast muffins. Meanwhile, in small bowl, mix chicken spread with thyme; spread on hot muffins; keep warm while poaching eggs.

When eggs are done: With slotted spoon, drain each egg and place on muffin half; sprinkle with chives. Makes 6 servings.

—————◆—————

HAM-AND-POTATO CASSEROLE

butter or margarine	⅓ cup diced green pepper
5 or 6 large potatoes, cooked, peeled, thinly sliced	⅓ cup diced canned pimientos
salt	3 eggs
seasoned pepper	½ cup milk
1 12-ounce can chopped ham	1 4-ounce package shredded Cheddar cheese (1 cup)

About 1 hour and 15 minutes before serving: In well-buttered 1½-quart shallow baking dish, arrange one-third of potato slices, overlapping slightly. Sprinkle with salt, seasoned pepper.

Preheat oven to 375°F. Cut ham into 10 slices; arrange half on potatoes in dish; sprinkle with half of green pepper and pimiento. Top with another third of potatoes, rest of ham slices, green pepper and pimiento. Top with remaining potatoes. Dot with butter. Bake 10 minutes.

Meanwhile, combine eggs with milk and ¼ teaspoon salt; spoon over casserole mixture; continue baking 40 to 45 minutes. Sprinkle with cheese; bake until bubbly. Makes 4 servings.

TUNA LOAF WITH CUCUMBER SAUCE

1 cup milk
3 eggs, slightly beaten
18 saltine crackers, finely crushed
1 cup finely chopped celery
3 6½- or 7-ounce cans tuna, drained
2 tablespoons grated onion
¼ teaspoon pepper
salt

2 medium cucumbers, peeled,
   seeded and chopped
2½ tablespoons butter or
   margarine
2½ tablespoons flour
1½ teaspoons grated lemon peel
1 teaspoon lemon juice
2 egg yolks

About 1 hour and 15 minutes before serving: Preheat oven to 350°F. In large bowl, combine milk, eggs and crackers; let stand 5 minutes, stirring occasionally. Stir in celery, tuna, onion, pepper and ¾ teaspoon salt. Pour mixture into well-greased 9½″ by 5″ by 3″ loaf pan. Bake 1 hour or until table knife inserted in center comes out clean. Set on rack to cool slightly.

About 15 minutes before serving: Prepare Cucumber Sauce: In small saucepan, simmer cucumbers in 1 cup water until tender-crisp. Drain; reserve liquid, adding enough water to make 1¾ cups. Set aside.

In medium saucepan over medium heat, melt butter; add flour; stir until smooth. Slowly add cucumber liquid; cook, stirring, until thickened. Add 1 teaspoon salt, lemon peel, juice and cooked cucumbers; cook just until boiling.

In small bowl, beat egg yolks slightly; stir in some of hot liquid, then slowly add mixture to saucepan. Cook, stirring, until thickened; do not boil.

With spatula, loosen tuna loaf; invert onto serving platter. Pour some of sauce over loaf; pass remainder. Makes 8 servings.

◆━━━━━━◆

CHICKEN IN ORANGE GRAVY

⅓ cup regular all-purpose flour
½ teaspoon salt
½ teaspoon paprika
½ teaspoon garlic salt
1 4½- to 5-pound roasting chicken,
   cut up
6 tablespoons salad oil
1 3-ounce can whole mushrooms

¼ teaspoon nutmeg
2 teaspoons granulated sugar
1 10½-ounce can condensed
   cream-of-mushroom soup
½ cup canned chicken broth
1 cup orange juice
3 cups diagonally sliced, pared
   carrots

About 1 hour before serving: Blend together flour, salt, paprika and garlic salt; coat chicken.

In large skillet, in hot salad oil, sauté chicken pieces until golden. Meanwhile, drain mushrooms, reserving liquid; add mushrooms to chicken; sprinkle chicken with nutmeg and sugar.

In bowl, thoroughly combine reserved mushroom liquid, mushroom soup, chicken broth and orange juice; pour over chicken. Bring to boil; simmer, covered, 25 minutes. Place carrots over top of chicken; cook 20 minutes or until carrots are tender. Skim off surface fat if any. Makes 6 servings.

VEGETABLE TIP: Place 3 acorn squash, halved and seeded, cut side down, in baking dish. Combine 2 cups apple juice, 1¼ teaspoons salt, ⅛ teaspoon each cinnamon, mace and pepper; pour into dish. Bake in 350°F. oven 45 minutes. Turn; spoon juice over tops; bake 10 minutes or until tender. Spoon juice into squash centers to serve. Makes 6 servings.

APPLE-SPICED ACORN SQUASH

FRIDAY

*Tuna Loaf
with Cucumber Sauce**

Buttered Peas

*Cling-Peach Halves
with
Creamy French Dressing*

Butterflake Rolls

*Ice-Cream Parfaits
with Vanilla Wafers*

Tea   Coffee

SATURDAY

*Chicken
in Orange Gravy**

Mashed Potatoes

*Apple-Spiced
Acorn Squash**

Chicory-Pear Salad

Spice Cake

Tea   Coffee

1 6-pound whole fish (such as red snapper, bass, silver salmon, king mackerel, bluefish or whitefish)

1 tablespoon lime juice

butter or margarine

1 medium onion, minced

½ cup minced celery

1¼ cups packaged herb-seasoned stuffing mix

1 4-ounce can slivered toasted almonds

1 4-ounce package shredded Cheddar cheese (1 cup)

¼ cup chopped parsley

½ teaspoon nutmeg

1 teaspoon salt

½ cup milk

toothpicks

1 cup dry white wine

lemons for garnish

romaine for garnish

parsley sprigs for garnish

About 3 hours before serving: Wash fish well. Brush cavity with lime juice; refrigerate 1 hour.

Meanwhile, make stuffing: In skillet, in ¼ cup butter, melted, sauté onion and celery until tender. In large bowl, combine stuffing mix, almonds, cheese, parsley, nutmeg and salt; add onion mixture and milk, mixing thoroughly. Preheat oven to 375°F.

Drain lime juice from fish; pat cavity dry with paper towels. Fill with stuffing; close and secure with toothpicks.

Combine 1 cup melted butter with wine.

Lay fish in foil-lined roasting pan. Bake 1½ hours, basting every 15 minutes with a little butter and wine mixture. When fish flakes easily when tested with fork, with 2 pancake turners, lift to platter. Garnish with lemons, romaine and parsley; remove toothpicks.

To serve, cut top of fish into squares just down to bone; serve with some of stuffing and gravy. Lift off bones; serve lower section of fish. Makes 12 servings.

VEGETABLE TIP: Heat cooked zucchini slices, small whole canned carrots, small cooked white onions with butter, salt, seasoned pepper and a little orange juice.

DESSERT TIP: If you have a home freezer or refrigerator-freezer, make tiny scoops of lemon sherbet; freeze on tray for several hours. Just before serving, roll each ball in sugar-coated cereal. Place several in a dessert dish; spoon crushed, thawed frozen strawberries over each.

———◆———

CHEESEBURGER TURNOVERS

1 pound ground beef chuck

2 teaspoons instant minced onion

1 teaspoon seasoned salt

⅛ teaspoon seasoned pepper

2 8-ounce packages refrigerated buttermilk biscuits

5 slices process Cheddar cheese

About 30 minutes before serving: Preheat oven to 425°F. In skillet, combine chuck, onion, seasoned salt and pepper; sauté 5 minutes or until chuck is brown.

On pastry board, with lightly floured rolling pin, roll 2 of the biscuits, slightly overlapping, into 6″ by 5″ oval. On half of oval, pile 3 tablespoons chuck mixture; top with half slice of cheese. Fold other half of biscuit over cheese; moisten edges with water; pinch together to seal. Prick top of turnover with fork; lay on ungreased cookie sheet. Repeat with rest of biscuits.

Bake turnovers 8 to 10 minutes or until brown. Makes 4 servings.

REGAL BAKED FISH

ONION FLAT BREAD

1 13¾-ounce package hot-roll mix
½ teaspoon salt
1 cup shredded Cheddar cheese
1 to 2 teaspoons butter or

margarine, melted
dehydrated onion flakes
poppy seed

About 4 hours before serving: Make hot-roll mix as label directs but add salt and cheese; let rise until double.

Press raised dough into well-greased, lightly floured 15½" by 10½" by 1" jelly-roll pan. Brush with melted butter; press generous amount of onion flakes into dough; sprinkle with poppy seed. Let rise again until double.

Preheat oven to 375°F. Bake 20 minutes or until golden. Cool in pan 5 minutes; remove to rack to cool. Makes 16 squares.

TUESDAY
Broiled Chicken Livers
Onion Flat Bread*
Spanish-Rice
Brown-Sugar-Topped
Grapefruit Halves
Tea   Coffee

menus for Winter / 185

SAUSAGE INDIENNE

WEDNESDAY
Vegetable Soup
*Sausage Indienne**
Succotash
Tossed Green Salad
*Capped Custards**
Tea   Coffee

1 pound pork-sausage meat
1 cup uncooked oatmeal
½ cup finely chopped pecans
½ teaspoon curry
⅛ teaspoon ginger

⅛ teaspoon ground cloves
1 cup pineapple juice
1 tablespoon honey
1½ teaspoons cornstarch

About 30 minutes before serving: In large bowl, combine sausage, oatmeal, pecans, curry, ginger and cloves; shape into 4 thick patties. In medium skillet over medium heat, brown patties; spoon off fat.

In small bowl, combine pineapple juice and honey; pour over patties. Cover and simmer 20 minutes, turning once. Place patties on warm platter. Blend cornstarch with 1 tablespoon cold water; stir into pan liquid and cook, stirring constantly, until slightly thickened. Serve sauce over patties. Makes 4 servings.

CAPPED CUSTARDS

Make up one 3-ounce package egg-custard mix as label directs for 4 individual custard-cup servings but omit nutmeg. Just before serving, remove spoonful of custard from center of each; drop in teaspoon of jelly or chocolate sauce; replace custard caps. Top with whipped cream, if desired. Makes 4 servings.

GOLDEN CHICKEN BREASTS

THURSDAY
Pineapple Punch
Golden
*Chicken Breasts**
Harvard Beets
*Hot-Savory Corn**
*Lemon Surprise**
Tea   Coffee

4 large whole chicken breasts, boned, skinned
1 cup mayonnaise or salad

dressing
2 teaspoons prepared mustard
1 teaspoon Worcestershire

About 1 hour and 10 minutes before serving: Place chicken breasts, boned side down, in greased 15½″ by 10½″ by 1″ jelly-roll pan. Preheat oven to 400°F.

In bowl, combine mayonnaise, mustard and Worcestershire; spread over top and sides of chicken. Cover with foil. Bake chicken 45 minutes; remove foil and bake 15 minutes longer or until golden. Makes 4 servings.

VEGETABLE TIP: Heat drained canned whole-kernel corn with melted butter to which minced garlic, celery salt and pepper have been added.

LEMON SURPRISE

1 3¼-ounce package lemon-pudding-and-pie-filling mix
granulated sugar
2 eggs, separated

7 packaged ladyfingers
2 tablespoons currant jelly
2 tablespoons graham-cracker
crumbs (optional)

About 4 hours before serving: In saucepan, combine pudding mix, ⅓ cup granulated sugar and ¼ cup cold water. Stir in egg yolks and 2 cups cold water; cook as label directs.

Beat egg whites until foamy; add ¼ cup granulated sugar, one tablespoon at a time, beating well after each addition. Continue beating until stiff peaks form; gradually fold in pudding.

Split ladyfingers and line bottom of 8″ by 8″ by 2″ baking dish with them. Spread ladyfingers with jelly; top with pudding, then with graham-cracker crumbs. Refrigerate 3 hours. Cut into squares. Makes 9 servings.

PARMESAN FLOUNDER FILLETS

About 20 minutes before serving: In shallow dish, combine 6 tablespoons grated Parmesan cheese and 3 tablespoons flour. Use to coat 1½ pounds flounder fillets on both sides. In large skillet over medium heat, sauté fish, in 3 tablespoons butter or margarine, until golden on both sides, 4 to 6 minutes altogether. Remove to platter with butter; sprinkle with chopped parsley. Makes 4 servings.

DESSERT TIP: To prepare pineapple, grasp by crown; cut off rind all around, from top down; remove eyes, if desired. Cut fruit into ¼-inch crosswise slices; reassemble in pineapple shape.

FRESH PINEAPPLE

MEAT-STUFFED MANICOTTI

butter or margarine	¼ teaspoon nutmeg
1 cup finely minced celery	grated Parmesan cheese
½ cup finely minced onions	12 packaged manicotti
½ cup finely minced, drained, canned mushrooms	½ cup packaged seasoned bread crumbs
1 pound boned shoulder of veal, ground	2 egg yolks
salt	1 tablespoon canned tomato paste
seasoned pepper	¼ cup white wine
3 tablespoons flour	1 10¼-ounce can meat sauce for spaghetti
2¼ cups milk	

Early in day: In large skillet over low heat, in ½ cup butter, sauté celery, onions, mushrooms, veal, 1 teaspoon salt, ½ teaspoon seasoned pepper, 20 minutes, stirring often.

Meanwhile, make Bechamel Sauce: In saucepan, melt 3 tablespoons butter; stir in flour, milk, ½ teaspoon salt, ⅛ teaspoon seasoned pepper, nutmeg. Cook, stirring, until thickened; add 3 tablespoons Parmesan cheese; remove from heat.

To 6 quarts boiling water, add 1 tablespoon salt, 4 manicotti; boil rapidly 8 minutes; then remove with slotted spoon to greased bowl. Repeat, cooking 4 manicotti at time, until all are used.

To veal, add crumbs, yolks, paste, wine; stuff into manicotti. Place half of Bechamel Sauce in 13" by 9" by 2" baking dish; top with half of meat sauce. Lay manicotti over this; cover with foil; refrigerate along with rest of sauces.

About 45 minutes before serving: Preheat oven to 400°F.; pour rest of Bechamel Sauce over manicotti, then rest of meat sauce. Bake, covered, 30 minutes or until tender. Sprinkle with Parmesan. Makes 6 servings.

CREAMY PEACH CAKE

Day before: Prepare 1 package orange-chiffon-cake mix as label directs; bake in 10-inch tube pan; cool.

Make up two 3 or 3¼-ounce packages vanilla-pudding-and-pie-filling mix as label directs; cool; add 1 teaspoon almond extract; fold in 2 cups heavy or whipping cream, whipped. Drain one 29-ounce can cling-peach slices; reserve 8 for garnish; fold rest of peach slices into pudding.

Hollow out cake, leaving shell about ¾-inch thick. (Use cake pieces another day.) If desired, sprinkle with ¼ cup Grand Marnier. Spoon pudding into hollow. Refrigerate cake until serving time. Garnish with peaches. Sprinkle with confectioners' sugar. Makes 10 to 12 servings.

FRIDAY
Parmesan Flounder Fillets*
Tartar Sauce
French-Fried Potatoes
Fresh Pineapple*
Tea   Coffee

SATURDAY
Meat-Stuffed Manicotti*
Hot Italian Bread
Ripe Olives, Fennel, Pimientos, Carrot Sticks
Creamy Peach Cake*
Demitasse

APPETIZER TIP: Mash 2 ripe, peeled and pitted avocados to smooth pulp. Add 1 cup sour cream, ½ teaspoon monosodium glutamate, ½ teaspoon salt, 2 tablespoons horseradish and 1 small onion, grated. Beat well. Makes 2 to 2½ cups.

CHEESE DOLLARS

1 roll nippy process cheese food, crumbled
½ cup butter or margarine
⅛ teaspoon salt

1⅓ cups sifted regular all-purpose flour
¼ teaspoon paprika

About 3 hours before serving: In small bowl, with electric mixer at low speed, beat cheese with butter until just blended; beat in salt, flour and paprika. On lightly floured board, knead ball of dough into roll about 2 inches wide. Wrap in waxed paper; refrigerate 1 hour.

Preheat oven to 350°F. On cutting board, with sharp knife, cut dough crosswise into thin slices. Bake on cookie sheets 10 minutes or until light brown; cool. Serve with dip. Makes about 36.

MEATBALL STEW WITH BURGUNDY

1 10-ounce package frozen peas with onions
1 24-ounce can meatball stew

¼ teaspoon seasoned pepper
1 teaspoon instant minced onion
3 tablespoons Burgundy

About 25 minutes before serving: Cook peas with onions as label directs. Meanwhile, in saucepan, simmer stew, pepper, instant minced onion and Burgundy about 15 minutes.

Add peas with onions; heat and serve. Makes 4 servings.

SPINACH-EGG-AND-BACON SALAD BOWL

In small bowl, combine 1½ tablespoons chopped chives, 2 tablespoons minced onion, 2 tablespoons chopped dill pickles, 2 chopped hard-cooked eggs, 1 teaspoon prepared mustard, ½ teaspoon seasoned salt, ¼ teaspoon seasoned pepper, 6 tablespoons salad oil and 2 tablespoons cider vinegar. Beat until blended. Pour over one 10-ounce bag washed spinach, tough stems removed. Add 6 cooked, crumbled bacon slices. Toss well. Serve at once. Makes 6 servings.

HAM AND ENDIVES AU GRATIN

8 Belgian endives, roots trimmed
butter or margarine
⅓ cup lemon juice
salt
¼ cup flour

dash cayenne
2 cups milk
¾ cup grated sharp Cheddar cheese
8 thin slices baked ham
paprika

In large skillet, arrange endives in ¼ cup butter, melted, lemon juice, 2 tablespoons water; sprinkle with ¼ teaspoon salt. Cover; simmer 30 minutes. (Add a little water if needed.)

Preheat oven to 450°F. In saucepan, melt ¼ cup butter; remove from heat. Stir in flour, cayenne, milk; bring to boil, stirring; reduce heat; add ½ cup of the cheese; simmer over low heat until cheese melts.

Drain endives; wrap each with ham slice, leaving ends uncovered. Arrange in baking dish; cover with sauce; top with remaining cheese and paprika. Bake 15 minutes. Makes 4 servings.

SUNDAY
Avocado-Onion Dip*
Cheese Dollars*
Baked Ham
Au Gratin Potatoes
Peas and Mushrooms
Cherry Pie
Tea   Coffee

MONDAY
Meatball Stew with Burgundy*
Crisp French Bread
Spinach-Egg-and-Bacon Salad Bowl*
Fruit   Cheese
Coffee

TUESDAY
Ham and Endives au Gratin*
Baked Potatoes
Stewed Tomatoes
Green Salad
Holiday Cupcakes*
Tea   Coffee

CELERY AMANDINE

HOLIDAY CUPCAKES

3 cups sifted all-purpose
  flour
1¼ teaspoons baking soda
½ teaspoon salt
½ teaspoon cinnamon
½ teaspoon nutmeg
¼ teaspoon ground cloves
1 cup dark raisins

1 cup diced mixed candied fruits
1 cup chopped walnuts
1 cup shortening
1½ cups granulated sugar
2 eggs, unbeaten
1 cup sherry
½ cup honey

Preheat oven to 325°F. Grease bottoms of thirty 3-inch cupcake-pan cups. Sift flour with next 5 ingredients; stir in raisins, fruits and nuts.

In large bowl, with electric mixer at medium speed, mix shortening with sugar, then with eggs until light and fluffy, about 4 minutes. At low speed, beat in alternately, just until smooth, fruit mixture, sherry and honey. Fill cupcake-pan cups two-thirds full. Bake 50 minutes or until cake tester inserted in center comes out clean. Makes 30 cupcakes.

SWISS VEAL WITH LIMAS

¼ cup flour
salt
⅛ teaspoon pepper
2 pounds veal steak, 1-inch thick
2 tablespoons salad oil

2 medium onions, sliced
½ medium green pepper, slivered
1 cup tomato juice
1 10-ounce package frozen limas,
  partially thawed

Early in day: Mix flour, 1 teaspoon salt and pepper. With edge of plate, pound into veal. In large skillet, in hot salad oil, sauté veal until well browned on both sides; remove to 10″ by 6″ by 2″ baking dish. In same skillet, sauté onions and green pepper; stir in tomato juice; pour over veal. Cover with foil; refrigerate.

About 1¾ hours before serving: Preheat oven to 350°F. Bake veal, covered, 40 minutes. Uncover; add limas; sprinkle with 1 teaspoon salt. Cover; bake 45 minutes or until veal is tender. Makes 4 servings.

CELERY AMANDINE

Sauté ⅓ cup blanched whole almonds in 2 tablespoons butter until golden. Add 4 cups sliced celery, 1 chicken bouillon cube, 1 tablespoon instant minced onion, ½ teaspoon sugar, ⅛ teaspoon each garlic powder, ginger. Cover; cook about 10 minutes; stir often. Makes 4 servings.

WEDNESDAY
Swiss Veal with Limas*
Buttered Noodles
Celery Amandine*
Stewed Prunes
Milk ˴ Coffee

CHILI-CHEESE BEEF STEAKS

THURSDAY

Hot Consommé

Chili-Cheese
Beef Steaks*

Mashed Potatoes

Mixed-Greens Salad

Fruit Medley*

Tea   Coffee

3 tablespoons flour
2 teaspoons salt
2 teaspoons chili powder
¼ teaspoon pepper
2 pounds beef round steak, 1-inch thick, cut into 6 pieces
¼ cup shortening
2 cups chopped onions
1 16-ounce can whole tomatoes
1 4-ounce package shredded sharp Cheddar cheese (1 cup)

About 2 hours before serving: Combine flour, salt, chili powder and pepper. Trim excess fat from meat; place meat on board and sprinkle with some of flour mixture. With mallet or edge of plate, pound mixture into meat. Turn and repeat on other side.

Preheat oven to 350°F. In large skillet, in hot shortening, brown meat well on both sides; remove to board. In drippings, brown onions; stir in remaining flour mixture.

Into large shallow casserole, spoon onion mixture. Arrange meat on top; add tomatoes (and their liquid). Cover and bake 1½ hours or until tender. Spoon any fat from casserole. Sprinkle meat with cheese. Bake 5 minutes longer or until cheese is melted. Makes 6 servings.

FRUIT MEDLEY

Thaw package of frozen mixed fruit in quick-thaw pouch. Slice 2 bananas. Arrange layers of fruit and bananas in dish. Sprinkle with fresh lemon juice. Makes 4 servings.

TUNA CREOLE

FRIDAY

Tuna Creole*

Hot Fluffy Rice

Brussels Sprouts

Green Peas

Celery   Olives

Fudge Cake

Tea   Coffee

2 6½- or 7-ounce cans tuna
1 medium onion, sliced
1 cup diagonally sliced celery
1 medium green pepper, slivered
2 8-ounce cans tomato sauce with cheese
½ teaspoon salt
¼ teaspoon chili powder
¼ teaspoon thyme leaves
1 teaspoon granulated sugar
¼ teaspoon Tabasco
1 3-ounce can sliced mushrooms, undrained

About 25 minutes before serving: Drain off oil from tuna into large skillet; in it sauté onion, celery and green pepper until tender-crisp.

Stir in tomato sauce with cheese, salt, chili, thyme, sugar, Tabasco and mushrooms; simmer, uncovered, 10 minutes. Add tuna and heat. Makes 6 servings.

ITALIAN HERO SANDWICHES

SATURDAY

Mugs of
Cheddar-Cheese Soup

Italian
Hero Sandwiches*

Butterscotch Sundae

Milk   Coffee

12 sweet Italian sausages
2 tablespoons olive or salad oil
2 medium onions, thinly sliced
5 green or red peppers, seeded and cut into ½-inch strips
4 hard rolls, about 5-inches long

About 45 minutes before serving: In large skillet, place sausages with ¼ cup water. Cover; simmer 5 minutes. Remove cover; continue cooking 15 minutes or until sausages are browned, turning frequently.

In another large skillet, in hot oil, sauté onions just until limp; then add peppers and continue cooking over medium heat, stirring occasionally, until peppers are tender, about 10 minutes. Add cooked sausages.

Split hard rolls in half lengthwise. Place some of pepper and onion mixture on bottom halves; top each with 3 sausages; cover with roll tops. For easier eating, cut each roll in half. Makes 4 sandwiches.

CURRY SOUP

SUNDAY

Curry Soup*

Parmesan Twists*

Roast Duckling

Baked Yams

*Fresh
Brussels Sprouts*

*Warm Plum Pudding
with Whipped Cream*

Tea   Coffee

2 10½-ounce cans condensed
  cream-of-chicken soup
1 soup can water
1 soup can milk
2 tablespoons butter or margarine

1 tablespoon curry
½ apple, unpared
½ avocado, peeled
lemon juice
chopped chives (optional)

About 15 minutes before serving: In saucepan, combine soup, water and milk. Add butter and curry; heat until bubbly.

Meanwhile, cut apple and avocado into thin slices; brush with lemon juice.

Top each serving of soup with apple and avocado slices and chives. Makes 8 servings.

PARMESAN TWISTS

About 25 minutes before serving: Preheat oven to 425°F. Grease well five 17″ by ¼″ wooden skewers.

Open one package refrigerated buttermilk biscuits (10 in all) as label directs. Between palms of hands, roll one biscuit into strip 7 inches long; wind this strip loosely around skewer, pressing each end against skewer to hold.

On same skewer, with another biscuit strip, make second twist, starting 2 inches beyond end of first. Repeat with remaining biscuits and skewers.

Bake twists on ungreased cookie sheet 10 to 12 minutes or until well browned. Remove from skewers; brush with beaten egg yolk; sprinkle with about 1 teaspoon grated Parmesan cheese. Serve piping hot. Makes 10.

DEEP-DISH SUPPER PIE

MONDAY

Deep-Dish Supper Pie*

Whole Green Beans

Mixed-Fruit Salad

*Hot Chive-Buttered
Italian Bread*

*Cheese-Crowned
Pumpkin Pie**

Tea   Coffee

1 12-ounce can luncheon meat
1 tablespoon butter or margarine
¼ cup minced onion
¼ cup minced green pepper
½ cup fine dried bread crumbs
2 tablespoons grated Parmesan
  cheese

1 15-ounce container ricotta cheese
¼ teaspoon basil
½ teaspoon salt
⅛ teaspoon pepper
3 eggs
paprika

About 1 hour and 15 minutes before serving: Preheat oven to 375°F. Chop luncheon meat very fine. In medium saucepan over low heat, in melted butter, cook onion and green pepper until onion is tender. Remove saucepan from heat; add luncheon meat and bread crumbs; mix well; press mixture into bottom of greased 1½-quart round casserole.

In large bowl, combine cheeses. With electric mixer at medium speed, beat until smooth; add basil, salt, pepper. Add eggs, one at a time, beating until thoroughly blended.

Pour cheese mixture over meat layer in casserole; sprinkle with paprika. Bake 45 minutes or until cheese is golden. Remove from oven; cool 5 to 10 minutes so cheese layer can set.

With sharp knife, cut into 4 wedges. Makes 4 servings.

CHEESE-CROWNED PUMPKIN PIE

1 9-inch unbaked pie shell
1 8-ounce package sliced Cheddar
  cheese

2 eggs
1 13-ounce can evaporated milk
1 18-ounce can pumpkin-pie filling

CURRY SOUP

Early in day: Refrigerate unbaked shell 30 minutes. Meanwhile, let cheese stand at room temperature until very soft and pliable; carefully separate slices; roll up each, jelly-roll fashion; lay, seam side down, on cookie sheet; cover; refrigerate.

Preheat oven to 425°F. In bowl, beat eggs; stir in undiluted milk and pumpkin-pie filling until blended; pour into chilled shell.

Bake pie 10 minutes; reduce heat to 350°F. and bake 45 minutes or until filling is firm; cool. Snip each cheese roll into thirds. Arrange on pie. Cut pie into 8 wedges with a cheese roll on each. Makes 8 servings.

STUFFED BURGERS ON BUNS

2 pounds ground beef round
¼ cup prepared mustard
8 large stuffed green olives, minced
salt and pepper
6 hamburger buns, buttered

About 20 minutes before serving: Preheat broiler if manufacturer directs. Shape meat into 12 thin patties. In small bowl, combine mustard and olives; place heaping spoonful in center of each of 6 patties. Top with rest of patties and pinch edges together to seal.

Place patties on broiler pan; sprinkle with salt and pepper. Broil 6 to 8 minutes; turn; season; broil until of desired doneness. During last few minutes, toast buns. Serve burgers on buns. Makes 6.

CHICORY SALAD SPECIAL

1 8-ounce container plain yogurt
½ garlic clove, minced
2 tablespoons minced onion
2 tablespoons catchup
2 teaspoons basil
1 teaspoon granulated sugar
½ teaspoon salt
1 large head chicory, torn into pieces

In small bowl, stir yogurt with next 6 ingredients; toss with chicory in salad bowl. Makes 8 servings.

DESSERT TIP: Place 1 slice chocolate ice cream between 2 slices cake, sandwich-fashion; cut in half crosswise. If desired, top with nuts.

TUESDAY

*Stuffed Burgers on Buns**

*Chicory Salad Special**

Barbecue-Potato Chips

Pickles

*Chocolate Ice-Cream Bars**

Milk   Coffee

SAUERKRAUT SOUP

WEDNESDAY

Sauerkraut Soup*

Hot Rolls

*Apricot-Topped
Rice Pudding**

Milk   Coffee

1 teaspoon salt
½ teaspoon caraway seed
½ teaspoon chervil
16 small white onions, peeled
1 cup sliced celery
4 carrots, pared, sliced diagonally
1 16-ounce can sauerkraut, undrained

1 tablespoon granulated sugar
1 9-ounce package frozen whole green beans, thawed
2 pounds frankfurters, sliced ½-inch thick
1 large tomato, diced
2 10¼-ounce cans frozen cream-of-potato-soup, thawed

About 45 minutes before serving: In large kettle, place 3 cups boiling water, salt, caraway seed, chervil, onions, celery, carrots, sauerkraut, sugar. Simmer, covered, 15 minutes.

Stir in beans and rest of ingredients. Cover; cook, stirring occasionally, 15 minutes or until vegetables are tender. Makes 10 servings.

APRICOT-TOPPED RICE PUDDING

1 quart milk
1 cup uncooked regular white rice
salt
1 vanilla bean*
12 dried apricots

granulated sugar
¼ cup butter or margarine
4 eggs, separated
1 teaspoon grated lemon peel
⅛ teaspoon cream of tartar

About 3 hours before serving: In double-boiler top, over direct heat, bring milk just to boiling; stir in rice and ½ teaspoon salt; add vanilla bean. In double boiler, over boiling water, cook over low heat until thickened, stirring occasionally, 30 to 40 minutes or until rice is soft and liquid absorbed. Chill about 1 hour. Remove vanilla bean.

Meanwhile, in small saucepan, cook apricots with 1 cup water for 5 minutes. Add ¼ cup sugar and cook 5 minutes more; drain.

Preheat oven to 350°F. In large bowl, with electric mixer at medium speed, cream butter with ¾ cup sugar and egg yolks until fluffy; then stir in rice mixture and lemon peel. Beat egg whites with ¼ teaspoon salt and ⅛ teaspoon cream of tartar until stiff but not dry; carefully fold into rice.

Pour into well-buttered 12″ by 8″ by 2″ baking dish; bake 30 minutes. Arrange apricots on rice; bake 10 minutes more. Serve warm or cold. Makes 12 servings.

* For vanilla bean you may substitute 2 teaspoons vanilla extract.

———◆———

CORN FRITTERS, NORTHERN STYLE

THURSDAY

Ham Steaks

*Corn Fritters,
Northern Style**

Buttered Spinach

*Quick-Set
Fruit Salad**

Cheese and Crackers

Tea   Coffee

3 egg yolks
1⅔ cups drained canned whole-kernel corn
½ teaspoon salt

⅛ teaspoon pepper
¼ cup flour
3 egg whites, stiffly beaten
6 tablespoons shortening

Beat egg yolks until light; mix in corn, salt, pepper, flour. Fold in egg whites. Drop by tablespoonfuls into hot shortening in skillet. Cook on both sides until brown. Makes 6 servings.

QUICK-SET FRUIT SALAD

Dissolve one 3-ounce package blackberry-flavor gelatin in 1 cup boiling water. Stir in one 12-ounce package frozen mixed fruits, ⅛ teaspoon salt and 1 tablespoon lemon juice; let stand, stirring often, until fruit is thawed and gelatin slightly thickened. Pour into 4 individual molds; chill until set. Unmold; serve on greens with mayonnaise.

CRAB-MEAT SPREAD

In medium bowl, combine two 7½-ounce cans Alaska King crab, drained; ½ cup mayonnaise; 2 teaspoons horseradish; 2 tablespoons lemon juice; 2 tablespoons chopped green onions and ½ to 1 teaspoon salt; mix well. Cover; refrigerate. Makes about 2 cups.

FRIED RICE

1½ cups uncooked regular white rice	1 garlic clove, minced
salad oil	2 medium onions, chopped
1 pound lean pork, cut into julienne strips	4 green onions, chopped
	3 eggs, beaten
	soy sauce

About 45 minutes before serving: Cook rice as label directs.

In large skillet, heat 2 tablespoons salad oil; sauté pork until tender, about 8 to 10 minutes, turning frequently; remove. In same skillet, in 2 tablespoons salad oil, sauté garlic, onions and green onions until golden. Add eggs; cook, stirring, until just set, but not dry; remove.

In same skillet, in 2 tablespoons salad oil, toss rice until hot. Add 3 to 4 tablespoons soy sauce, pork, egg mixture; blend well. Serve with soy sauce. Makes 6 servings.

AVOCADO APPETIZERS

3 small avocados	6 tablespoons sour cream
lemon juice	6 teaspoons red caviar
1 13-ounce can jellied chicken consommé, chilled	cracked ice for serving
	6 lemon wedges

About 20 minutes before serving: Halve avocados lengthwise; remove pits. Brush with lemon juice. Spoon jellied consommé into avocado centers; top each with 1 tablespoon sour cream and 1 teaspoon caviar.

Arrange on cracked ice; serve with lemon wedges. Makes 6 servings.

ORANGE PORK CHOPS

6 pork chops, 1-inch thick	2 tablespoons shortening, melted
2 tablespoons flour	¾ cup orange juice
1 tablespoon seasoned salt	6 whole cloves
1½ teaspoons curry	¾ teaspoon coarsely chopped orange peel
¾ teaspoon paprika	6 thin orange slices
½ teaspoon pepper	

About 1 hour and 15 minutes before serving: Trim excess fat from chops. Combine flour, seasoned salt, curry, paprika and pepper; reserve 1 tablespoon; roll chops in remaining mixture.

In large skillet over high heat, brown chops in shortening; reduce heat; add orange juice, cloves and orange peel. Cover; simmer 45 minutes or until tender, turning chops occasionally. During last 5 minutes, add orange slices.

Remove chops and orange slices to warm platter. Skim off excess fat. Strain remaining liquids; discard cloves and peel. Return 1 cup liquid to skillet (add water to make 1 cup if necessary). Combine reserved flour mixture and 2 tablespoons cold water. Pour slowly into liquid; cook, stirring constantly, until slightly thickened. Spoon over chops. Makes 6 servings.

ORANGE PORK CHOPS

FRIDAY
Crab-Meat Spread*
Melba Toast
Chicken Chow Mein
Fried Rice*
Chow Mein Noodles
Snow Peas
Pineapple
Upside-Down Cake
Green Tea

SATURDAY
Avocado Appetizers*
Orange Pork Chops*
Baked Acorn Squash
Coleslaw
Hot Biscuits
Coconut-Custard Pie
Tea   Coffee

1 5-pound boned, rolled lamb shoulder

salt and pepper

½ cup apple jelly, melted

¾ cup butter or margarine

1½ cups diced celery

1½ 8-ounce packages herb-seasoned stuffing

2 medium apples, diced

2 teaspoons dill weed

3 cups apple juice

2 tablespoons flour

About 3¾ hours before serving: Preheat oven to 325°F. Rub lamb with 5 teaspoons salt and ½ teaspoon pepper. Place on rack in shallow open roasting pan; insert meat thermometer into center of meat; roast (see chart, page 220). During last ½ hour, baste meat generously with apple jelly. Let stand 20 minutes before carving.

About 1¼ hours before serving: To make stuffing: In medium skillet over medium heat, in 1 tablespoon of the butter, cook celery 5 minutes or until tender-crisp. In large bowl, combine celery, stuffing, apples and dill. In same skillet, heat 2 cups of the apple juice with remaining butter until melted; toss with stuffing mixture. Place in greased 2-quart casserole; bake with lamb for 1 hour.

Just before serving: Make gravy: Skim excess fat from lamb drippings; stir in flour. Gradually add 1 cup apple juice and ¾ cup water, stirring constantly; cook until mixture thickens. Makes 6 to 8 servings with enough lamb for French Stuffed Cabbage on Tuesday.

FLUFFY SWEET POTATOES

1½ cups dried apricots

2 18-ounce cans vacuum-packed sweet potatoes

½ cup milk

2 eggs

¼ cup butter or margarine, melted

1½ teaspoons salt

1 teaspoon grated lemon peel

About 1 hour before serving: Cook apricots as label directs; drain.

Preheat oven to 350°F. In large bowl, with electric mixer at low speed, mash apricots; beat in potatoes, milk, eggs, butter, salt and lemon peel until light and fluffy; pile into greased 1½-quart casserole. Bake 30 minutes. Serve hot. Makes 8 to 10 servings.

DESSERT TIP: In small saucepan, heat 3 tablespoons milk with 2 tablespoons butter or margarine; stir into 2 cups sifted confectioners' sugar until smooth. Blend in 1 teaspoon grated lemon peel and 3 tablespoons lemon juice. Spread over fruitcake. Garnish with mixed candied peels and maraschino cherry halves.

VEGETABLE TIP: Cook two 10-ounce packages cut green beans as label directs but add 1 small onion, sliced. Drain; toss with 2 tablespoons butter. Makes 6 servings.

WHIPPED-CREAM CHOCOLATE CAKE

Sprinkle ½ teaspoon unflavored gelatin over 2 tablespoons cold water in small bowl to soften. From 1 cup heavy or whipping cream, remove 2 tablespoons; scald; pour over gelatin, stirring until dissolved. Refrigerate until consistency of unbeaten egg white. Beat until smooth. Whip remaining cream; add dash salt, 2 tablespoons confectioners' sugar, ½ teaspoon lemon juice; fold in gelatin mixture. Use to fill and frost top of two 8- or 9-inch chocolate-cake layers.

FRENCH STUFFED CABBAGE

1 medium green cabbage	2 tablespoons fresh bread crumbs
1 tablespoon butter or margarine	½ teaspoon salt
¼ cup minced onion	dash pepper
1 egg	1 carrot, sliced
¼ pound pork-sausage meat	1 onion, thinly sliced
1 cup chopped cooked lamb	2 bacon slices
1 cup cooked rice	1 16-ounce can tomatoes
1 garlic clove, minced	

In large saucepan, in boiling salted water to cover, simmer whole cabbage 5 minutes. Plunge into cold water; drain well.

Preheat oven to 400°F. Make stuffing: In small skillet over medium heat, in butter, cook onion until tender. In medium bowl, beat egg; add sausage, lamb, rice, cooked onion, garlic, crumbs, salt and pepper; mix thoroughly; set aside.

In deep 3-quart casserole, arrange carrot and onion slices in layer. Place 2 20-inch lengths of string crisscross on top of vegetables. Set cabbage, stem end down, on top of string. With knife, from center of cabbage, cut out 3-inch round core to about 2 inches from bottom; fill cavity with stuffing.

Lay bacon across top of cabbage. With string, tie cabbage head firmly, pulling leaves up over stuffing. Pour tomatoes around cabbage. Cover and bake 1½ hours. Remove string; cut in wedges. Makes 6 servings.

——◆—◆——

SAUCE TIP: Combine ½ cup vinegar, 1 tablespoon butter or margarine, 1 egg, slightly beaten, 1 tablespoon sugar, 2 tablespoons prepared mustard, 1 tablespoon paprika. Cook over low heat, stirring, until just thickened. Serve with Boiled Tongue. Makes about ½ cup sauce.

WINTER VEGETABLE SALAD

1 medium rutabaga, diced	1 pint fresh Brussels sprouts
1 cup Italian or French dressing	1 16-ounce can julienne beets

Early in day: In saucepan, cook rutabaga in 1 inch boiling, salted water until tender-crisp; drain. Marinate in ⅓ cup of the dressing.

Cook fresh Brussels sprouts in 1 inch boiling salted water until tender-crisp (cook frozen sprouts as label directs); drain; cut in halves. Marinate in another ⅓ cup dressing. Drain beets well; marinate in remaining ⅓ cup dressing. Cover all; refrigerate, tossing occasionally.

Just before serving: Drain vegetables. Makes 6 servings.

——◆—◆——

PINEAPPLE-BEEF LOAF

½ cup fresh bread crumbs	1½ teaspoons salt
¼ cup milk	¼ teaspoon pepper
1 pound ground beef chuck	1 4-ounce can mushroom slices,
2 teaspoons Worcestershire	drained
1 egg, slightly beaten	1 8¼-ounce can pineapple slices,

Preheat oven to 375°F. In bowl, let bread crumbs and milk stand 5 minutes; with fork lightly mix in chuck, Worcestershire, egg, salt, pepper and mushrooms.

Pack meat into 8½″ by 4½″ by 2½″ loaf pan; bake 50 minutes; remove from oven; let stand 5 minutes. Pour off juices. Unmold onto heated platter. Lay pineapple slices on top. Makes 4 to 6 servings.

WINTER VEGETABLE SALAD

TUESDAY
French Stuffed Cabbage*
French Bread
Shoestring Carrots
Eclairs
Tea   Coffee

WEDNESDAY
Boiled Tongue
Quick Mustard Sauce*
Parslied Potatoes
*Winter
Vegetable Salad**
Hot Rolls
Stewed Figs
Holiday Cookies
Tea   Coffee

THURSDAY
Pineapple-Beef Loaf*
Buttered Spinach
Sesame Wafers
*Chinese Cabbage-Radish
Salad*
Butterscotch Pudding
Milk   Coffee

About 20 minutes before serving: Into medium bowl, pare and slice 1 cucumber. Into same bowl, section 2 large peeled grapefruit; add 1 quart bite-size salad greens and ¼ cup chopped chives. Toss with bottled garlic-flavored French dressing. Makes 6 servings.

VEAL POT ROAST

1 4- to 5-pound boned, rolled shoulder of veal	2 tablespoons butter or margarine
1 bay leaf	½ pound medium mushrooms
¼ teaspoon thyme leaves	2 tablespoons flour
2 teaspoons salt	½ 10-ounce package frozen peas
½ teaspoon seasoned pepper	2 egg yolks
3 carrots, pared, halved crosswise	2 tablespoons lemon juice
½ pound small white onions	fresh dill for garnish

About 3¼ hours before serving: In hot Dutch oven, sauté veal until lightly browned on all sides, 10 to 15 minutes. Pour off all fat; add ¼ cup water, bay leaf, thyme leaves; sprinkle on salt and seasoned pepper. Cover tightly; simmer 1¼ hours.

Add carrots and onions and simmer, covered, 1 hour or until veal and vegetables are tender. Remove to heated platter; keep warm. In skillet, in butter, sauté mushrooms 5 minutes.

Pour drippings from Dutch oven into measuring cup; add enough water to make 2 cups liquid. In Dutch oven, stir small amount of this liquid into flour; add rest of liquid, then peas. Cook, stirring, until thickened, and peas are tender. Add mushrooms; heat.

Beat egg yolks slightly; stir in some of hot liquid and lemon juice. Return to Dutch oven and cook, stirring, until thickened. (Do not boil.)

Arrange mushrooms around meat; pour some of sauce over meat and vegetables. Snip dill over vegetables. Pass rest of sauce. For easier serving, slice meat; reassemble on platter; then garnish with mushrooms, vegetables, sauce and dill. Makes 8 servings.

HOLIDAY BAKED PUDDING

2½ cups sifted regular all-purpose flour	1 cup granulated sugar
1 teaspoon double-acting baking powder	1 cup chopped apple
	1 cup fresh bread crumbs
1 teaspoon salt	1 cup chopped dates
½ teaspoon cinnamon	1 cup ground beef suet
½ teaspoon ground cloves	½ cup chopped walnuts
2 eggs	½ cup light molasses
	1 cup buttermilk

Preheat oven to 325°F. Sift together flour, baking powder, salt, cinnamon and cloves.

In large bowl, with electric mixer at medium speed, beat eggs until frothy; gradually add sugar, beating until mixture is thick and lemon-colored. Stir in apple, bread crumbs, dates, suet, walnuts and molasses; alternately add flour mixture and buttermilk, stirring well.

Pour batter into greased 2-quart casserole; cover; bake 2½ hours or until cake tester inserted in center comes out clean. Serve warm, right from casserole. Makes 12 servings.

To do ahead: Bake; cool; wrap in foil, refrigerate. To serve, reheat, wrapped, at 325°F. for 1 hour.

MARINATED SIRLOIN STEAK

SUNDAY
Marinated Sirloin Steak*
French Fries
Tossed Green Salad
Nesselrode Pie*
Tea   Coffee

About 3 hours before serving: In large shallow baking dish, place one 4-pound sirloin steak, cut 1½ inches thick; pour ½ cup red wine over steak. Cover; refrigerate 2 hours, turning steak once or twice.

About 40 minutes before serving: Preheat broiler if manufacturer directs. Drain marinade from steak; reserve. Sprinkle steak with 1 tablespoon seasoned salt and ¼ teaspoon seasoned pepper. Gash fat edge of steak at inch intervals, to keep it from curling.

Broil, basting occasionally with marinade. (To check doneness, make small gash in center of meat.) Makes 6 servings.

NESSELRODE PIE

1½ cups finely ground walnuts	2 teaspoons grated lemon peel
granulated sugar	6 egg whites
1 envelope plus 1 teaspoon unflavored gelatin	1 4-ounce jar diced mixed candied fruits (about ½ cup)
1½ cups milk	whipped topping or whipped cream
½ teaspoon salt	
6 egg yolks	candied pineapple, cut in slivers
2 tablespoons rum	

Early in day: Preheat oven to 400°F. Combine walnuts and 2 tablespoons sugar. With back of spoon, press mixture to bottom and sides of 10-inch pie plate. Bake 8 minutes or until light golden.

Meanwhile, in double boiler top, soften gelatin in milk; add ¼ cup sugar, salt and slightly beaten egg yolks; stir until blended. Cook over simmering water, stirring constantly, until mixture is thickened and coats metal spoon. Remove from heat; stir in rum and lemon peel. Place waxed paper directly on surface of gelatin mixture; refrigerate until just cool but not firm.

In large bowl, with electric mixer at high speed, beat egg whites until foamy; gradually add ¼ cup sugar, beating until stiff but not dry. Gradually fold gelatin mixture and diced candied fruits into egg-white mixture. Pile lightly into crust; chill until firm, about 1 hour.

Spread whipped topping or cream on pie; garnish with candied pineapple. Refrigerate until served. Cut into wedges with knife dipped in warm water. Makes about 10 servings.

COUNTRY DINNER

MONDAY
Hot Beef Broth
Assorted Crackers
Country Dinner*
Applesauce
Gingerbread Cookies
Coffee   Tea

about 20 small carrots, pared	2 4-ounce cans Vienna sausage, drained
2 tablespoons butter or margarine, melted	5 servings hot fluffy instant mashed potatoes
5 or 6 small wedges of green cabbage	seasoned pepper
2 tablespoons butter or margarine	warm bottled French dressing

About 30 minutes before serving: In Dutch oven, in about 1 inch salted water, on rack, simmer carrots 15 minutes or until tender-crisp; remove to heated platter; pour melted butter over them; keep warm. In same Dutch oven, simmer cabbage wedges for 5 minutes or until tender-crisp; drain; add to platter.

In same Dutch oven, in butter, sauté sausages until nicely browned on all sides. Mound potatoes in center of platter. Sprinkle carrots and cabbage with seasoned pepper; stick sausages into potatoes. Pass dressing to pour over cabbage wedges. Makes 4 servings.

CREAMY SHRIMP-AND-MUSHROOM SOUP

1 10½-ounce can condensed
   cream-of-mushroom soup
1 10½-ounce can condensed
   cream-of-asparagus soup

½ cup sherry
⅔ cup milk or light cream
1 cup cooked shrimp, shelled,
   deveined, cut in half lengthwise

In medium saucepan, combine undiluted soups; gradually add 1 soup can water, sherry, milk and shrimp. Heat just to boiling, stirring occasionally. Makes 4 servings.

SALISBURY STEAK WITH ONION SAUCE

2 tablespoons salad oil
5 medium onions, sliced
3 tablespoons soy sauce
½ teaspoon granulated sugar

1 tablespoon cornstarch
1½ pounds ground beef chuck
1 teaspoon salt
¼ teaspoon pepper

In medium skillet over medium heat, in salad oil, cook onions 2 minutes, stirring. Add 1½ cups cold water, soy sauce and sugar; bring to boil; cook over medium heat 10 minutes or until onions are tender. Dissolve cornstarch in ¼ cup cold water; slowly stir into onions until sauce thickens. Set aside and keep warm.

Preheat broiler if manufacturer directs. In medium bowl, with 2 forks, mix chuck with salt and pepper; shape into 4 patties. Place on broiler rack; broil 4 minutes on each side or to desired doneness.

Spoon some of cooked onions on top of each patty; serve hot. Makes 4 servings.

VEAL PAPRIKA

2 pounds veal stew meat
2 tablespoons shortening, melted
2 beef bouillon cubes
3½ cups boiling water
1 medium onion, sliced
2 teaspoons paprika

1 teaspoon salt
¼ teaspoon pepper
1⅓ cups regular white rice
1 3- or 4-ounce can sliced
   mushrooms
1 pint sour cream

About 1½ hours before serving: In large skillet over medium heat, in shortening, sauté veal until well browned on all sides.

Add bouillon cubes, boiling water, onion, paprika, salt and pepper. Simmer, covered, 45 minutes.

Stir in rice and undrained mushrooms. Cover; simmer 25 minutes or until rice is tender. Stir in sour cream; heat through. Add salt if needed. Makes 8 servings.

BREAD TIP: With tines of dinner fork, lightly puncture edge of each English muffin all the way around; gently pull apart. Toast under broiler; spread with butter and sprinkle with celery or poppy seed. Slide under broiler a minute or two longer.

LEMON FRUIT PIE

Early in day: Make and bake a 9-inch pie shell. Make up one 3¼-ounce package lemon pudding-and-pie-filling mix as label directs for lemon meringue pie.

PARSLIED NOODLE CASSEROLE

In bowl, with electric mixer at high speed, beat 2 egg whites until foamy; gradually add ¼ cup granulated sugar while beating until stiff. Fold in hot pie filling, then one 16-ounce can fruit cocktail, well drained. Pour into shell. Refrigerate until serving time. Makes 8 servings.

CHICKEN-AND-SAUSAGE BAKE

1 medium onion, minced	thighs)
½ teaspoon oregano	1 pound sweet Italian sausage
6 whole chicken legs (including	1 tablespoon chopped parsley

Preheat oven to 450°F. Sprinkle onion, oregano, 2 tablespoons water over bottom of 13″ by 9″ by 2″ baking dish. Arrange chicken legs on onion. Cut sausage into 1-inch diagonal slices; lay on chicken.

Bake, uncovered, 45 minutes or until chicken is fork-tender, turning sausage once; baste occasionally.

Transfer chicken to large platter; garnish with sausage. Skim fat from liquid in baking dish; pour liquid over chicken. Sprinkle with parsley. Makes 4 to 6 servings.

PARSLIED NOODLE CASSEROLE

½ pound bow-tie noodles	onion
butter or margarine	¼ cup chopped parsley
1½ teaspoons seasoned salt	2 eggs, beaten
⅛ teaspoon seasoned pepper	¾ cup milk
1½ teaspoons instant minced	

About 1½ hours before serving: Cook noodles as label directs; drain. Preheat oven to 375°F.

In large bowl, combine hot drained noodles with 1½ tablespoons butter, seasoned salt and pepper, onion, parsley. Turn into greased 1-quart casserole; dot with 1 tablespoon butter.

Combine beaten eggs with milk; pour over noodles in casserole; bake 40 minutes. Makes 4 servings.

VEGETABLE TIP: In skillet, grate 6 pared medium beets. Sprinkle with ½ teaspoon salt, ⅛ teaspoon each garlic salt and pepper; dot with 2 tablespoons butter. Simmer, covered, 20 to 30 minutes. Makes 4 servings.

SATURDAY
Tomato Juice
Chicken-and-Sausage Bake*
Parslied Noodle Casserole*
Buttery Shredded Beets*
Hard Rolls
Rum-Raisin Ice Cream
Tea   Coffee

HAM-AND-TURKEY GALA

1 4-pound all-white-meat turkey roll
1 5-pound canned ham
½ cup peach preserves
¼ cup currant jelly
Paprika Onions (below)

Early in day: Roast turkey roll as label directs; cover and refrigerate.

About 1½ hours before serving: Preheat oven to 350°F. Remove any gelatin from ham; slice ham ¼-inch thick. Use center slices only; refrigerate end slices for Ham Hash, page 206. Slice turkey roll into ¼-inch thick slices. In foil-lined shallow open pan, alternately secure turkey slices and ham slices through center of long skewer. If skewer isn't long enough, start with another one from the other end. Roast 30 minutes.

In small saucepan over medium heat, stir peach preserves and currant jelly until blended; use to generously glaze meat; continue roasting 30 minutes. Place meat on warm platter; remove skewers. Garnish with Paprika Onions. Makes 10 to 14 servings.

Paprika Onions: Drain one 15½-ounce can whole white onions. In small skillet, sauté onions in ¼ cup butter, melted, 5 minutes or until heated. Sprinkle with paprika and 2 tablespoons finely chopped parsley. Use as garnish for Ham-and-Turkey Gala.

PEPPER-CORN-CASSEROLE

1 small green pepper
½ cup finely chopped onions
¼ cup butter or margarine
¼ cup flour
2 teaspoons salt
½ teaspoon dry mustard
2 cups milk
2 16-ounce cans whole-kernel corn, well-drained
1 cup packaged herb-seasoned stuffing croutons
2 eggs

About 1 hour and 20 minutes before serving: Preheat oven to 350°F. Slice two rings of green pepper; reserve; finely chop remaining pepper. In large skillet, sauté chopped green pepper and onions in butter 5 minutes or until soft. Add flour, salt and mustard and cook, stirring, until blended. Gradually stir in milk; cook over medium heat, stirring, until thickened and smooth. Remove from heat; stir in corn and croutons. Beat eggs slightly; stir in. Pour into greased 2-quart casserole. Arrange reserved green-pepper rings on top. Bake 55 minutes or until top is golden. Makes 8 to 10 servings.

SALAD TIP: Combine 1½ cups creamed cottage cheese with ¾ cup bottled creamy Caesar salad dressing; cover; refrigerate.

Wash two 10-ounce packages fresh spinach; break into salad bowl; toss with enough dressing to coat the leaves. Refrigerate leftover dressing for another day.

CUSTARD-MINCEMEAT PIE

unbaked 9-inch pie shell
1 18-ounce jar prepared mince-meat, drained (about 1¼ cups)
1½ cups milk
2 eggs, slightly beaten
¼ cup granulated sugar
1 teaspoon vanilla extract
½ teaspoon nutmeg

Early in day: Preheat oven to 350°F. Into pie shell spoon mincemeat. In small bowl, mix well milk and remaining ingredients; pour over mincemeat; bake 45 minutes or until custard is set. Cool or serve warm. Makes 8 to 10 servings.

HAM HASH

About 30 minutes before serving: With medium fine blade of food grinder, grind together 4 pared medium raw potatoes, 1 medium onion, 1/2 seeded green pepper and 1 cup diced cooked ham. Add 1/4 teaspoon salt, 1/8 teaspoon pepper. In large skillet, melt 3 tablespoons butter or margarine. Add ham mixture; cook over low heat, covered, 15 minutes, or until potatoes are cooked and hash is browned on bottom. Remove from heat; uncover; loosen edges with spatula. Turn onto platter. Makes 4 servings.

FRUIT-COCKTAIL CAKE

1 package lemon-cake mix
1 17-ounce can fruit cocktail, undrained
1 2-ounce package whipped-topping mix

Early in day: Preheat oven to 350°F. Make cake mix as label directs but add another egg—3 eggs in all. Substitute fruit cocktail with its syrup for water called for in cake mix.

Turn batter into well-greased and lightly floured 10-inch tube pan. Bake one hour or until cake tester inserted in center comes out clean. Cool in pan 20 minutes; unmold onto rack to cool completely.

Prepare topping mix as label directs. Frost cake. Makes 10 to 12 servings.

BROCCOLI WITH CREAMY MUSTARD SAUCE

About 15 minutes before serving: Prepare two 10-ounce packages frozen broccoli spears as label directs; drain.

Meanwhile, in small saucepan, stir 1 cup sour cream with 1 tablespoon prepared mustard, 1 tablespoon minced onion, 1/4 teaspoon salt and 1/8 teaspoon pepper. Heat over low heat, stirring frequently. Sprinkle with 1 tablespoon chopped green onions. Serve sauce with broccoli. Makes 6 servings.

SAUSAGE-AND-CAULIFLOWER CASSEROLE

1 10-ounce package frozen cauliflower
1 1/2 8-ounce packages brown-and-serve sausage links
2 tablespoons butter or margarine
2 tablespoons all-purpose flour
1/4 teaspoon salt
3/4 cup milk
1 4-ounce package shredded Cheddar cheese (1 cup)
1/4 teaspoon Worcestershire
1/4 cup bread crumbs

About 20 minutes before serving: Cook cauliflower as label directs; drain. Brown sausage links as label directs; remove; keep warm. Preheat broiler if manufacturer directs.

In skillet over low heat, melt butter; stir in flour and salt until blended. Gradually stir in milk and continue cooking, stirring constantly, 5 minutes or until sauce thickens. Remove from heat; add cheese and Worcestershire, stirring until cheese melts.

In bottom of shallow 1 1/2-quart baking dish, place half of links; top with cauliflower, then with remaining links. Pour sauce over all; sprinkle with bread crumbs. Broil a few minutes until hot and bubbly. Makes 4 servings.

MONDAY
Ham Hash*
Green Beans with Almonds
Assorted Pickle Tray
Fruit-Cocktail Cake*
Milk   Tea

TUESDAY
Broiled Hamburgers
Baked Potatoes
Broccoli with Creamy Mustard Sauce*
Cheesecake
Milk   Coffee

WEDNESDAY
Sausage-and-Cauliflower Casserole*
Mashed Potatoes
Tomato Aspic
Tapioca Pudding
Milk   Coffee

BAKED BUTTERY POTATO SLICES

About 1 hour before serving: Preheat oven to 350°F. In 12" by 8" by 2" baking dish, melt ⅓ cup butter or margarine in oven. Slice 6 pared, medium potatoes ⅛-inch thick and arrange in melted butter; sprinkle with 1 teaspoon salt and dash pepper. Bake 40 to 45 minutes or until potatoes are fork-tender. Makes 6 servings.

———◆———

CHICKEN WITH MINCEMEAT

1 3-pound broiler-fryer, cut up
2 tablespoons olive oil
1½ teaspoons salt
pepper
1 28-ounce can peeled whole
   tomatoes
1 teaspoon oregano
¼ teaspoon garlic powder

¼ teaspoon crushed red pepper
⅛ teaspoon black pepper
1⅓ cups (half 28-ounce jar)
   ready-to-use mincemeat, flavored
   with brandy and rum
½ cup dry red wine
1 4-ounce can mushroom stems
   and pieces, drained

About 1¼ hours before serving: Wash, then dry, chicken pieces. In large heavy skillet or Dutch oven over medium heat, in hot oil, sauté chicken pieces until well browned. Sprinkle with ½ teaspoon salt and dash pepper. Cover and cook over medium heat 35 to 45 minutes or until chicken is almost tender.

Meanwhile, in medium saucepan, combine tomatoes (break up with wooden spoon), 1 teaspoon salt, oregano, garlic powder, red pepper, black pepper, mincemeat, wine and mushrooms. Bring to boil; simmer, uncovered, 15 minutes or until slightly thickened, stirring occasionally.

Drain off any excess fat from chicken. Add sauce to chicken. Cook 5 to 10 minutes or until chicken is tender. Makes 4 servings.

APPLE-NUT BREAD

Early in day: Grease, then flour well, 1-pound tall coffee can. Preheat oven to 375°F. Make up 1 package apple-cinnamon muffin mix as label directs; stir in 1 cup coarsely chopped walnuts.

Pour batter into coffee can; bake 40 to 45 minutes or until cake tester inserted in center comes out clean. Remove to rack.

Cool 10 minutes; loosen with spatula; remove from can. Makes 1 loaf.

———◆———

MEAT TIP: Prepare beef stew as usual, but during last half hour add ½ cup dry red wine and ½ pound sliced mushrooms.

FROZEN CREAM VESUVIO

1 4-ounce jar diced mixed candied
   fruits (½ cup)
2 tablespoons rum
1 cup heavy or whipping cream

½ cup chopped pistachio nuts or
   roasted diced almonds
3 pints vanilla ice cream,
   softened

Early in day: Mix fruits and rum in small bowl; let stand 1 hour. Whip cream until stiff; fold in fruits and ¼ cup nuts. Line 2½-quart bowl with 2 pints ice cream. Spoon fruit mixture into center. Spoon rest of ice cream over top. Cover with foil; freeze.

About 1 hour before serving: Dip bowl of ice cream into hot water for a moment; unmold onto serving plate. Sprinkle with ¼ cup nuts; freeze until served. Makes 12 servings.

THURSDAY
Pork Chops
Spiced Apple Rings
Baked Buttery
Potato Slices*
Buttered Parsnips
Grapefruit Halves
Tea   Coffee

FRIDAY
Chicken
with Mincemeat*
Hot Fluffy Rice
Buttered Peas
Apple-Nut Bread*
Chocolate Pudding
Tea   Coffee

SATURDAY
Beef Stew
in Red Wine*
Hot Garlic Bread
Big Green Salad
Frozen Cream Vesuvio*
Demitasse

COMPANY SAUERBRATEN

1 6-pound beef chuck roast	1 pint wine vinegar
2 medium onions, sliced	2 tablespoons shortening
2 bay leaves	10 small gingersnaps, crumbled
6 whole cloves	½ pound bow-tie noodles
12 peppercorns	½ cup chopped parsley
2 teaspoons salt	

Day before: Place roast in large bowl with onions, bay leaves, cloves, peppercorns, salt, vinegar and 1 cup water. Cover; refrigerate overnight, turning roast once or twice in marinade.

Early in day: Drain roast thoroughly, reserving marinade. In Dutch oven, in hot shortening, brown roast on all sides; add marinade; simmer, covered, about 3 hours or until roast is fork-tender; cool; chill in Dutch oven, turning roast once or twice.

About 30 minutes before serving: Skim all fat from marinade in Dutch oven, remove and slice roast. Strain marinade; return to Dutch oven with gingersnaps; cook until dissolved.

Add sliced roast to gravy in Dutch oven; cover; cook about 10 minutes or until hot.

Meanwhile, cook bow-tie noodles as label directs; drain; toss with parsley; arrange on large heated platter; top with meat and gravy. Makes 10 servings.

CHARLOTTE MARTINIQUE

Day before serving: Grease 3-quart tubeless fluted mold with salad oil. Line bottom and sides with one 3-ounce package ladyfingers, split. Pack mold with 2½ quarts strawberry-parfait ice cream, slightly softened. Cover top with foil; freeze.

2 hours before serving: Make up one 2-ounce package whipped-topping mix; place in pastry bag fitted with rosette tube. Unmold ice cream onto cake stand. Garnish with rosettes; freeze until a few minutes before serving. Makes 12 servings.

———◆———

RICE-AND-BEEF CASSEROLE

2 tablespoons butter or margarine	1 16-ounce can whole tomatoes
¾ cup chopped onions	1 10½-ounce can condensed
1 pound ground beef chuck	cream-of-mushroom soup
1¼ teaspoons seasoned salt	1 cup packaged precooked rice
¼ teaspoon instant minced garlic	3 slices Cheddar cheese, each
¼ teaspoon oregano	cut into 4 strips
¼ teaspoon thyme leaves	3 stuffed olives, sliced
1 teaspoon Worcestershire	

About 30 minutes before serving: Preheat broiler if manufacturer directs. In medium skillet, in butter, brown onions with chuck. Add seasoned salt, garlic, oregano, thyme, Worcestershire, tomatoes, undiluted soup, rice; simmer 5 minutes, stirring occasionally.

Spoon mixture into 1½-quart shallow baking dish; arrange cheese strips crisscross over top. Broil 5 minutes or until cheese is bubbly; garnish with olive slices. Makes 4 servings.

SALAD TIP: In jar, combine 1 cup salad oil, ⅓ cup granulated sugar, ⅔ cup lemon juice, 1½ teaspoons salt, 2 teaspoons paprika and 1 teaspoon minced onion. Cover; shake well. Makes 1⅔ cups dressing.

SUNDAY

Pickled Herring,
Sliced Wurst

Pumpernickel Bread

*Company Sauerbraten**

Buttered Red Cabbage

*Charlotte Martinique**

Tea   Coffee

MONDAY

Rice-and-Beef
*Casserole**

Romaine Salad with
*Lemon Dressing**

Italian-Style
Green Beans

Tangerines and Pears

Milk   Tea

CHARLOTTE MARTINIQUE

PORK-AND-BEAN STEW

1 pound dried white kidney beans or navy beans	2 pounds boneless pork shoulder, cut into 1-inch cubes
salt	1 cup chopped onions
1 onion, studded with 3 cloves	1 garlic clove, minced
2 celery stalks	1 cup tomato purée
1 bay leaf	1/4 teaspoon pepper
2 tablespoons shortening	

About 3 hours before serving: In large kettle, boil beans with 2 quarts water and 1 tablespoon salt for 2 minutes. Remove from heat; let stand one hour. Add onion studded with cloves, celery stalks and bay leaf; cover; simmer one hour.

Meanwhile, in Dutch oven or large heavy kettle, in hot shortening, thoroughly brown pork and onions. Spoon off any excess fat. Add 1½ teaspoons salt, garlic and 1½ cups water; cover; simmer 40 minutes. Stir in tomato purée and pepper; continue cooking until meat is tender, about 20 minutes more.

Drain beans, removing onion, celery and bay leaf. Stir beans into pork and simmer about 10 minutes longer, stirring once or twice. Makes 6 servings.

ONION-RYE ROLLS IN LOAF

About 1/2 hour before serving: Preheat oven to 425°F. In top of oval loaf of unsliced rye bread, make 11 evenly spaced crosswise cuts almost to bottom crust. Spread each cut surface with butter. Insert thin onion slice in every other slit; cover with foil; place on cookie sheet. Bake 15 minutes or until hot. To serve, cut through slits that have no onion. Makes 6 servings.

TUESDAY
Pork-and-Bean Stew*
Onion-Rye Rolls in Loaf*
Chinese Cabbage Salad
Cherry-Flavor Gelatin with Whipped Topping
Milk   Tea

SUNNY CITRUS STEAK

WEDNESDAY
Sunny Citrus Steak*
Hashed-Brown Potatoes
Broccoli
Sesame-Seed Rolls
*Chocolate-Glazed
Angel-Food Cake*
Tea   Coffee

1 3- to 4-pound beef chuck steak,
   1½ inches thick
¼ cup shortening
2 large onions, sliced
4 teaspoons salt

2 teaspoons light brown sugar
1 teaspoon pepper
1 cup grapefruit juice
1 large grapefruit, sectioned
1 large orange, sectioned

Preheat oven to 350°F. If necessary, trim excess fat from steak. In extra-large skillet with ovenproof handle, in melted shortening, brown steak on both sides. Add onions, salt, sugar, pepper and juice; cover; bake 1½ hours or until meat is fork-tender. Add fruits to meat during last 5 minutes of cooking; heat through. Remove meat, fruits and onions to warm platter. Thicken juices with mixture of 3 tablespoons flour and ½ cup water. Makes 6 to 8 servings.

HOT FRANK-AND-POTATO-SALAD CASSEROLE

THURSDAY
*Hot Frank-
and-Potato-Salad
Casserole**
*Raw Vegetable
Relish Tray*
Crusty Rolls
Apple Pie with Cheese
Milk   Coffee

Preheat oven to 400°F. Combine 4 cups thinly sliced, cooked potatoes; 1½ teaspoons salt; dash pepper; ⅓ cup salad oil; 3 tablespoons vinegar. In greased 1½-quart casserole, layer 1½ cups canned or cooked green beans, potato mixture, ¼ cup thinly sliced onion, 4 sliced frankfurters. Cover; bake 30 minutes. Makes 4 servings.

GRANNY'S INDIAN PUDDING

1½ quarts milk
¾ cup corn meal
¾ cup finely chopped, *not
   ground,* beef suet
¾ cup light molasses
1 egg, beaten
1 teaspoon salt

½ cup butter or margarine
1 teaspoon cinnamon
½ teaspoon ground cloves
¼ teaspoon nutmeg
½ teaspoon ginger
1½ cups light or dark raisins
vanilla ice cream

FRIDAY
*Broiled Crab Claws
with Lemon Butter*
Baked Potatoes
Succotash
*Granny's
Indian Pudding**
Tea   Coffee

About 4 hours before serving: Preheat oven to 300°F. In large saucepan over low heat, bring 1 quart milk just to boiling. Gradually stir in corn meal; boil over low heat, stirring, until thickened. Add suet and next 9 ingredients. Turn into greased 3-quart casserole. Bake, uncovered, set in pan of hot water, 30 minutes. Pour on remaining ½ quart milk (2 cups); *don't stir.* Bake 3 hours.

Serve warm or cold, topped with ice cream. Makes 12 servings.

To do ahead: Bake pudding day before; chill. To serve, reheat in pan of hot water in 300°F. oven about 45 minutes.

CHEESE BREAD

Early in day: In large bowl of electric mixer, thoroughly mix 2 cups regular all-purpose flour, 2 tablespoons granulated sugar, 2 teaspoons salt, 2 packages active dry yeast.

In small saucepan, combine 1 cup milk, ¾ cup water, 1 tablespoon butter or margarine and 4 drops red and 3 drops yellow food color. Heat over low heat until just warm (butter or margarine does not need to melt).

With electric mixer at medium speed, gradually add liquid to dry ingredients; beat 2 minutes, scraping sides of bowl occasionally. Add ¾ cup flour, or enough to make thick batter; beat at high speed 2 minutes, scraping sides of bowl occasionally. Stir in two 4-ounce packages shredded

CHEESE BREAD

Cheddar cheese (2 cups) and enough flour (2½ to 4 cups) to make a soft dough. Turn onto lightly floured surface; shape into ball; knead until smooth and elastic, about 10 minutes. Place in large greased bowl; turn, to grease top; cover and let rise in warm place (80°F. to 85°F.) free from drafts, until doubled in bulk, about 1 hour. Punch dough down; turn onto floured surface; cover with bowl; let rest 15 minutes. Shape into 2 balls, kneading each until smooth. Turn into 2 greased 1-quart round casseroles; brush tops with melted butter; cover with clean towel or waxed paper. Let rise again until doubled in bulk, about 40 minutes.

Preheat oven to 375°F. Bake breads 35 to 40 minutes or until they sound hollow when rapped with knuckles. Cool on rack 5 minutes; remove from casseroles. Cool completely on racks. Makes 2 loaves.

SATURDAY
Baked Ham
Mashed
Sweet Potatoes
Cauliflower
*Cheese Bread**
Napoleons
Tea   Coffee

SUNDAY

Eggnog

*Cornish Hens
with Apple-and-Orange
Stuffing**

Frozen Asparagus

Buttered Beets

Relish Tray

Petits Fours

Tea   Coffee

MONDAY

French Toast

Pan-Fried Ham

*Broiled Mixed Fruits**

Lemon Whipped Dessert

Pretzels

Milk   Tea

TUESDAY

*Corned-Beef Hash
with Poached Egg*

*Poppy Braid**

*Waldorf Salad
with Spanish Peanuts*

Danish Pastries

Tea   Coffee

WEDNESDAY

*Pork Chops Italiano**

Baked Potatoes

*Frozen-Spinach
Soufflé*

Spanish Melon

*Lemon-Nut Crunch
Cookies*

Milk   Coffee

CORNISH HENS WITH APPLE-AND-ORANGE STUFFING

8 thawed 1-pound Cornish hens	1 8-ounce package herb-seasoned
seasoned salt and pepper	stuffing
butter or margarine	½ cup minced celery
1 cooking apple, chopped	1 tablespoon grated orange peel

About 1¾ hours before serving: Preheat oven to 400°F. Season hens inside and out with seasoned salt and pepper.

In medium bowl, melt 2 tablespoons butter in 1 cup hot water; add apple, stuffing, celery and orange peel. Use to stuff birds. Place birds, breast side up, on rack in roasting pan; brush with melted butter. Roast, uncovered, basting occasionally with melted butter, 1 hour 15 minutes or until drumsticks move easily up and down. Makes 8 servings.

BROILED MIXED FRUITS

1 16-ounce can cling-peach halves	3 tablespoons brown sugar
1 15½-ounce can pineapple rings	⅛ teaspoon ground cloves
3 tablespoons butter or margarine,	⅛ teaspoon salt
softened	1 large banana, cut into chunks

About 20 minutes before serving: Preheat broiler if manufacturer directs. Drain fruits; place on broiler pan.

In bowl, mix butter, sugar, cloves and salt; spread some on canned fruits. Broil a few minutes until hot. Spread rest of mixture on banana; place on pan; broil until hot. Makes 6 servings.

POPPY BRAID

2 7-ounce cans butter-	1 egg, well beaten
crescent flaky rolls	2 teaspoons poppy seed

About 40 minutes before serving: Preheat oven to 375°F. On lightly floured surface, unroll one can dough, keeping rolls intact; pinch together perforations. Unroll second can of dough and lay on top of first, pinching together perforations; roll all into rectangle 15″ by 8″. Cut this into 3 lengthwise strips; roll strips between palms, then braid together, sealing ends with a little egg. Brush with egg; sprinkle with poppy seed. Place on cookie sheet. Bake about 25 minutes or until golden.

PORK CHOPS ITALIANO

4 pork chops, about 1″ thick	2 large green peppers, cut in
seasoned salt	¾″ strips
pepper	2 8-ounce cans tomato sauce
½ pound small fresh mushrooms	½ bay leaf
1 tablespoon salad oil	1 tablespoon lemon juice
1 medium onion, chopped	⅛ teaspoon sage
½ garlic clove, sliced (optional)	

Trim excess fat from chops, sprinkle with seasoned salt and pepper. In large skillet, brown chops; drain off excess fat. Place chops in 2½-quart casserole; add mushrooms. Preheat oven to 375°F.

In same skillet, in oil, sauté onion, garlic and green peppers until golden; add tomato sauce, 1 teaspoon seasoned salt, ⅛ teaspoon pepper, bay leaf, lemon juice and sage; simmer, covered, until vegetables are almost fork-tender. Pour this sauce over chops and mushrooms.

Cover; bake 1 hour or until chops are fork-tender; skim off fat. Makes 4 servings.

FRENCH MIMOSA SALAD

1 head Boston lettuce
3 tablespoons chopped parsley

2 hard-cooked eggs
French or Italian dressing

Arrange washed, chilled lettuce leaves in bowl; sprinkle with parsley. Press egg whites, then yolks, through sieve over salad. Pass dressing. Makes 4 servings.

FUDGE CUTS

2 squares unsweetened chocolate
½ cup shortening
1 cup granulated sugar
2 eggs, well beaten
½ cup sifted regular all-

purpose flour
¼ teaspoon salt
1 teaspoon vanilla extract
½ cup finely chopped walnuts

Preheat oven to 400°F. Grease two 8″ by 8″ by 2″ pans. In double boiler, melt chocolate and shortening; remove from water. Mix in sugar, eggs, then flour, salt, vanilla; stir well. Pour into pans; top with nuts. Bake 12 minutes or until done. Cool in pan. Cut into 2-inch squares. Makes 32.

FRIED CLAMS

About 30 minutes before serving: Beat 1 egg with 2 tablespoons water. Drain 1 quart shucked raw soft-shell clams, removing any bits of shell. Dip each clam into egg, then into packaged dried bread crumbs, corn meal or fine cracker crumbs.

In deep skillet, fry clams in 1½ inches of salad oil at 365°F. until nicely browned on all sides. Drain on paper towels. Serve on toast with lemon wedges or Quick Tartar Sauce. Makes 4 servings.

QUICK TARTAR SAUCE

Combine 1 cup mayonnaise with 1 to 2 tablespoons each minced pickle, chopped parsley, bottled capers, chopped onion or chopped green or stuffed olives. Makes about 1¼ cups.

GREEN BEANS IN HERB SAUCE

1 tablespoon margarine
1 large onion, thinly sliced
1 large stalk green celery,
  thinly sliced
1 tablespoon parsley flakes
¼ teaspoon garlic salt (optional)

¾ teaspoon salt
generous dash black pepper
1 tablespoon cornstarch
1 9-ounce package frozen cut
  green beans

About 25 minutes before serving: In a medium saucepan, in margarine, sauté onion, celery and parsley flakes until onion is golden.

Meanwhile, mix garlic salt, salt, pepper and cornstarch; slowly stir in 1 cup water to form a smooth paste. Add this mixture and green beans to onion; cover; gently boil 10 minutes or until beans are tender-crisp and sauce has thickened slightly. Makes 4 generous servings.

BROILED MIXED FRUITS

THURSDAY
Broiled Hamburgers
with Mushrooms
Herb Rice
French Mimosa Salad*
Fudge Cuts*
Milk   Coffee

FRIDAY
Cream-of-Celery Soup
Fried Clams*
Quick Tartar Sauce*
French Fries
Green Beans
in Herb Sauce*
Lemon Tarts
Tea   Coffee

CHAFING-DISH MEATBALLS

SATURDAY

Chestnut-Stuffed Goose*

*Hot Sauerkraut
with Caraway Seed*

Mashed Potatoes*

Brussels Sprouts

Hot Finger Rolls

Danish Rum Cake*

Tea   Coffee

CHESTNUT-STUFFED GOOSE

1 pound large chestnuts	1 4- to 5-pound ready-to-cook
1 tablespoon shortening	goose
3 cups fresh bread crumbs	3 tablespoons honey
1 teaspoon salt	2 tablespoons butter or margarine
1 teaspoon minced onion	3 ½-inch-thick apple slices, halved
½ teaspoon chopped parsley	¼ cup honey
¼ cup butter or margarine, melted	watercress
1 egg, slightly beaten	6 cooked prunes

Day before or early in day: Preheat oven to 325°F. Cut gash in shell of each chestnut. Arrange in 10-inch skillet with ovenproof handle; add shortening; bake 15 minutes. Remove shells and inner skin; cook chestnuts in boiling salted water, to cover, 5 to 10 minutes or until tender; drain. Reserve 6 chestnuts for garnish; chop rest fine (about 2 cups). Refrigerate.

About 3½ hours before serving: Preheat oven to 325°F. Combine chopped chestnuts, bread crumbs, salt, onion, parsley, ¼ cup butter, egg and 3 tablespoons water. Toss lightly. Stuff neck and body of goose; fasten neck skin to back with skewer; close body opening. Place goose on rack in shallow roasting pan.

Roast 2¾ to 3 hours; turn oven heat to 425°F.; roast 10 minutes longer. When goose is done, remove from oven; brush with 3 tablespoons honey. Place in center of heated oval platter and keep warm.

In small skillet, in 2 tablespoons butter, sauté apple slices until tender and golden; remove. Pour ¼ cup honey into skillet; add reserved chestnuts; sauté until glazed. Place chestnuts and watercress on breast of goose. Garnish with apples and prunes. Makes 4 servings.

VEGETABLE TIP: Sauté minced onion in butter for 5 minutes or until golden; add to hot mashed potatoes. Serve sprinkled with paprika.

DANISH RUM CAKE

margarine	½ teaspoon salt
1¼ cups pecans, finely ground	1⅔ cups granulated sugar
2 cups sifted all-purpose flour	5 eggs, well beaten
½ teaspoon double-acting	¼ cup light rum
baking powder	Rum Frosting (below)

About 3 hours before serving: Preheat oven to 325°F. With 2 tablespoons melted margarine, grease 9-inch tube pan. Line with waxed paper; grease again. Sprinkle about ⅓ cup of the ground pecans around bottom and sides of pan.

Into medium bowl, sift together flour, baking powder and salt.

In large bowl of electric mixer, at medium speed, beat 1 cup margarine and sugar until light and fluffy (about 10 minutes), scraping sides of bowl and beaters occasionally.

At low speed, add flour mixture; blend thoroughly. Add eggs and mix at medium speed until *just* blended. *Do not overbeat.* Stir in rum and remaining ground pecans. Turn batter into prepared pan. Bake 1 hour and 10 minutes or until cake tester inserted in center comes out clean. Let cake rest in pan 10 minutes.

Remove cake from pan; remove waxed paper. Cool completely on rack. Frost with Rum Frosting; decorate with pecan halves, if desired.

Rum Frosting: In medium mixing bowl, whip 1 cup heavy or whipping cream with 1 tablespoon confectioners' sugar, sifted. Fold in 1 tablespoon rum.

CHAFING-DISH MEATBALLS

1½ pounds ground beef chuck
½ cup packaged dried bread
  crumbs
1 teaspoon salt
¼ teaspoon pepper
1 egg, slightly beaten
½ cup milk

¼ cup shortening
2 tablespoons flour
2 cups canned tomato juice
¾ cup bottled barbecue sauce
1 20½-ounce can pineapple chunks,
  drained
stuffed olives

Early in day: In bowl, with two-tined fork, toss together chuck, bread crumbs, salt, pepper, egg and milk until well blended. Shape into ½-inch balls. Place in shallow pan with shortening; refrigerate.

About 1½ hours before serving: Preheat oven to 350°F. Bake meatballs 30 minutes. In saucepan, combine flour and tomato juice until smooth. Add barbecue sauce and ¼ cup water; blend well. Set aside. Drain off excess fat from meatballs; pour on tomato sauce; bake 45 minutes longer.

Spoon meatballs into chafing dish. Place pineapple chunks and olives here and there. Spoon sauce over all. Makes about 48 meatballs.

VEGETABLE TIP: To 3 cups hot, seasoned, mashed yellow turnips, add 2 tablespoons butter, ⅔ cup shredded process Cheddar cheese, 1 table-spoon minced onion and ½ teaspoon bottled thick meat sauce. Mix well.

───◆─◆───

LAMB STEW

2 tablespoons all-purpose flour
seasoned salt
½ teaspoon seasoned pepper
4 pounds lamb stew meat
¼ cup salad oil
2 medium onions, chopped

2 garlic cloves, minced
½ teaspoon thyme leaves
4 medium tomatoes, cut into
  wedges
2 green peppers, cut into 1-inch
  squares

About 2½ hours before serving: Combine flour with 1 tablespoon seasoned salt, seasoned pepper; coat lamb on all sides.

In Dutch oven over medium heat, in hot salad oil, brown lamb on all sides; add onions and garlic; brown a few minutes longer. Add thyme, 1 cup water. Simmer, covered, 1½ hours or until lamb is almost tender, stirring occasionally. If necessary, add a little more water during cooking. Skim off excess fat.

Add tomatoes and green peppers; sprinkle with ½ teaspoon seasoned salt. Cook 15 minutes or until vegetables are tender. Makes 6 servings.

───◆─◆───

VEAL DINNER SPECIAL

1 9- or 10-ounce package frozen
  chopped broccoli in cream sauce
  or au gratin
1½ cups packaged precooked rice
1 envelope instant beef broth

1 tablespoon parsley flakes
8 roast veal slices
¼ cup light cream
3 tablespoons grated Parmesan
  cheese

About 40 minutes before serving: Preheat oven to 400°F. Heat broccoli *just to thaw.*

Cook rice as label directs but add beef broth to water; toss rice with parsley. Spread over bottom of 10″ by 6″ by 2″ baking dish; arrange veal slices, overlapping, on top of rice. Mix cream with broccoli; pour over veal; sprinkle with Parmesan. Bake 15 minutes or until bubbly and brown. Makes 4 servings.

SUNDAY

*Chafing Dish
Meatballs**

Roast Veal

*Mashed Yellow Turnips**

Peas and Onions

Hot Rye Bread

Eggnog Ice Cream

Tea   Coffee

MONDAY

*Lamb Stew**

Parslied Potatoes

*Artichoke Hearts
with Mild Garlic
French Dressing*

*Sesame-Seed
Crackers*

*Coffee
Whipped Dessert*

Tea   Coffee

TUESDAY

*Veal Dinner Special**

*Whole-Cranberry
Sauce*

*Assorted-Cracker
Basket*

*Fresh-Fruit
Bowl*

Tea   Coffee

SKILLET-BARBECUED FRANKS

3/4 cup catchup
1 tablespoon Worcestershire
1 teaspoon chili powder
1/2 teaspoon salt

1 teaspoon sugar
dash Tabasco
1 cup water
8 to 12 frankfurters

In skillet, combine all ingredients except franks; bring to boil; add franks; reduce heat; simmer 15 to 20 minutes. Makes 4 to 6 servings.

———◆———

CROUSTADIN

1/2 pound bacon slices
1 pound liverwurst (6 slices, about
    1/2-inch thick)
flour

1 tablespoon butter or margarine
6 French bread slices, 1/2-inch thick
lemon wedges
chopped parsley

About 30 minutes before serving: In skillet, fry bacon until crisp; remove; drain off all but 3 tablespoons drippings.

Sprinkle both sides of liverwurst with flour; sauté in drippings until brown; remove from skillet; drain off drippings.

In same skillet, heat butter until brown; in it, lightly toast bread on both sides; top each with liverwurst slice, then with bacon slices. Squeeze on lemon juice; sprinkle with parsley. Makes 4 to 6 servings.

ACCOMPANIMENT TIP: Drain one 20 1/2-ounce can pineapple tidbits; toss with 1/2 teaspoon curry powder and 2 cups flaked coconut. Cover; chill. Spoon into relish dish. Makes 6 to 8 servings.

———◆———

PRALINE RING

1/2 cup butter or margarine
1 cup packed brown sugar
1/2 cup broken pecans or walnuts

2 1/2 cups corn, bran or wheat flakes
vanilla ice-cream balls

About 1/2 hour before serving: Chill 5-cup ring mold. In saucepan, boil butter with sugar just 2 minutes. Add pecans and cornflakes; with fork, toss to coat. Press lightly into mold. Refrigerate 10 minutes; unmold; fill with ice cream. Makes 6 servings.

———◆———

TUNA CURRY

3 6 1/2- or 7-ounce cans tuna
1 medium onion, chopped
1 medium apple, pared, chopped
6 tablespoons flour
2 1/2 teaspoons curry
1 1/2 teaspoons salt
1 teaspoon granulated sugar

1/4 teaspoon ginger
2 cups milk
1 beef bouillon cube
1 tablespoon lemon juice
3 cups hot fluffy rice
salted peanuts (optional)

Early in day: Into medium saucepan, drain oil from 2 cans tuna. In oil, sauté onion and apple until tender. Stir in flour, curry, salt, sugar and ginger; gradually stir in milk and 1 cup water; add bouillon cube.

Cook over medium heat, stirring, until sauce is thickened and comes to boil.

Stir in all the tuna; add lemon juice. Heat.

Serve over rice sprinkled with peanuts. Makes 6 servings.

WEDNESDAY
Skillet-Barbecued
Franks*
Buttered Noodles
Mixed-Vegetable Salad
with French Dressing
Orange Gelatin
Chocolate Cookies
Milk   Tea

THURSDAY
Croustadin*
Limas and Carrots
Pineapple Relish*
Baked Custard
Nut Cookies
Milk   Tea

FRIDAY
Cheese Ravioli
Chicory
with
Creamy Onion Dressing
Italian Rolls
Praline Ring*
with Vanilla
Ice-Cream Balls
Demitasse

SATURDAY
Fresh-Fruit Cup
Tuna Curry*
Mixed-Greens Salad
Hot Apple Pie
Milk   Coffee

EGGS EN GELÉE

Day before serving: Cut 24 hard-cooked eggs in half lengthwise. Moisten yolks with French dressing. Fill whites; press halves together. Place each egg in muffin-size foil baking cup, set in shallow pan.

Soften 2 envelopes unflavored gelatin in ⅔ cup water; stir into two 10½-ounce cans hot condensed beef consommé. With star aspic cutter, cut 24 stars from 4 canned pimientos, split.

Spoon gelatin over each egg until cup is almost full. Garnish with stars and slices of ripe olives. Refrigerate. Makes 24 servings.

STANDING RIB ROAST SUPREME

1 7-inch, 7-rib standing rib roast (about 16 to 18 pounds)	2 teaspoons seasoned salt
3 cups grated carrots	½ teaspoon seasoned pepper
2 cups coarsely chopped celery leaves	carrot curls for garnish
	parsley sprigs for garnish

About 5 to 6 hours before serving: Preheat oven to 325°F. Roast meat as directed (see chart, page 220). Two hours before roast is done, cover with mixture of grated carrots, celery leaves, seasoned salt and pepper; continue roasting.

During last hour, cover meat loosely with foil, leaving thermometer uncovered. Continue roasting until meat is of desired doneness.

When roast is done, let stand 15 minutes. Cut crosswise, starting at backbone, between third and fourth rib bones. Arrange halves on platter. Garnish with carrot curls and parsley. Makes 24 to 28 servings.

CRISP POTATO TREE

Early in day: Cook 8 pounds unpeeled medium white potatoes in boiling water 10 to 15 minutes until partially done; peel; cover; refrigerate.

About 1 hour before serving: Cut potatoes lengthwise in half; cut each half into 3 or 4 lengthwise wedges. In large skillet, in 1 cup hot salad oil, fry some wedges until golden; drain; keep warm in 325°F. oven. Repeat process. Sprinkle potatoes with salt.

To serve: Arrange in tree-like pattern, as pictured. Makes 20 to 24 servings.

PUMPKIN MOUSSE

7 envelopes unflavored gelatin	2 teaspoons nutmeg
2 cups orange juice	2 teaspoons ginger
2 29-ounce cans pumpkin	1½ teaspoons salt
2 cups granulated sugar	½ gallon vanilla ice cream, softened
1 tablespoon ground cloves	whipped cream
4 teaspoons cinnamon	

Early in day: Make foil collar for 2-quart soufflé dish: Cut 35-inch piece of 12-inch-wide foil; fold in half lengthwise; butter lightly. Wrap around outside of dish so collar stands 3 inches above rim. Fasten with cellophane tape.

Sprinkle gelatin on orange juice to soften. In large pan, heat pumpkin with next 6 ingredients. When mixture is hot, stir in gelatin until dissolved; set aside.

In large mixing bowl, with electric mixer at medium speed, beat ice cream smooth; gradually stir into pumpkin mixture; blend. Pour into soufflé dish; chill 5 hours or until set; remove collar; garnish with whipped cream. Makes 20 to 24 servings.

SPECIAL-DAY DINNER
Eggs en Gelée*
Standing
Rib Roast Supreme*
Crisp Potato Tree*
Romaine-Red-Onion
Salad
Pumpkin Mousse*
Tea   Coffee

The Grand Feast
of Winter

A festive holiday menu, packed with pleasant surprises, awaits guests at this party. Eggs en Gelée (at lower left), a very special appetizer, taste as good as they look. Standing Rib Roast Supreme, the king of meats, is roasted, then split in half for serving. The Crisp Potato Tree is made from partially cooked potatoes, cooled, then sliced, fried and stacked in a tree shape. For the salad, crisp romaine and red-onion slices are tossed with a favorite dressing. And as a rich but light ending to this elegant feast, a make-ahead Pumpkin Mousse with a delightfully different blend of orange and spices.

Cut	Approx. Weight Pounds	Oven Temperature Degrees F.	Meat Thermometer Reading Degrees F.	Approx. Roasting Time Min. per lb.
BEEF*				
Standing Rib†	4 to 6	325	140 (rare)	26 to 32
			160 (medium)	34 to 38
			170 (well)	40 to 42
Standing Rib†	6 to 8	325	140 (rare)	23 to 25
			160 (medium)	27 to 30
			170 (well)	32 to 35
Standing Rib†	16 to 18	325	140 (rare)	15 to 18
			160 (medium)	18 to 20
Rolled Rib	5 to 7	325	140 (rare)	32
			160 (medium)	38
			170 (well)	48
Rib Eye (Delmonico)	4 to 6	350	140 (rare)	18 to 20
			160 (medium)	20 to 22
			170 (well)	22 to 24
Tenderloin (whole)	4 to 6	425	140 (rare)	45 to 60 (total time)
Tenderloin (half)	2 to 3	425	140 (rare)	45 to 50 (total time)
Rolled Rump	4 to 6	325	150–170	25 to 30
Sirloin Tip	3½ to 4	325	150–170	35 to 40
VEAL*				
Leg	5 to 8	325	170	25 to 35
Rolled Shoulder	4 to 6	325	170	40 to 45
PORK—Fresh*				
Loin				
Center	3 to 5	325	170	30 to 35
Half	5 to 7	325	170	35 to 40
End	3 to 4	325	170	40 to 45
Roll	3 to 5	325	170	35 to 45
Picnic Shoulder	5 to 8	325	170	30 to 35
Rolled	3 to 5	325	170	35 to 40
Leg (fresh ham)				
Whole (bone in)	12 to 16	325	170	22 to 26
Whole (boneless)	10 to 14	325	170	24 to 28
Half (bone in)	5 to 8	325	170	35 to 45
PORK—Smoked*				
Ham (cook-before-eating)				
Whole	10 to 14	325	160	18 to 20
Half	5 to 7	325	160	22 to 25
Shank or Butt				
Portion	3 to 4	325	160	35 to 40
Ham (fully cooked)				
Whole	10 to 14	325	130	10 to 15
Half	5 to 7	325	130	18 to 24
LAMB*				
Leg (bone-in)	5 to 8	325	175–180	30 to 35
Leg (rolled)	3 to 5	325	175–180	35 to 40
Shoulder (bone-in)	5 to 7	325	175–180	30 to 35
Shoulder (rolled)	4 to 6	325	175–180	40 to 45
POULTRY				TOTAL TIME
Broiler-Fryer‡	1½	400	——	1 hour
"	2	400	——	1 hour, 10 min.
"	2½	375	——	1 hour, 15 min.
"	3	375	——	1 hour, 30 min.
Roaster‡	3½	375	185	1 hour, 45 min.
"	4	375	185	2 hours
"	4½	375	185	2 hours, 15 min.
"	5	375	185	2 hours, 30 min.
Capon‡	6 to 8	350	185	3 to 3½ hours
Cornish Hen	1 to 2	400	——	1 hour
Duckling‡	4 to 5	325	——	2½ to 3 hours††
Goose‡	4 to 6	325	185	2¾ to 3 hours
"	6 to 10	325	185	3 to 3¾ hours
"	10 to 14	325	185	3¾ to 4¾ hours

* Meat continues to cook after removal from oven. To permit roast to "set," remove it from oven when thermometer registers 5° to 10° lower than desired doneness. (The larger the roast, the higher the temperature rise after removal from oven.)

† Ribs which measure 6 to 7 inches from chine bone to tip of rib.

‡ For stuffed poultry, allow about one half hour more.

†† Increase oven temperature to 400°F. during last 30 minutes.

INDEX
A–B

Italic type indicates tips; **boldface type** calls attention to special categories, such as Budget Dishes, Do-Ahead Dishes, etc.

V–Z